THAT WOMAN
FROM
MISSISSIPPI

Norma Watkins

ISBN: 978-1-936946-95-2

The Nautilus Publishing Company
426 S Lamar Blvd. Suite 16
Oxford, MS 38655
Tel: 662-513-0159
www.nautiluspublishing.com

First Edition

Front cover design by Wil Oakes
Cover photo credit to Fran Fevrier
Interior design by Sinclair Rishel

Photo credit to Fran Fevrier for photos on pages 39, 150, 154, 180, 213, 231, and 266 (top).

Library of Congress Cataloging-in-Publication Data has been applied for.

Printed in the USA

10 9 8 7 6 5 4 3 2 1

To Les

"I decided to write about lust and gluttony, the only deadly sins that are worth the trouble."

— Isabel Allende

"With enough courage, you can do without a reputation."

— Margaret Mitchell

BEFORE

1

"I have to leave," my lover said.

My mind refused to take in the words. I had not thought past playing at this dangerous game, meeting at his house on warm evenings when I was supposed to be at the college library, or where we were tonight, hiding in the darkest corner of a restaurant parking lot on the far side of town. He'd brought fried catfish and hush puppies to eat in the car. My fingers were greasy.

"I've taken another job in Florida," he said.

This is how happiness ended, with four words in a parking lot.

"I want you to come with me."

I must have heard wrong. "What did you say?"

"We can go together. The new job is with Legal Services, working with migrant farmers south of Miami, using the law to protect the downtrodden, the way I do here in Mississippi."

I interrupted. "I can't leave."

He took my greasy fingers and wiped them clean, sex with a paper napkin. "You have to come."

I pulled my hands away. "I can't. I have a husband. I have four children."

The brown eyes pleaded. "You don't love him the way you love me."

These last months I had been extra kind at home, a patient and slightly distant wife, a sweet and forgiving mother. Hiding this huge secret in my head and waiting for the next chance to see Bruce. I shook my head. I loved Fred, of course—he was the father of my children—but not the way I loved Bruce, not with this lava flow of feeling.

"And I've never loved anyone the way I love you. Don't you see how lucky we are, how rare this is? We can't afford to throw it away."

"I can't leave."

"If it's the children you're worried about, you won't be giving them up. As soon as we get settled, we can send for them."

"Maybe I could come in the fall."

"You have to come with me, or it won't work."

"Why not?"

"Unless we leave together, you won't come."

He was right. The idea of walking out of my life was too terrifying to contemplate with him. I would never get up the nerve to do it alone. "When do you have to go?"

"I should be on the road by the first week in July."

Three weeks.

Writing these words, my throat closes the way it did that June night in 1966. Common sense battling temptation.

2

In the spring of 1965, a swashbuckling crew of civil rights lawyers took on the misery of Mississippi's troubles, working to save us from our bigoted selves. Using the courts, they chipped away at a century of Jim Crow laws, attacking wrongs our black residents dared not question. Well-meaning white people like me watched admiringly. We spent our time talking big and doing nothing, too scared to fight.

During the day, the lawyers worked on constitutional challenges. At night, we invited them to dinner in our suburban homes. This felt heroic, as if we were helping solve the problem by feeding the people who did.

I met Bruce Rogow at one of those dinners.

Seeing him felt like a recognition: he stood on the far side of the room, dark-haired and smiling, fierce nose, broad shoulders, the person I was meant to be with, ten years and four children too late. We sat together at dinner. With a voice like warm caramel, he talked his way under my skin. I liked the look of his hands on the silverware and the way his hair fell over his forehead. He read the same books I did, and when I spoke, he appeared to listen. What did I want to do with my one and only life? I told him I would get my bachelor's degree in June and go on to graduate school.

He looked across the room at Fred Craig, the man I was married to. "Either you've got a very understanding husband or a marriage that's in trouble."

I felt exposed, as if those dark, observant eyes saw past the polite words to the place where I hid my dissatisfactions: the daily dullness of keeping house, marriage to a conservative man, the secret of our terrible sex.

I wasn't exactly lying about graduate school. I wanted to be an English professor, like my model at Millsaps College, who stood before us in his tweed jacket with what felt like the breadth of literature and life's meaning at his fingertips. I had been offered fellowships to go away for a master's degree, but Fred said I should have thought of that sooner. He said I made the choice to be a wife and mother and that's what I was. He'd agreed to undergraduate school because Millsaps was close by. He'd put up with years of my studying and running off to the library. Now I wanted to run off to the University of Arkansas. It was out of the question.

Instead of answering Bruce's question about my marriage, I told him how disgusted I was with our brutal state, where blacks were forced into menial jobs and murdered for trying to vote. He refused to join me in my Mississippi-hating. The South was a good place, and lawyers like him were here to make it better.

I called him the next day, using some pretense.

"You want to see me again," he said. "I want to see you, too."

The man saw right through me. I tried inviting him to dinner.

"I don't want to get to know your husband and your family. I want to know you."

We went for a picnic near the zoo, a place no one I knew would go in the middle of a weekday. I took tuna sandwiches. My mouth was too dry to swallow, but I admired the appreciative way Bruce ate. He told me about the night he'd been assaulted by white boys for being in a car with a Negro woman. He ran a red light to escape and was pulled over by the police. He followed them to the station, and while he was inside, the boys turned his car upside down. He tried to file a complaint but got cited for running the light.

I loved these stories. He was the first white man I'd ever known who defended black people in court and dated Negro women. Listening to him felt like being part of a movement I was too frightened to join. We had a second picnic, more talk, a kiss this time. He took me to the house he rented with other lawyers in the black section of town. I had never entered this part of Jackson except to pick up our cook. There was a big gray dog inside the front door. Bruce said it was good to have a big dog if you worked in civil rights. He gave me a tour of the rooms, the dog clicking along behind us: bare living room, kitchen with a rackety refrigerator. I followed him down the hall to a bedroom. I went willingly, hand-in-hand with the fascinating stranger.

We met whenever he could get away from his life and me from mine. We had endless talk and exciting, sinful sex. Being in love with him was like tumbling off a cliff and discovering I could fly. I liked the careful way he removed his clothes, the look of his long, lean body, and the care he took with mine. I liked the way our talk of books and ideas moved into lovemaking and back into talk. He was the handsomest man I'd ever seen, smart, funny, and brave, doing the hard work against segregation I was too terrified to try. This paragon of manhood liked me. After each of our encounters, I went back to my life. I never thought past the present guilt, which was bad enough.

3

For two weeks, I tugged myself back and forth. In the real world, I served supper, helped with homework, kissed children to sleep, and smiled at the man I'd married. Inside, an endless dialogue:

Of course you can't leave. Put it out of your mind.

You could go to graduate school.

And desert my children? It's out of the question.

Bruce says the children will come later.

I would be leaving them now.

You could stop being afraid. Speak your mind. Help the people you're too afraid to help here.

My whole life is in this town. I can't walk away from my life.

You would be with Bruce. The most remarkable man you've ever met wants you.

I can't.

Lust tugged and reason pulled back. Somewhere, in a mythical land where women were free, I would be given time served and released. I had done my duty—married and given birth to four healthy children. A hundred years ago, I'd be dead from infection or childbirth. This was my turn.

I never admitted to these dark thoughts, not even to Bruce.

4

On a hot afternoon in late June, I decided.

After the riots and killings over admitting James Meredith as the first black student at the University of Mississippi, he went on to finish college (accompanied by federal marshals) and graduate. In June 1966, he began an almost solitary march from Memphis to Jackson to support black voting rights. He called it The March Against Fear, but on the second day out, a white gunman fired three shotgun blasts from the roadside. Wounded, Meredith left the march to recover. Every faction of the civil rights movement came together to finish it for him, from Martin Luther King's non-violence to Stokely Carmichael's enough-of-this-shit, whitey. By the time they reached Jackson, Meredith had recovered enough to rejoin them. The march grew to fifteen thousand people, and along the way, four thousand blacks registered to vote.

The marchers were scheduled to arrive on Sunday afternoon, June 26. I wanted to be there. The area around the State Capitol was blocked off. Behind the barriers, a crowd of white people jeered, holding signs that read "No Commies Wanted" and "Go Home, Nigger."

I stood in the street, trying to figure out where to go. A policeman walked over, eyes hidden behind sunglasses.

"Are you with them?" He indicated the crowd behind the barriers.

I shook my head.

"Them?" The snaking line of marchers drew closer.

"No."

"Pick one or the other, lady. You can't stand here in the middle."

I was trapped in a state with no middle.

I drove home, thinking about what had happened, along with every atrocity I stood by and watched without acting. I was trapped in a city that let Medgar Evers bleed to death in his driveway, shot for going on Jackson television to speak against segregation. Trapped in a state that did not rage when three missing civil rights workers were dug out of a landfill, assassinated for the crime of coming here. Our leaders said they should have known better. They said the same thing about fourteen-year-old Emmett Till when his mutilated body was pulled out of the river. Murdered for speaking to a white woman. He should have stayed home in Chicago where he belonged. Trapped inside a family who called me a communist for wanting to integrate the schools.

My father was part of both our white hate groups: the Citizens Council, a gentlemanly Ku Klux Klan that tracked and punished any black person who got out of line, and the Sovereignty Commission, a huge spy operation keeping files on anyone, black or white, who spoke against separation of the races. At family dinners, Daddy sat at the head of the table, listening with amusement to my arguments for change. You will grow out of your naive idealism, he told me. You will come to see the world for what it is.

Trapped in marriage to a man who liked the world the way it was.

Trapped by a decision I made at nineteen.

Life waited out there, life with its unknown freedoms, and Bruce Rogow was willing to take me.

From a pay phone next to the post office, I telephoned. I told Bruce yes, I would go. He said we would leave the next Friday. I drove home and fried pork chops for supper.

5

I had to tell Fred. I was so scared I thought I might have a heart attack before I got the words out. We were in our bedroom on Monday morning, three children off to school, the youngest playing in his room.

"I need to go away for a little while."

Fred stopped making up his side of the bed.

"I'm worn out. I want some time to myself."

His blue eyes darkened with suspicion. "Go away where?"

It was hard looking at him. "I'm not sure."

"For how long?"

"I don't know."

"When were you thinking of doing this?"

"Friday?" My voice rose like I was asking for permission.

"Are you planning on coming back?"

"I'm not sure." I took a breath. "I may not be able to do this any more." I indicated the room and meant the marriage. "I have to get away for awhile and think."

His voice turned cold. "Know this. If you leave me, you're leaving all of us, and if you try to divorce me, I'll make sure you never see these children again."

Was that true? Could he keep me from seeing the children? I felt rattled by fear.

He turned to go. "Do what you want, but be aware of the consequences."

"Wait."

He stopped. I saw a flicker of hope in his eyes.

"I need some money."

He shook his head in disbelief. "You want me to pay you to leave?"

"You have all the money. I only need five hundred dollars."

"I'll bring you a check tonight." He went out the door, his face hardened into what looked like hatred.

I fell on the bed, hugging a pillow, quaking at what I had done. I had never been physically afraid of Fred, but I had never tried to leave him either. He acted as if I were stealing something he owned.

On Wednesday, I told Fred's parents, Pop and Sug, We stood in their den, a room Fred built and I helped decorate. I gave my excuses about being worn out and needing time away. Pop was almost deaf. Sug had to keep shouting what I said. I told them I was going alone. Nobody heard about Bruce. With every word, Sug's eyes grew more unfriendly. By the end, she'd become a stranger.

On Thursday, I told Mother. She threw a fit. I had everything a woman wanted. What was I thinking? When she saw she couldn't change my mind, she stamped her foot and wept. I was ruining her life in this town, destroying everything she'd worked for.

I waited until my father got home from the law office to tell him. I led him into the living room and stumbled out my story. He put his hands on my shoulders. "We love you, baby. Do what you have to do." I hugged him, dampening his shirt with my tears. He understood; he was the only one who understood. He had tried to leave Mother once and been dragged home by duty. I remember being fourteen and too happy to have him back to care what he wanted.

For those four days, I lived inside a shivering bubble of determination, trying to pretend nothing was wrong in front of the children and ignoring Fred's silent anger. I slept in my younger son's bedroom, listening to Fred sob through the wall. When he grew quiet, I held my breath, waiting for him to come and kill me. Open the small pocketknife he carried and jab, jab, jab until I was dead. No jury in Mississippi would convict him.

6

I didn't tell the children until Friday. I heard the back door slam when Fred left to check his construction jobs.

I waked Clay first. He was almost nine and could dress himself. He was also the slowest. The girls slept in twin beds built along a wall in their large room. Linden, four, woke up happy. This was the way she greeted every new day: another chance to go school, another chance to learn. Allison was crankier. They washed their faces and brushed their teeth. I dressed Linden while she talked about the coming day at pre-school.

"I could draw you a picture."

"That would be wonderful."

"Of a rabbit."

Would I ever see this picture? She leaned warm against me as I tried to comb the tangles out of her straight brown hair. She liked to play with her hair until it knotted.

Allison stared at herself in the mirror. "I hate wearing a uniform."

"I know you do, sweetie." The gray jumper and forest green jacket were boxy. At six, my number one daughter knew exactly how she wanted to look, and St. Andrew's gray and green weren't it.

"You could send me to a different school."

"St. Andrew's is the best." The Episcopalians didn't teach bigotry as part of the school curriculum. Would Fred allow them go there after I left? I thought of not being here to hug them in the mornings, to dress them and comb their hair, and felt hollow with grief.

I said, "You love your school."

Allison stared. "Why are you shaking?"

"I'm not." I took a breath. "Turn around and let me get the back."

"And I hate having bangs," she said.

"Look at yourself." I faced her toward the bathroom mirror and kissed the top of her blond head. "You're perfect."

Clay had managed to get himself into a white shirt, striped tie, gray pants, and green jacket. I re-tucked his shirt and brushed his dark hair "My big boy, dressing yourself."

"I'm almost nine."

"You are nine going on twenty."

He smiled with pride.

I grabbed Thomas out of his crib. At two, he still had his baby smell, warm from sleep, thick, blond curls soft under my cheek.

"Thomas, Thomas, Thomas." I spoke into his hair, making him giggle. "Don't let anyone call you Tom or Tommy, okay? You're Thomas, nothing but Thomas."

He laughed in delight and pulled out of my arms, running up the hall.

They gathered around the breakfast table. I got out bowls, poured cereal and milk and four glasses of orange juice.

I looked at them, happily eating, talking over each other the way they did every day, and had done since they were old enough to speak: two brown-haired, brown-eyed children; two blond, blue-eyed children; two boys, two girls. You would think we had planned it.

After today, I wouldn't be here: no waking, no warm hugs, no breakfast. I couldn't reconcile what I was doing. One part of me might leave with Bruce, but surely the mother would stay. I had been here, fixing breakfast and combing hair, every day of their lives, except for a week in Jamaica and one month in New York.

New York City had given me my first taste of escape. I went with my friend Kay to visit two friends who were studying there. We got a sublet in Greenwich Village and hardly slept. We went to plays, drama classes, and bars. I walked the crowded, noisy streets, watching black and white people mingle as if it were nothing, seeing women who appeared happy without men.

My throat hurt, looking at my children, imagining not being able to look at them.

"Are you crying, Mama?" Allison, ever observant.

I wiped my eyes on the tail of my shirt. "No, love. Finish up."

When they were ready, mouths wiped, Clay's shirt tucked in again, I gathered them at the back door. "Before your rides get here, I need to tell you something." I took a breath. "When you come home from school today, I won't be here. I'm going away for a little while." The words echoed, as if they came out of someone else's mouth. "But Marie will be here." Marie had been my nurse and was now my children's. "Daddy will be here, and Pop and Sug. Everything will be the same." I listened to the stranger mouthing these lies.

Allison stared as if I had lost my mind. "Where will you be if you're not here?"

"Away, darling."

"Mothers don't leave."

She was right. Mothers did not leave, and what kind of monster did that make me? I tried again. "It's just for a little while." I felt the way I did telling them the doctor's shot wouldn't hurt.

Clay said, "If you're not here, how will I talk to you?"

My defenses shredded. Clay loved to talk, and I loved listening. "I'll call, I'll write. I promise."

"Will you be back for my birthday?"

In my haste to get away and my fear at being stopped, I had forgotten he would turn nine on July 20. "I may not be, baby, but I'll make it up to you. I'll send you nine presents, one for each year."

"Me, too." Linden jumped up and down at the idea.

Her ride came. My younger daughter gave me a neck-squeezing hug and ran out the door.

Clay and Allison's carpool arrived. I hugged them. Allison looked at me with disbelief. Clay held on, tears in his eyes. I had broken his heart.

Only Thomas remained, clinging to my leg. Trying not to cry, I ruffled his hair.

Marie came in, put on her apron, and began washing the breakfast dishes. Thomas ran to her.

My suitcase was in the trunk of the car. Scraped raw, I dressed, hugged Thomas until he pulled away, and told Marie I was going out for a little while.

She knew, and her dark look let me see what she thought of me. If I were still a child, she'd grab me by an arm and tell me to stay in my room until I learned how to behave. I was an adult now, and she couldn't stop me.

I got in the car and stared at my hands on the wheel. Listened while my heart tried to pound through my ribs. I could change my mind. Go inside and claim to have a headache. Lie on the gold velvet bedspread until Fred got home for lunch. Apologize.

I backed down the driveway. This was a new car, a navy blue Pontiac convertible with red leather upholstery. Fred gave it to me for graduation. My plan was to drive it to the dealer and leave it behind.

Bruce thought this was silly. It was my car and in better shape than his old Triumph.

I had packed a few clothes and shipped my books. I didn't want to take anything else that belonged to Fred Craig.

7

I waited for Bruce on a corner of South State Street, sweating with fear. Someone would spot me and call my husband. I would be hauled home like a bad child.

This was Mississippi, where a wife did not leave her husband and children. Husbands left their wives, and we blamed the wife. She must have done something wrong, gotten fat and stopped caring. No one blamed the husband. We shook our heads over the shame of it and held tighter to our own.

Every person who knew me, and plenty who didn't, would have an opinion of what I was doing.

Left her husband and children, can you imagine?

Picked up and walked out.

I heard she left for graduate school.

Going back to college at her age. What for, I ask you?

What use does a thirty-year-old woman with four children have for another degree?

I was about to do a terrible thing, but somewhere under the fear, I suspected I might be saving my life. If I stayed, I would end up drowning my rage and resentment in alcohol the way my mother did. Leaving was better than staying here, powerless and afraid.

Bruce pulled up in the small blue convertible, smiling, delighted to find me on this corner. "I was afraid you wouldn't come."

"Here I am." I tried to match his joy.

The top was down. The sun gleamed on the big dog's gray coat. Bruce put my suitcase in back, and the person who used to be me got in front.

Anybody could see us in this car. "Could we put the top up?"

Top up, windows down, I let the wind blow my hair. Terrified and elated, I stared at the road south where my new life waited.

8

Growing up in Jackson, I used to try to kiss my elbow. If you succeeded, superstition held, you turned into a boy. Boys got to roam the neighborhood, while my sister and I were confined to a fenced yard. Boys could play in the creek where we were forbidden to go. Boys possessed the single quality I most longed for—freedom.

Mississippi was a man's world in the '40s and '50s. Married women couldn't buy or sell property, open a charge account without their husband's permission, or serve on a jury. Married women couldn't teach or sign a contract. White females ranked higher than black people, but we were kept in our place by rules and flattery, bestowed with allowances and borrowed honor. If you married an important man, you became the moon to his sun, glowing in reflected light. We weren't allowed to be president of the bank, but we could do the moon's work: lead the Junior League, run the Altar Guild.

Mother got to be the wife of Governor Ross Barnett's personal attorney, even after Daddy no longer wanted her. She planned a daily menu with Annie, our cook, and spent idle afternoons drinking over a bridge table. This was how the well-off wives of Jackson used their days. Growing up, I saw no way out. If I couldn't be a man, the next best thing was to marry one. Marriage got you out from under your mother and into place of your own, which sounded almost like freedom.

I met Fred Craig my sophomore year at Ole Miss. He was a college graduate, home from two years in Korea. He had a real job and was ready for marriage. I did what Southern women are taught to do from birth—chased him until he caught me. I was nineteen, a child, and I grew up in that marriage. By twenty-seven, I had given birth to four children without experiencing a single orgasm. Fred told me things would get better, but when they didn't, he told me I was frigid. If I were, I wouldn't care so much. Wouldn't lie there afterwards, frustrated and furious.

I went back to college, lost my religion, discovered liberal politics, and realized I was stuck: wedded for life to a conservative who didn't know how to make love.

Marriage did not set me free, nor did having children. With each lurch toward freedom, I trapped myself more. I tried cutting my way out of the briar patch with organization. Our house ran like a factory. I made Fred's breakfast every morning, the same breakfast: juice, cereal, egg over easy, bacon, toast, and coffee. I got the older children off to school and the younger one playing. In the afternoons, when all four were home, we had quiet time from two to four. Everyone went to his or her room to read or nap. On the two days I had help, I took college classes and volunteered. Supper was served promptly at six or Fred got a stomachache. By seven o'clock, the children were bathed. By eight they were read to, prayers said, and lights were out. By eight thirty, Fred was asleep under *Time* magazine, and I began studying at the dining room table.

I loved being back in college, but I had stretched it out as long as possible. In June, I would have to graduate, and I wanted more: I wanted to go to graduate school. I wanted to live in a place where women and black people could be people.

In Mississippi, Nigras (as we called them, though we spelled it Negroes) were fired, beaten, and murdered for stepping out of line. Fred instructed me to stay clear of the whole civil rights mess. If I did something silly like take to the streets, he would lose the rich clients whose houses he built. The cowardly me was terrified of making a scene that might get me arrested. I satisfied my queasy conscience by fuming over bigotry with my six liberal friends.

The 1960s were the first years of the birth control pill, and I no longer had to fear getting pregnant. On the side, discreetly, I searched for fulfillment. There must be a man out there who could show me the secret. I didn't dare ask my friends. Maybe other people talked about their sex lives. We did not. With four children in eight years, Fred and I must be going at it like rabbits, or that's what I hoped people thought. Into this stew of discontent stepped Bruce Rogow.

I was married for ten years – you'd think I'd have enough sense to know being with another man wasn't the same as being free, but I didn't. I had found a new man, liberal and unafraid, and this one would make all the difference.

On that hot July afternoon, headed south out of Jackson, I told myself to stop shaking and be glad. I was fleeing racism, sexism, violence, repression, and my family's backward politics. I was leaving a state I hated and headed to freedom with the man I adored. The tarnished side of that shiny coin were the children I had left behind.

I convinced myself running was the only way, but there is always a choice. I was thirty, and any noble reasons I gave myself for desertion were inextricably mixed with lust.

Until I could manage my children's rescue, they were in good hands. They had Fred who, whatever his other faults, was a terrific father. They adored their nurse, Marie. They had two sets of grandparents, a nice home, friends, and good schools. Once I freed myself, I would free them.

Looking back, I am astonished at how the itch for sexual fulfillment and a desire to escape can blind you to consequences.

DURING

9

Bruce had a week to report to his new job in Miami. My only requirement that first day was to get safely out of Mississippi.

We took the coast road over to Mobile, past houses shaded by verandas and enormous, wind-twisted oaks. The Triumph was crowded with suitcases, the two of us, and a large, gray Weimaraner. On a Southern highway filled with American cars, we stood out.

No one knew where I was going, but this did not ease my anxiety. I kept checking over my shoulder, past Yosserian's flapping ears, to see if we were being followed. When I told everyone goodbye, I said I was traveling alone. Not one soul who knew me would believe this. I could barely find my way to South Jackson.

Was that a Buick behind us? It could be Uncle Doug's car. Mother might have put him on my trail. I twisted to check. The round face over the steering wheel could be Uncle Doug. I scooted down in the seat.

Bruce said, "What are you doing?

The black car passed us, and I sat up. "Nothing."

I had never belonged to myself. At nineteen, in an enormous wedding, I was handed from my father to Fred. I was property, chattel, and part of me expected to be caught and sent home to the city where my family had lived for a hundred years. I was the daughter of Mr. and Mrs. Tom Watkins, the wife of Fred Craig, mother to Clay, Allison, Linden, and Thomas. In 1966 Mississippi, a thirty-year-old, married woman did not run off to find a new life with a Jewish civil rights lawyer. I was allowed days filled with tennis, bridge, and tasteful, noncontroversial volunteer work, but not this. Never this.

I checked my watch by the dashboard light. I should be in the kitchen on Audubon Park Lane, cleaning up after dinner. Before I left, I prepared frozen meals, wrote menus, and turned down pages in *The Joy of Cooking*, thinking if I left behind the things expected of a wife, they wouldn't notice my absence.

Bruce spotted a lighted roadside diner, and we stopped for coffee and pie. A man came in, a man in a suit with a fedora pulled low over his eyes. He sat at the counter and stared at me. A detective, I decided, ducking my head, a private eye Fred hired to follow me. I couldn't swallow.

"If you're not going to finish that pie, I'll eat it." Bruce was happy, thrilled to be on the road with the woman he loved.

I passed him my plate, keeping an eye on the man, who paid for his coffee as soon as the waitress put it down, ready to come after us when we left.

The bill was $3.85. Bruce left a quarter tip.

"Is that enough?"

He put down another dime. I let him go ahead and added two quarters, wondering if this was how life together would be, me hanging back in restaurants.

Hurrying out, I watched the man at the counter. He didn't get up and hadn't come out when we pulled onto the highway. Safely back on the road and hidden by darkness, I breathed easier. There was no one in front of us and no one behind. I relaxed enough to confess. "I keep thinking someone's following us."

"You could be right." Bruce had on his teasing voice. "We're breaking real laws."

My heart resumed its worried bumping. "Which ones?"

"Wouldn't be so bad for me. Fornication is only a misdemeanor, but you—" He shook his head in regret. "Adultery, I'm afraid, is a felony."

I slid back down in the seat, holding my knees. "Why didn't you tell me that before?"

"They hardly ever prosecute."

We were coming up behind a highway patrol car. "Slow down," I said.

"I'm going the speed limit."

"Don't get too close. What if he stopped us?"

Bruce shook his head in exasperation, but eased his foot off the gas and let the patrol car pull away.

Lying next to him in the small Alabama motel where we stopped the first night, I brought up my fears again. "What if there was a knock on the door?" I meant the detective, the man in the fedora.

"I wouldn't answer it."

That seemed so simple, I wondered why I hadn't thought of it. No one back home would dream of not going to the door, letting a phone ring unanswered, or asking a guest to leave, no matter how late the hour.

"Quit worrying," Bruce said. "You didn't tell anyone about us but that Episcopal priest, and priests are sworn to silence."

I had told the priest at my church the truth. I wanted one person to know, in case—I wasn't sure what I meant by in case—in case my body was found in a crushed blue Triumph convertible.

It was hard to make Bruce understand my fears. "The priest said if I left with you, I would suffer from guilt for the rest of my life."

"Plenty of men leave their wives. Nobody tells them they're going to suffer the rest of their lives."

"It felt like being cursed."

Bruce kissed the side of my face. "You're not cursed. We're here, and we're together."

"Then why do I feel I so miserable?"

"You need to look at the big picture."

"In the big picture, I'm nothing."

"Exactly."

"Is that supposed to make me feel better?"

"Men leave their children all the time."

I whispered my misery. "Women don't."

"Think of it this way—you're ahead of your time."

Which for some crazed reason relieved the pain. I was not evil—I was ahead of my time.

In the moments when we weren't laughing together or reading to one another or making love, my mind trotted like a bird dog back to the children. What were they doing? Were they all right? Did they miss me? Especially Thomas. I could see him, the curls on his blond head, the determined look he got, stomping around, knowing exactly where he wanted to go. He was only two and a half. What if something happened to him when I wasn't there? At a gas station the next morning, I went to a pay phone and called home.

Thomas's baby voice answered. "Hello."

My chest seized. Answering the phone was his newest achievement. I wanted to snatch him through the line, but I didn't make a sound.

"Hello, hello, hello." Sounding just like himself.

I hung up. He was all right. The pain was so terrible, I wondered if you could die from a broken heart.

10

On the second day, we reached Gainesville. Bruce had gone to law school at the University of Florida and wanted to show me around. He took me by the motel where he'd worked as a desk clerk. He said not to believe clerks when they said they didn't have a room. They always had a room. If a hotel claimed they didn't, you were supposed to say: What if the President showed up? When they admitted, yes, they would find a room for the President, you said, give me that room.

I listened, nodding, knowing I would never do such a thing. I loved Bruce's nerve. That might have been what I loved most about him, the way he ignored boundaries I had been brought up to consider impenetrable. This nerve made him a great civil rights advocate. When a Mississippi judge accused him of being a Yankee carpetbagger, Bruce put on a Southern accent and told the judge he'd had to travel north to get to Mississippi. To him, insults were mistakes made by otherwise well-meaning people. Barriers were opportunities.

We parked the car on the university campus and headed to the law school. I was flattered he wanted to bring me here. The place looked a lot like Ole Miss, where I'd spent two years smiling until my mouth hurt, trying to be a good Southern girl.

"This is the library." Bruce led me into a large room where young men sat at tables, heads bent over heavy books. One person spotted me and began stomping his feet. Another joined, and another, until there was a thunder of feet on the floor.

I stood frozen. Every man stared at me, and the faces were not friendly.

"What are they doing?"

Bruce whispered, "Women aren't allowed in here."

I pulled him out the door. Behind us, the thunder faded.

"Then why did you take me in?"

"I wanted you to see where I spent most of my time."

"But you knew."

He lifted his shoulders in a shrug, grinning. "I thought you would get a kick out it."

I walked ahead of him to the car, hot with embarrassment from being stomped out of that room. "I can't believe women aren't allowed in a Florida law school—it's 1966. My aunt is a lawyer. Don't you believe women should have the freedom to be whatever they want?"

"I just freed you, didn't I?"

Change of subject, unfair fighting, embarrassing someone you loved. I didn't know where to begin. "Saying you freed me is like hearing my mother brag how well she treats colored people because she buys our cook orthopedic shoes. Are you saying you're good to your female the way Mother is good to her Negro?"

"One battle at a time, okay? It's just a tradition."

I couldn't afford to have doubts; I had given up everything for this man, but I kept reliving the feeling in that room. Mississippi was bad, and Florida wasn't looking much better.

If only I'd known: two places we passed, wide spots in the road now, had been—under Spanish rule—small forts, where free blacks, Indians, and whites lived in peace together. With the Spanish gone, both places were destroyed. Those settlements represented what white Southerners feared most: a mingling of the races and people of color with property and weapons.

11

We made our way east to A1A and started south along the coast: Daytona Beach, New Smyrna, Titusville. We drove slowly, stopping to look at anything that caught our eye: stands selling carvings made from coconuts, beach shops with flapping displays of Hawaiian shirts. It was like a honeymoon for miscreants—him the lesser, me the felon.

We were in no hurry. We had five days to get to Miami. Around three each afternoon, we began searching for a place to spend the night. We liked one-story family motels with rooms facing the ocean, pastel paint peeling, and signs out front winking a red "Vacancy." We parked where the dog couldn't be seen from the office. I stayed in the car with the Weimaraner while Bruce asked if they took pets. Yossarian didn't look like a pet. He was enormous, and he looked like trouble, like dog piss on the carpets, chewed furniture, and howling in the night. In truth, he was a calm and placid animal, as long as Bruce was around.

In Titusville, we made love in a dim room on a nubby cotton bedspread, went for a swim, showered, and ate dinner at a nearby restaurant. When night fell, we walked the beach, listening to the waves rush up and away, the water phosphorescent in the darkness. Back in the room, we made love again and readied ourselves for sleep. Bruce curled behind me, one hand cupping down there. How different this was. I'd never had a man hold onto the warmth of lovemaking. Note the reticence: I cannot, even now, say the names of parts of the body. Growing up, it was "his thing" and "down there," neither of which we were supposed to touch.

I spent ten years with Fred without once feeling sexual pleasure. He was happy. He climbed on top, climaxed in seconds, collapsed to the side, thanked me, and fell asleep. At first, we tried talking about the trouble, but neither of us knew what to do. We were victims of ignorance and denial. Be patient, he told me.

Sex with Bruce was madly exciting. From watching Fred, I knew what an orgasm looked like and had become adept at faking them. With Bruce, the thrill was so enormous I didn't have to fake. This must be it.

The dog shifted at the bottom of the bed, and I moved my legs to give him room. I felt self conscious making love in front of Yossarian, but he was polite about our acrobatics, turning his head toward the wall, or scooting out of the way when we threatened to roll on top of him. He slept at the end of the bed, a heavy third body, fastening the covers on top of our legs. I'd never slept with a dog before.

Bruce stirred beside me. I said, "Why won't Yossarian be still?"

"He's just trying to get comfortable."

"What's he doing down there?"

"Circling the tall grass." Bruce's voice was warm in my ear. "It's an inherited memory. Dogs once roamed the plains at night. Before they slept, they circled the tall grass, flattening a resting place."

"On the end of the bed?"

"It's tall grass to Yossarian."

And tall grass to me, this new world, nothing but tall grass as far I could see. The dog began to lick his balls. I pulled a pillow over my ear to block the wet sloshing.

I wish I could claim I adored the dog as much as I did his owner. I acted as if I cared about Yosserian because I wanted Bruce to think me a perfect companion, but I didn't love the dog. He was large and clumsy; his nails scratched, and he smelled of—dog. He was always there, in the way of our perfect two-ness. I was pretty sure Yossarian felt the same about me.

I woke from dreams of home and looked at Bruce sleeping beside me, a dark, curly presence. The first time I saw him, I thought he was beautiful, but what I really loved was his foreignness. He looked and sounded nothing like a Southern man. With his hooded eyes and that beak of a nose, he seemed to fear no one, and he made fun of everything I grew up considering sacred. Even asleep, he looked confident, his nose a prow against the pillow.

His eyes opened. Disconcerting the way he moved from oblivion to awareness in an instant. He smiled. "You're beautiful in the morning."

I shook my head. No woman looked beautiful in the morning.

He stroked my arm. "You are much prettier without makeup. You don't need that stuff women wear in Mississippi to look good. I like you better the way you are now."

Makeup and going to the beauty parlor twice a week were two of the habits I'd left behind. Visible signs of freedom, masks I no longer needed to wear. "Mother would say I'm letting myself go," I told him. "She'd say it's too bad I stopped caring."

"Take my word for it. You look better now than you ever did in Jackson. Like the outfit you had on when I met you."

I remembered getting dressed that night, sliding the red silk over my hips, admiring my body, thinking no one would guess I had four children. Vain thoughts while I imagined the stranger I would meet at dinner. Dressing for his eyes, not my husband's.

I made a disappointed face. "I wore that dress for you."

Bruce lifted the hair from my forehead and kissed my eyes. "You had on some kind of girdle underneath."

"A panty girdle to hold my stockings up." I sounded defensive. "That's how we were raised. You wore a panty girdle to keep your skirt from cupping under your behind and getting butt sprung."

"Butt sprung?"

"That's when your skirt pooches out from sitting. We had to give our clothes to the help when that happened." I caught myself: what a bigoted thing to admit. "If you wear a girdle," I hurried on, "everything gets held in." The meaning of my words hit me. Women were expected to keep not only our behinds in check, but our lust and dreams, along with any desires to be more than a wife and mother.

Bruce ran his hands down my sides. "I like being able to feel your body when I touch you, not rubber underwear."

He wanted all the layers peeled away. For the first time in my life, I was invited to be myself. If I peeled away the layers, would there be anything at the core?

He turned me toward the mirror on the opposite wall. "See how much better you look?"

I saw a tanned face with dark eyes, white teeth, and straight hair falling to my shoulders. I didn't like looking at my reflection. Seeing my face reminded me of what I'd done, and I didn't want to start the day in misery. I turned and straddled Bruce, helping him inside. For ten years, my body had belonged to someone else, there to make children, to make Fred happy, to make dinner. Now it was mine, and I gave it willingly to Bruce Rogow. "Look how well we fit," I said.

He made a satisfied sound.

"Don't you wish we could stay like this and never have to separate? I could ride around holding onto you with my legs. You could have your suits made bigger."

"People would talk." His breath was hot against my hair.

"Let them." I fell back, head off the side of the bed. He rose above, moving me and the mattress, which sang in protest. The pressure felt wonderful. When he came, crying blindly above me, I felt an answering warmth.

"Did you come?" He pulled me up.

"Of course." Had I? Was that coming? I didn't know. "Can I ask you something?"

"Anything."

Anything. What a marvelous thing to hear. Fred spent the first ten minutes after every party going over the things I shouldn't have said. With Bruce, nothing was hidden, no knowledge withheld. "In Mississippi, my father said the civil rights lawyers weren't there to help people, but to sleep with Negro women. Which was it?"

Bruce gave me a goose in the ribs. "The sleeping, of course."

He was joking, but I suspected not entirely. He'd dated a lot of Negro women, and that fact alone made him almost an alien. From birth, we'd been taught that any social contact between the races was abhorrent. For all my progressive ideas, I had never been attracted to a black man. The taboo was too great. Yet, here I was, sleeping with a man who'd made love to Negro women, a man who'd put his body inside the forbidden race. I wanted to ask him if they were different. Were they better in bed? The question was too bigoted to speak.

Bruce and I showered together in the dim sandy-floored bathroom. At the end, he turned cold water on us. I screamed.

"You should do this every time you shower," he said. "It's good for the skin."

In my personal opinion, it turned a nice shower into torture, but part of my new life was adapting to different ways. "I was screaming with pleasure," I lied. I wanted badly to be the person he thought he'd saved.

We dressed and walked out with Yossarian into a sun so white and hot my eyes stung. The light washed away all color. Squinting, I saw a row of palm trees lining the beach, as insubstantial as a mirage. The water moved languidly along the shore, stainless steel against a pale sky. On the sand, people lay motionless, melting greasily into their towels, contours wavering in the heat. We ate breakfast, packed the car, and got back on the coast road south.

12

During those first days, I watched to see if Bruce's character and habits matched mine. In Jackson, our meetings had been in dark corners of restaurant parking lots or hidden away inside his rented house. This was the first time we'd been together in everyday life.

I glanced in the backseat for probably the hundredth time at the only household goods he'd brought along: a matching wastebasket and towel set. The basket was straw, woven from two brilliant and equally hideous shades of fuchsia. The towels matched, hot pink carved with maroon roses, towels I wouldn't willingly hang in a bathroom. I wondered if another woman chose them.

I was afraid to ask. Bruce was Jewish, my first Jewish boyfriend. Criticizing his stuff might indicate anti-Semitism so deep and horrible, I would be dropped off onto the side of A1A. Even to think such a thing was bigoted. Why did I associate ugly towels with being Jewish? In Jackson, Mississippi, my experience with Jews had been limited. There were ninety-nine Jewish families, or so we were told, and according to my mother, not one of them had a son who would marry me. To her it was simple: no sense wasting your time. Perfectly lovely people, she'd say. "I used to date one of the Perlinsky boys up in Canton, but it couldn't come to anything. We both knew that." She always made it sound as if the Jews wouldn't marry us, but I wondered if that was code for the reverse.

Farther south at dusk, the two of us swam in the warm Atlantic, hanging weightless in water as warm as my skin. I lay on my back, facing the sky. Floating with my ears underwater, no sound penetrated except a distant seashell roar. The sky was an upturned bowl of deep gray. If I faced away from the shore, I became a mote in an endless sea. In the big picture I was nothing, as Bruce pointed out, so why was I here? Seized by hope, I closed my eyes. I could blink away this dream and wake in my own bed. Walk along the dark hall and check on the sleeping children. When I kissed them, their eyes would open. "Mama," they'd whisper before sinking back into sleep. Tears slid into the ocean.

Bruce swam silently up beside me. He stood in the chest-deep water, holding me against him, letting me feel his cool length. I wrapped my legs around his waist, and he gave me a kiss, sweet and salty, pushing the sad thoughts out of my head. He slid his hands under my bathing suit and pulled it aside, making room. I lay in the water and let my upper body float. Bruce pushed the top of my suit up and kissed each breast. We floated quietly, fastened together, as the sky turned black above, and the stars winked on.

13

The priest was right about guilt. I didn't know how divorced men felt, but beneath each day, sadness flowed like an underground river. I was amputated from my past, operating blindly in this new world, where I seesawed between joy and despair. There was enormous happiness in spending time with Bruce: the fun of discovering someone as a grownup, with full-sized beds to sleep in and restaurants to try, endless talk about books, his life, my life, what we believed and despised, the things we might accomplish together. And then there were my children, farther away with each mile. I swung between delirious joy at being with Bruce and anguish over what I'd done.

Driving, Bruce noticed my despondency. "Thinking about the kids again?"

I nodded.

"Don't worry. They'll come and live with us."

He was an attorney; he must know about these things. I reminded myself of the good parts: I was in a blue convertible next to a man I loved and on my way to graduate school. This was my new life, and I wanted to believe Bruce: I would get the children; things would turn out; this was the best of all possible worlds. Right-thinking people like us would make it better.

Which didn't keep me from checking on reality. At the next roadside phone, I called my best friend, Patricia Derian. Like everyone else in Mississippi, I had lied to her, saying I was going away to rest and be alone. Standing at a pay phone on a sandy roadside, I told her the truth, where I was and who I was with, swearing her to secrecy.

There was a long silence. When she spoke, her voice was stern, the same voice she'd used when I complained of being too scared to help black people and she said I was old enough to have the courage of my convictions.

Patt said, "You may be walking the beaches under the moon with your new lover, but your son cries himself to sleep every night asking for his mother."

I stopped breathing; she meant Clay and the words pierced me. "Patt—please."

"You need to hear the truth."

I asked if he was okay, and she said he was not okay. He would be okay, of course, eventually, but he wasn't yet. They were bringing him to their house as much as possible to take his mind off things.

Her son, Craig, and Clay were best friends. I listened, ears ringing from the hurt. "Next time he comes over," I told her, "tell him how much I love him."

I had left in a kind of blind optimism. Bruce kept saying everything would work out, but he'd never met my children. They weren't real to him. When he said men left their children, he spoke as a bachelor.

Even in the eyes of people who admired me, like Patricia, I was a bad person, an uncaring mother, a cheating wife. How could a good person do a bad thing, and if I had ever been a good person, could I be one again? Could you earn your way back to goodness, not by returning, but by doing good in another place?

I couldn't bear the thought of Clay crying himself to sleep. Through tears, I spotted a bus stop across the road. I could take my suitcase out of the blue Triumph and go home. Walk over, wait for the next bus north, and get on it.

Walk away.

Bruce held the car door open. Yosserian jumped in the back. Bruce motioned for me. I couldn't go back, not yet. I had worked too hard to escape. Return meant spending my days like my mother and my nights with Fred. If I went home to Jackson, I would be treated the way white men treated everyone who threatened their dominance: a foot on the neck for Negroes, a not-so-heavy foot for women.

I got in the car, smiling, wiping my eyes. "Clay really misses me."

Bruce reached over and gave me a squeeze. "Of course he does. I miss you every time you're out of my sight, but you'll see, everything will be fine."

At Vero Beach, we rode the waves. The ocean was rougher here. I didn't know about this sport, and Bruce showed me. We swam far out and waited. If we caught the incoming wave right—flattening ourselves and lifting ahead of the crest—our bodies shot toward land, riding the wave's force until it dumped us on the shore, separated and battered by churning sand. In the dizzy ride, all sense of direction vanished. The world had no up or down. It was all gray water and helpless tumbling. Then came a thump, my body bounced along the sand, scraping knees, thighs, shoulders.

I was terrified. These rides, like giving birth, seemed to be taking a frightful chance. Each one was a dare thrown at fate. Instead of having a new baby or hitting the bumpy shore, I would be dead.

Down the beach, Bruce came up, gasping, laughing, searching for me. "Wasn't that great?"

14

We arrived in Miami at night in the rain. The pulse of traffic intensi-
fied. I had never seen rain like this, sheets of water slamming the windshield
and drumming the convertible's roof. Nothing visible except the taillights
of cars in front of us and headlights coming the other way. Bruce said in the
summer, thunderstorms like this rolled through south Florida almost every
day.

We pulled into a motel on Biscayne Boulevard and made a wet dash for
our room. It had a gritty floor and a sagging bed. The dog shook himself,
flinging water.

Bruce looked around and made a face. "Not much, but it's just for one
night."

We were short of cash. I had left Mississippi with seven hundred dollars.
Bruce paid most of the bills, and I chipped in. I had barely enough left to
cover summer school tuition at the University of Miami. I smiled my game-
girl smile. If I couldn't stand up to a little grit, what was I doing here?

We woke to sunshine, put the top down, and headed south for a town
called Homestead, where Bruce's new job waited. It was a long drive down
Dixie Highway. Bruce grinned when he told me the name, as if I should feel
a kinship.

I looked out my window at rows of ugly, flat-roofed shops. "In the old
days," I told him, "we'd get teary-eyed singing 'Dixie.' Everyone mourning
the lost South."

Bruce sang the first verse. I waited him out. He had a good voice.

"We sang that at football games instead of the national anthem. It's become the South's hymn of defiance—live segregated or die trying."

"Still a nice song," Bruce said.

"I went to an Ole Miss game once where Governor Ross Barnett spoke to the crowd." I imitated his gutteral drawl: "'I love our state. I love her people.' The crowd roared, and we knew which people he meant. James Meredith, trying to get in Ole Miss, wasn't one of them. Barnett said, 'Red birds mate with red birds, and blue birds mate with blue birds. God didn't mean them to mix, and he doesn't mean us to either.'"

Bruce smiled in delight. "I wish I'd been there."

"What would you have done?"

"Enjoyed the moment."

The ranting I despised tickled Bruce, and I might be remembering wrong. I wasn't sure Barnett said that thing about birds, but I didn't take it back. I had made Bruce laugh. I loved doing that. "Why is this called the Dixie Highway?" I said.

"I have no idea. Miami's nothing like the rest of the South."

I hoped he was right.

I quit talking, too busy staring out the window at what passed for scenery: a Shell station hugging a donut place next to a barbeque stand. A car dealership waving hundreds of tatty flags in the hot breeze; a gym shouting in red neon "Iron Men Built Here," next to a hair-replacement salon. Flowers for All Occasions adjacent to a Colonial-styled funeral home that promised "Complete Memorialization."

"I didn't think Miami would be this ugly."

Bruce nodded in agreement. "Not all of it is. Just this part."

I didn't say what I really thought: I left Mississippi for this? My fantasies about living in Florida were fading fast. I thought everybody down here got to live on the water. Compared with Mississippi's stingy scrap of coast, Florida was a long finger, an entire state gloved in beaches. I knew exactly what I wanted: a cottage on the sand with palm trees and white curtains blowing in the breeze. I wanted to wake and swim in blue-green water like I'd seen in Jamaica, with no stingrays or jellyfish. I hadn't seen the ocean since yesterday, and there was no smell of the sea here. Dixie Highway smelled like hot grease.

Farther south, past another strip of stores called Cutler Ridge, the shops thinned. A railroad track ran along the highway, and we passed huge sheds. The air thickened with the smell of something terrible, as if the whole world were rotting. I held my nose, but the stink found its way in.

"Rotten limes," Bruce said. "These are packinghouses for beans, tomatoes, and limes. The one we're passing now is a juice plant. After they squeeze the limes, they throw the hulls out back to rot."

I saw the peels, gray mountains of them steaming in the morning sun. The tomato sheds were worse: hills of discarded tomatoes decayed behind the buildings, turning from red to black, choking the air for half a mile.

I covered my mouth and nose and told myself this stink was not a metaphor. Being an English major didn't mean everything stood for something else.

Bruce laughed at me hunched in my seat. "We're in the Redland now, farming country. This is where I'll work. This is where we'll live."

He was to be in charge of a rural office for Legal Services, a lawyer for poor people in the farmlands. He couldn't wait to defend the rights of migrant workers with the same zeal he'd defended Negroes in Mississippi: arrests, sit-ins, federal suits, class actions, constitutional issues. For him, this was the meat and potatoes of the law, and he was ready to dig in.

In Homestead, someone from his office had found us a cheap furnished apartment in a new complex. I looked around the two small rooms. The walls were so thin, they vibrated if you bumped them.

"Okay?" Bruce said.

"Fine."

"I'll find us something better after I get settled."

"It's fine, really." Lying through my teeth. I unpacked. When I tried to open a reluctant drawer in the fiberboard dresser, the whole thing threatened to topple. It was like the Three Little Pigs, except I'd traded my house of brick for one of straw.

Bruce grimaced. "Must not seem like much to you."

I smiled, putting on the face of the adventurer I wanted to be, telling myself to buck up. Don't think about the solid house Fred Craig built, the brick floors and pumpkin carpet. When Allison's Wells, where I grew up, burned to the ground with everything in it, my aunt, Miss Hosford, said it was all stuff, and stuff didn't matter. Except for the children, everything I'd left behind was only stuff.

Before Bruce got a secretary, I was his assistant. I helped decorate the almost windowless office down in Florida City, painting the concrete block walls a cheerful yellow, unpacking the framed photographs of his Mississippi colleagues and clients. I typed his legal papers, making awkward mistakes while he stood behind me, urging speed.

We went grocery shopping together, and I found grits. Bruce claimed he didn't like grits, and I told him he had never tasted mine. None of the restaurants in South Florida served them, which I found strange, since we were about as far south as you could get. Eggs were served with fried potatoes and catsup. Bruce told me to forget geography; Miami had been settled by Northerners. This was fine with me. I'd lived with Southerners my entire life, and I looked forward to a change.

Over breakfast (with my excellent cheese grits), sitting at the wobbly table in our apartment, we argued the law. Which approach would get Bruce into federal court where the judges were more liberal? How might the case of a Negro family turned away by a white trailer park be expanded into a class-action suit? It was like solving a puzzle, and sometimes I found a way through the legal thicket.

Bruce looked at me with admiration after one of these talks. "You've got a very good legal mind."

I flushed with pleasure, and realized I was doing it again. With Fred Craig, I helped start a construction company, and now I was playing lawyer. I loved burrowing into a man's soul, where work, I discovered, not romance, resided. I remembered my father's secretary, who saw more of him than Mother did. Mother ran the boarding house where my father paused to eat, sleep, and change clothes. His real life took place downtown at the law office. Days and evenings spent with knotty legal mysteries; no bills to pay or children to listen to; no slurred-voice, drinking wife—just worshipful Mildred and her steno pad. No wonder he fell in love with her.

Graduate school would change everything. I would emerge on the other side as an independent woman with a master's degree and a career. Meanwhile, it was immensely satisfying, after having Daddy tell me I could never be a lawyer because I was a too-emotional female, to bask here with Bruce in the glory of my good legal mind.

After Bruce hired a secretary, there was nothing for me to do. I had two weeks before the summer term began, and I spent the empty days reading inside the air-conditioned apartment, sitting with a novel in the unmade bed, looking out a tiny window onto a baked courtyard, worried that fumes from the cheap carpet and pressed wood furniture were poisoning me. Yossarian didn't like the place either. He stayed in the living room, chewing on the legs of the rented chairs, leaving dark teeth marks in the painted wood.

One evening, Bruce brought home a white kitten he'd found on the street outside his office. "To keep you company." I bathed the dirty little thing and named her Honeysuckle. Yosserian was fine with the new arrival and less bored with a darting ball of white fur to keep an eye on. A cat did not fill the hole left by my children, but she did purr between our pillows at night and cuddled with me while I read. Life felt less empty.

During the daylight hours, it was too hot to walk outside, the sun so bright on the paved streets, I could hardly open my eyes. Which was just as well: late in the afternoon when we did walk, I saw that many of the stores along the main street were closed and boarded. Homestead looked like a dying town.

For entertainment, we went to the small movie theater at the south end of Krome Avenue. It ran old "B" movies dubbed into Spanish. Every night, for twenty-five cents, they played a different movie for the migrant farm workers. We sat in a darkened room filled with the smell of people who had worked all day in the fields. Whole families crowded in, from grandpa to the tiniest baby, talking and laughing in Spanish, chewing sunflower seeds and spitting the hulls on the floor. Being there, Bruce said, made him feel like one of the people. It made me wish I understood Spanish and weren't so squeamish about smells.

I spent a lot of hours staring at the book I was reading, wondering what in the hell I was doing in Homestead, Florida. In my head, I returned to Audubon Park Lane, to the children running down the hall, hollering, "Mama, Mama." I sat in my former bedroom, deep in a book, with my legs pulled up in the chair that looked out on the garden. I missed having Clay read to me while I fixed supper, excited by words, with four-year-old Linden staring at the page, pretending to read.

Clay was having his ninth birthday, and I wouldn't be there. Instead of a mother, he'd get the box I mailed, with a wrapped gift for each year. I took a breath to relieve the pain. I missed looking in on Allison asleep. When my number-one daughter finally quit running, she slept as if someone had flung her at the pillow. I wanted to be there when the four of them jumped in bed on Sunday mornings, and Fred read the funny papers aloud. What had I done?

Bruce came home for dinner, his hair windblown, tie loosened. My heart expanded with love for him and the good work he did in the world. His face got such an eager, open look when he found me there waiting. I put my unhappiness away and got up to cook. We made love every night.

On Friday evening, a week after we arrived, we drove north to Key Biscayne for dinner with an older lawyer. He was head of the board of Legal Services, the man who'd gotten Bruce his job. He arrived with a mistress instead of his wife. Bruce warned me this might happen, but it was a harsh reminder of what I had become: no longer a wife, but the kind of woman you didn't introduce to your wife.

We ate outside next to Biscayne Bay at tables in the sand. The man kept ordering Black Russians, a drink I'd never heard of, but which tasted like dessert.

"When we're done eating," he said, "let's all take off our clothes and jump in the water."

I was shocked. The blond stewardess hanging on his arm bobbed her head in agreement.

I used my most proper voice. "No, thank you. I don't know you well enough to get naked."

The man looked at Bruce and laughed in a nasty way. "You sure picked a bourgeois one."

Bruce chuckled, but I saw his disappointment. This was a person he wanted to impress, and I had let him down. I sat through the rest of the evening, throbbing with embarrassment, insulted to be thought the kind of person who would get naked in front of a stranger, but mortified to be called bourgeois.

Driving home, I said, "Did you think I would take off my clothes in front of that man?"

"That just Toby," Bruce said. "It was a compliment. He thought you were cute, and he wanted to get a look at your bod."

"Did you want me to get undressed?"

"I don't want you to do anything that makes you uncomfortable."

Which wasn't an answer. In Mississippi, Fred would have leapt to my defense and challenged a man who made that kind of rude suggestion. I had come down from my pedestal and left the place where men protected their women, so why did I feel hurt?

In my old life as a Mississippi housewife, I understood the rules. Here, I was traveling blind.

Bruce and me in Miami, 1969

15

The English Department accepted me as a graduate student for the summer. Bruce drove me to the University of Miami to register for courses in Old English and the early American novel.

In 1966, the University of Miami was a cluster of forgettable modern buildings in a landscape of skinny palms. That was fine with me. This was a world away from Confederate flag-waving Ole Miss, with its shaded walks and white-columned buildings. Different was good.

When classes began, I caught a Greyhound bus from Homestead to Coral Gables each morning and home again at night. I liked riding the bus, where I relaxed and read. I had seen almost as little integration in Miami as in Mississippi, but on the Greyhound, the races mixed freely and without comment.

One morning I glanced across the aisle and saw a small black child sitting with what looked like his grandmother. He gave me a gap-toothed grin, and I smiled back. The older woman patted the boy's leg. "Don't be bothering the lady." A child again, I sat with my nurse Marie on the wide rear seat of a segregated Mississippi bus, happy to go anywhere she took me. On the Greyhound, I stared at my open book, grateful for the changes, grinning, as if having black people up front with me was some kind of personal achievement.

I had no sense of direction, and this did not improve at the university. For the first ten days, I found my way from where the bus dropped me off, to my classrooms, and back to the bus. I wore a path between these points, too afraid of getting lost to venture off course.

In the novel class, I sat at a desk near the front, taking notes and trying to look like a model graduate student. I didn't know a soul, and, apparently, no one wanted to know me. Anonymity was a relief, but it got lonely. I reminded myself how I hated the forced friendliness of Mississippi: "How are yew?"

people demanded in the grocery store. "Don't you look cute?" Here, nobody asked who I was or who I used to be. I thought of my aunt Miss Hosford, who once ordered me to the head of a long line in New Orleans, saying, "Go and tell them who we are." In Miami, the answer was no one. My accomplishments, my daddy the prominent attorney, the four sets of wedding china—all erased. I was starting new.

My fellow students were white, a fact I didn't question. Most were fresh out of college, and no one looked thirty. One day, a woman named Isabel spoke to me. She was tall and pale, with a slight accent which turned out to be Irish. She had been a high school teacher and had come back for a master's degree. She was thirty-two—hurray. She told me she'd been educated by nuns and lived with a husband and three daughters. This did not sound like the kind of person who would approve of my choices. When she asked questions, and she asked a lot of them, I gave away only as much as felt safe.

Taking me in hand, Isabel showed me around campus, expanding my horizons to the library, cafeteria, and post office. In the cafeteria, I tried my first bagel. Bruce talked about buying bagels in Jackson, at what he called the Seg Deli. I had read about them in novels, but this was the first one I'd actually seen. I knew about the hole in the middle, but I was shocked by the weight. I bit, and the bagel resisted. I sat there chewing. Nothing in the books mentioned tough. I expected bagels to be easier on the teeth, like donuts. I expected Miami to be easier, too, but it was turning out to be more like a bagel.

At Isabel's urging, I tried cheesecake, another dish I'd only read about. I did not admit my disappointment. The gooey slab on my plate was nothing people at home would describe as cake. Every surprise I ran into, I attributed to ignorance. In Mississippi, most of my life experience, like a lot of the words I knew and couldn't pronounce, came from books. The food here in Miami was as foreign in my mouth as walking under the skinny palms.

My clothes looked wrong, too. They looked like Junior League meetings, not graduate school. I tried to imitate Isabel, wearing skirts with white blouses and shirtwaist dresses. My pastel linen sheaths with their matching jackets, outfits I'd worn to dinners in Mississippi, were shoved to the back of our small closet.

One day in the cafeteria, Isabel said, "Why do you live so far away?"

She knew I was from the South and that I rode the bus from Homestead, but that's all she knew. Maybe the toasted bagel gave me confidence, or maybe I was tired of keeping secrets. Isabel waited, watching me with what looked like friendly curiosity. I told her the truth: "I live in Homestead because I'm with a civil rights lawyer. He works south of there, in Florida City."

She raised her eyebrows. "I wondered who the other half of that 'we' was." She looked at my left hand. "Not married though?"

"I am married." Here it came, and getting the words out was harder than I expected. "My wedding ring is at home in the jewelry box, but my husband is back in Mississippi."

Isabel leaned forward, eyes eager. "Curiouser and curiouser."

"I left him."

"For the lawyer?"

"That's not the worst part."

She hitched her chair closer.

She would either be okay with what I was about to say, or my friendship with this schooled-by-nuns lady was over. Blond stewardesses on the arms of married men might be the only females willing to be around me. "I left my four children."

Her brows went up, her chin down. "Did you indeed?" She leaned over the table, our noses practically touching. "Tell me everything."

I felt shaken by the relief of being able to talk to a woman. "It's the worst thing I've ever done." I told her about the civil rights mess in Mississippi and being too scared to do anything and too angry to stay. How I couldn't find a useful purpose outside of motherhood and wanted more.

She nodded in a way that encouraged me to go on.

I told her about meeting Bruce and falling in love and how he offered to take me away. I did not tell her the no-orgasm part. Nobody, no matter how close we got, was going to hear that.

Isabel had questions. How old were the children? Was I in touch with them? She seemed more inquiring than disapproving, as if I were a new species to investigate. "Will you get a divorce?"

I winced at the word. As a child, watching my father leave and make his forced return, I swore never to divorce. "I don't know. I guess."

"And marry the lawyer?"

I spouted my new philosophy. "Neither of us believes in the institution of marriage."

Walking back to the library, she took my arm. "My theory is, each of us is dominated by one of the seven deadly sins. Yours is gluttony."

I liked to eat, but gluttony?

"You want it all—a husband, lover, education, children, freedom—that's gluttony."

It did sound pretty gluttonous. But what was wrong with wanting it all— love and good work and children? Men got to have those things.

"My sin is envy." Isabel pulled me closer. "I want to know everything about the people who interest me. I like to dig so deep I almost become the person."

We parted at the library doors. She said, "I can't wait to meet this super-man who stole you away."

I took the elevator up to my carrel—which was, so far, the best part of school. As a graduate student, I was allowed through a gate next to the library's main desk. I rode a small elevator to the stacks, where only librarians, professors, and people like me could roam. Among the towering shelves of books were small study spaces—the carrels—each with a desk, a chair, a lamp, and a window—private, silent, with access to all of the books. I was permitted to wander through the shelves, pluck off any book I liked, and take it to my desk without checking it out.

I sat in the carrel. The intensity of Isabel's curiosity had been almost frightening, but she was my first Miami friend. I was willing to tell her almost anything she wanted to know.

16

To earn a master's degree in English, the university required a year of Old English, our mother tongue, from the fifth through the twelfth centuries. Old English looked and sounded as much like modern English as Finnish. Doggedly that summer, I translated lines from Beowulf: "weox under wolc-num, weorðmyndum þah," became, almost as nonsensically, "wex (waxed) under welkin (clouds), [in] mind's-worth (honor) thrived." In novel class, I slogged my way with Natty Bumppo through James Fenimore Cooper's *Deerslayer*, and ten other early American novels, each so dull it's a wonder the form survived. I worked hard, determined to prove myself. This was the world I'd chosen. I had given up everything for graduate school, and I would not fail. Success would prove to my parents, and to everyone else back home, that leaving hadn't been a mistake. After wearing out "I'm tired" as a reason for going away, my excuse for staying away was school.

I left Mississippi with a little over seven hundred dollars. I was able to pay for summer school, but I had no graduate assistantship for the fall and no more funds. I decided to write my father and ask for enough money to cover tuition. Daddy hated talking about money and preferred giving only when not asked, but I couldn't think of another option. I used general delivery at the university post office as my return address: "Could you lend me enough from whatever inheritance I may one day receive to go to school this fall?"

His response arrived on a day when Bruce picked me up at school. I opened the envelope in the car. My father wrote in heavy black ink on his law firm's stationery:

I will lend no financial support to this venture. If you are unhappy in your marriage, you can move across the hall. You can move across town. I will not help you to move across the country.

I stuffed the letter back in the envelope and turned toward the window so Bruce wouldn't see the tears.

"What did he say?"

"He said no." Rejection felt like I'd swallowed something that wouldn't go down. My father was the man I loved first. Thrilled when he returned safely from the war, I thought we'd be pals forever. But the civil rights movement came between us in 1954, and we argued through every meal for the next twelve years. When I left Mississippi, he seemed to be the only person who understood; his sympathy must have ended at the city limits.

The letter made me feel disowned, but then I had been, in a way, since birth. More than anything else in the world, my father wanted a son to carry on the Watkins name. Instead, he got three daughters. He never forgave our mother for having a hysterectomy while he was away in the Navy. He told me that was the moment he stopped loving her. He probably wouldn't have sent a son the money either.

Bruce patted my knee. "Don't worry. We'll figure it out."

Silently, I made a vow: as long as I lived, no matter what happened, I would never ask my father for another cent.

I smiled at Bruce, and the lump in my throat dissolved. He had that effect on me, living as he did in a state of total sunlit confidence.

Mother wrote as soon as she got hold of my university post office address. "I almost sent your Uncle Doug to get you, to bring you back here where you belong, back to your senses and your family." She used large indignant swoops of blue ink, a few lines to the page.

Reading that letter, I realized I hadn't been paranoid: they were trying to haul me home. What did "almost" mean? Was Uncle Doug in the car, ready to drive south? I tried to picture my uncle, fat and puffing, his hair carefully combed to the side, dark suit buttoned across a stomach that barely fit under the steering wheel of his newest Buick. I saw him coming into the university cafeteria on his short legs, straight to the table where I sat with Isabel. Conversations would cease. "Naw-a-mah," he'd say, pronouncing my name the way people did in Mississippi, with three syllables, "I've come to take you home."

Odd to be burdened with this fear as a grown woman, but we were raised to be subservient and to surrender to male authority. That sense of being someone else's property might have been enough to make me meekly follow my uncle to his car.

Doug Latimer was a formal, careful man, the richest and most undemonstrative of my uncles. He probably refused, telling Mother if Fred Craig didn't choose to drag his wife home, he wasn't going to.

I applied for a fellowship for the fall semester. To get one, I needed recommendations, and I had a brilliant idea. At Millsaps, I'd taken two creative writing classes from Eudora Welty. The college started an honors program my senior year, and I was selected as one of the first five students. Eudora served on my committee. With her guidance, I submitted poems and stories to the college literary magazine. Seeing my words in print went straight to my head. I would be an English professor and a writer. Maybe I would become a writer first.

Eudora Welty and I became friends, the sort of friends where one person is well known and the other fears over-reaching, but I was pretty sure she liked me.

I don't have the letter I wrote her, but I remember the tone, filled with false bravado to cover the shame of what I'd done. I told her I had run away to go to graduate school and to escape Mississippi's bigotry. In an excess of self-regard, I sent along the novella I'd written for the honors class, asking if she would pass it along to her agent. Eudora's typed response, dated July 29, 1966, reached me a few days later.

Dear Norma,

Your letter took me by surprise and has saddened me—I hope you are working things out.

As to what you wanted, I don't really know anything first-hand I could tell the gentleman about either what you'd be teaching or the way you'd teach it. About what I am familiar with, your writing, I thought you were an A student in an undergraduate class at Millsaps, but I've no idea what interest your work would have to the higher levels in the academic world—or to the world in general, which is something else. Your stories, like everything you do, have a pleasing energy and vitality about them, and a dash that, in the writing, may be a style some day—I'm not sure it is now.

And you don't need me to tell you you have a good mind. As to whether or not you have that indescribable but essential spark, the imagination, feeling for human beings, the extra thing that sparks a person to make a serious writer with real stories to tell—I don't think I could predict, it's too important and I wouldn't dare. I do feel your work, while good and entertaining and not without ambition, is still not anything "new," and I don't detect the wild streak of true and undeniable originality, though this is not to say it isn't buried somewhere under the surface. If you weren't, as I thought asking me what I thought of your writing on the after-graduation level, forget what I've said—I only offer the opinion for what it's worth. I don't claim and never did claim, as my class knew, to tell anybody how to write their stories, or even whether to write their stories, and I don't tell you that now either.

I sent back your ms. to the General Delivery address (the most depressing item about the letter you sent). I read it such a while ago now that I'm clear only in my impression that it was interesting, ambitious, and worth doing, but that some of the approach is perhaps a bit self-indulgent. I'm guilty of the same thing sometimes, so I know what it means and whereof I speak. I know you wrestled hard and long with it, and your own satisfaction to have brought it into form at last must be worth a lot and should be.

This letter is probably unsatisfactory to you, but you see if you ask people to be a party to what you call running away, it puts them in spot if they like you. I do like you and wish you well.* Take care.

Sincerely,

Eudora

(She signed the letter in pencil, and added a line in ink across the bottom)

*I could only write you what I thought was true.

Daddy's letter made me cry, but Eudora's made me sick to my stomach. In my arrogance, I had forgotten how much family meant to her. She never married and cared for a brother until he died. She still lived in her parents' house and told us the only reason she taught at Millsaps was to earn the money to keep her mother in a better nursing home. My carefree talk of running away must have been horribly offensive.

She said I was not a writer; she saw no sign I would ever be a writer. I took her at her word. Eudora Welty was one of the most beloved authors in America. If she said I didn't have talent, I must not have it.

I owned a small blue suitcase, part of a set I'd been given for high school graduation. All of the letters I received that first year after leaving Mississippi, letters telling me I'd made a mistake or threatening to drag me back, I read as fast as I could on the day they arrived, stuffed them into the blue suitcase, and never looked at them again. Eudora's letter joined the rest.

I continued working to become a professor, but I did not attempt another creative word for a decade.

17

Uncle Doug might have refused to come after me, but Bruce and I didn't want to take chances. We kept ourselves as private and anonymous as possible. Bruce received his mail at the office; I got mine at school. At home we had no telephone. I called the children each week from a pay phone at the Florida Pharmacy in Homestead.

If Fred answered during these weekly calls, I kept my voice neutral. "I'm fine, how are you? Are the children there?" The sarcasm in his voice made me cringe.

I tried to sound cheerful and spoke to each of the children, in order, by age. I asked Clay what he had done in school and if his bad leg hurt. He had a weak spot on his left femur and had broken this leg more than once. I asked Allison who was combing her hair. I giggled with Linden about the guinea pig she cared for at pre-school, and commiserated with Thomas over his bumped toe, sending kisses over the phone to make it better. All of them wanted to know when I was coming back. Each week I repeated what I said the week before: "As soon as I can, baby. Mama's in school."

I hung up, the torture over for another week. I hated going through Fred to speak to my children, and talking to them made me burn with guilt over not being there. Fred now combed Allison's hair and took Clay to the doctor to check his bad leg. Fred heard the children's stories of school and comforted Thomas over his toe. In between the calls, I could tell myself how terrific it was to be a graduate student, living with a man who understood my ambition, free to speak my mind as a liberal. Once a week I was reminded of what else I was: a mother who had deserted her children. I couldn't have it all, and I was a bad person for trying. Hanging up the phone some weeks, I felt like strangling myself with the cord.

For emergencies, I gave the family a telephone number in the dean of arts and sciences' office at the university. I never let any of them know where I lived. "It's lovely," I wrote in letters home. "I rent a house south of Miami, and I catch the Greyhound bus to school each day. The weather is warm, but no warmer than Mississippi. A small hurricane blew through last week with wind as loud as a train. I wasn't afraid, but the lights went out for hours, and I had to use a candle to study." In the letters, it was always "I," and this "I" lived alone. "I don't know how long I'll be at this place," I wrote. "Better to write me at school." I'm not sure they believed me, but everyone pretended. Only Patricia Derian and the Episcopal priest knew the truth about Bruce, and I trusted them to keep quiet.

I made two As in summer school, and the university awarded me a fellowship for fall: full tuition plus a stipend of a hundred dollars a month. I had done it—I was officially a full-time graduate student. The extra hundred dollars felt magnificent after a summer of penury. Best of all, the money was mine. For the first time as an adult, I would earn my own money.

18

I had been away from Mississippi for more than two months, calling and writing the children. I needed to see their faces and hold them. In the break before fall classes began, I decided to fly to Jackson for a long weekend. I felt terrified returning to the scene of my crime. Bruce was my anchor. If I went too far, the chain connecting us might break, and I would never find my way back.

I rehearsed the triumphs I could present to the family: I was a full-time graduate student. I had won a fellowship and was supporting myself (as far as they knew). These were all things they would have been proud of in a son, if you skipped over the leaving four children and a spouse.

Fred met me at the airport with the children. Seeing him standing there, tall and serious, the children clustered around him, I winced at the pain I had caused this man.

"Mama." Clay threw himself against me, with Linden and Thomas close behind. Allison stood back until I bent to hug her.

I brought out presents.

Thomas held onto my dress, calling to everyone who passed: "S'mama, s'mama."

Seeing them made me cry. They had grown and wore clothes I didn't recognize and which didn't quite fit. I couldn't look at them enough. Clay and Allison told me about school and what they ate now and who their friends were. Linden chimed in, her four-year-old life no less busy.

Fred stood back, a slight smile on his face. "How have you been?"

I nodded without quite meeting his eyes. "I'm fine. You?"

"We're managing."

His "we" meant the family I was no longer a part of. Letting me feel the burden I'd left him to carry.

To the people around us, I must have appeared a normal mother, returning home after a trip, the children thrilled to see her, the father impassive. Fred and I had not touched.

We were at baggage claim. "I'll get that." Fred picked up my bag, the way he always had. A white woman shouldn't carry anything heavier than her purse; her insides might fall out.

In the station wagon, I sat up front and twisted around to see the four of them.

"Why did you leave us?" Allison said.

My heart took a painful plunge. "I explained, honey. I needed to get away for a little while, and I'm in school now, the way you are."

"But you'll never leave again, will you?" Clay watched me, eyes filled with hope.

Breathe, I told myself. Do not look at Fred. "I don't know, love. I may have to."

His face grew sad.

Riding north, I repeated what I'd written about Florida, going on about the palm trees and coconuts, the dolphins they could ride when they came for a visit. Fred didn't respond. He pulled up in front of my parents' house and got my bag out of the back.

I saw the shock on the children's faces when they realized I wasn't coming home with them.

"Why can't you stay at our house?" Linden said.

"Because your dad and I have decided to be apart for a while."

"But why?" said Clay.

Why indeed. I felt as squashed as if someone had sat on me. "Don't worry. You'll all come and spend a night with me." Feeling beaten, I watched their questioning faces peering out the window, growing smaller as Fred drove away.

Mother looked pale and puffy. She'd been drinking too much before I left, and I suspected she was still at it. She stared at my straight hair and makeup-free face and said exactly what I predicted. "You've let yourself go." She asked not one question about my new life.

Our cook, Annie Carter, lit up when she saw me. "Don't you look fine?" Shouting as if I were across the street. She held out her big arms without blame or judgment. "Come over here and give me some sugar." Nothing about her life had improved. She still lived in a cramped apartment in public housing. Mother paid her ninety dollars a week for sixty hours of work. Her weight made her knees hurt and her ankles swell. Her orthopedic shoes had holes cut out for her bunions. None of this was cause for complaint; she was simply happy to see me. I walked into her arms and let myself be pressed into her deep bosom, breathing in the smell of starch and snuff. I wanted to hold on and cry. She was the most welcoming person I saw during the entire trip.

Daddy came in from work looking much the same, handsome and distracted. He gave me a hug and a peck on the cheek. "We missed you around here." He didn't mention not sending money for tuition, and I acted as if I didn't remember asking for it.

Annie called us to dinner. There were only three of us at the table. My middle sister, Mary Elizabeth, was married with her own house, and my younger sister, Sydney, was off at college. I had a hard time swallowing Annie's excellent roast beef. I felt grief being back in their house—a woman without a husband or her own house to go home to—exiled from her children. These were subjects none of us mentioned. I pushed the food around on my plate, chatted about Miami, and bragged about my fellowship.

I asked if it would be okay for the children to come and spend the night. Daddy said of course it would be okay. Mother wanted to know how I thought they looked. She was fishing. I was supposed to say they looked deprived without me. I said they looked good. It might have been the most awkward meal I ever sat through at that table. I couldn't have felt more like an outsider.

When it was over, Daddy drove Annie home and, as was his habit, went back to the office. I shut myself in my old bedroom, longing for Bruce and Florida. At the table, I had been careful never to mention Bruce's name. I tried not to think about him, for fear word of his existence might fall out of my mouth. Closed in my teenage bedroom, I yearned for him. He would have said something funny at the dinner table. He would have made them laugh.

My room looked exactly the way it did when I left to get married: the hideous wallpaper I'd selected at fifteen—dark green with white dogwood blossoms. The same dresser where I once sat for hours trying to lift one eyebrow, convinced this achievement would render me irresistible. My parents' marriage bed, the two windows looking out on King's Highway, the screen on the left still dented from the nights I sneaked out.

In college, when I came home during the holidays, Mother put a vase of flowers on top of the toilet as a welcome. No flowers for this visit. I lay in bed staring in misery at the ceiling. I had gotten married to leave this room. I shouldn't be back.

In the kitchen, I heard my mother cracking an ice tray in the sink: time to drink.

On Saturday, I borrowed her car and drove to my old house. Fred met me at the door, as impassive as ever. The children came up the hall, screaming in glee. I walked through the front rooms, looking at the brick floor, the pumpkin-colored Formica and carpeting, the cherry dining set Fred and I had chosen—every detail familiar and strange, as if years, not months, had passed since I lived here. I let Clay and Allison lead me down the hall. Clay's room first to see his newest books. My childhood books were still in his bookcase: sets of fairytales and myths, a row of red Tarzans. I admired his new Hardy boy mysteries and let Thomas pull me into his room. Here was the bed where I slept the last week, and I remembered my fear. Thomas demonstrated his new pull toy, a duck that went quacking around the floor.

The girls urged me away. A right turn down a glass-walled passage into the room we added for them. Allison showed me her new dress. Linden demonstrated the living arrangements of the visiting guinea pig.

After the children showed off their toys, the new clothes, and artwork, Fred told them to run outside and play. Here it came, whatever it was. We were in our old bedroom. The gold velvet bedspread was still on the bed. Everywhere my eyes fell reminded me of what I'd done. We'd been making up that bed when I told him I wanted to leave.

He sat in one of the chairs we bought instead of an engagement ring. I stretched out on the rug where I had been looking at a book with Thomas. Fred stared at me, then dropped to his knees and put his arms around me. I kept very still.

After a few moments, he pulled away. "I repulse you, don't I?"

I shook my head no. I had been trained to please men. Unable to do that now, or to tell the truth, I stayed quiet and hoped this would be over soon.

"Yes, I do. You can't stand for me to touch you. You're down there in Miami with your new lover, and you don't care anything about us."

I held my breath, pulse pounding in my throat. How did he know? I hadn't told anyone about Bruce but Patt Derian and the priest. Everyone else thought I was off in graduate school alone. Patt would never go back on her word, and a priest was sworn to secrecy. I kept my expression neutral, trying to hide my fear.

"You thought I didn't know." Fred's voice was triumphant. "The bus station in Miami called when your books arrived, so I knew where you were headed before you got there. I started asking around. The Bestermans told me who else left town that day. You thought you were being so clever."

I did think I was clever, or at least I had five minutes ago. The Bestermans were Carmen and her husband, the couple who'd given the dinner where I met Bruce. All those weeks on the telephone, Fred had been pretending ignorance, waiting to spring this. I thought I was devious, but he'd known about Bruce the whole time. I lay motionless on the rug in my marital bedroom, hooked like a fish. Fred glowered above me. I didn't try to defend myself; there was nothing to say.

I still had a chance, if I wanted to take it. Five minutes ago, Fred had embraced me. If I begged, if I got on my knees, wrapped my arms around his legs, and pleaded for forgiveness, I was pretty sure he'd take me back. The town would buzz for a few weeks, then move on to the next scandal. I would be considered eccentric, perhaps unstable, certainly not president-of-the-Junior-League material, but I would be folded back into the community. Once I might have surrendered to the pressure of Fred's disapproval. Not now. He was absolutely right about one thing: I couldn't stand for him to touch me.

I stood, pretending to brush myself off. "I was a terrible wife. Can't we just let each other go in peace?"

"We were a family," Fred said. "You didn't just leave me, you left us all. If you don't want to be with me, as far as I'm concerned, you're no longer part of this family. You're nothing."

The words stabbed. I wanted to be part of the family, just not his wife. I couldn't let him see how much he'd hurt me. I said, "I have to go now."

"Fine." His face was sharp and hostile, his voice thick with disgust. Here was the famous Craig stubbornness: Craig as in the crags of Scotland, and just as stony. Everything in life was black or white. You were either with them or against them. I would grow accustomed to this Fred over the next decades.

I wept, but not until I was inside my mother's car, driving half-blind back to my parents' house to hide in my old bedroom. There was a difference between leaving and being rejected, along with the added stink of being caught in a lie. Only a fool would believe I left Jackson by myself. I, who couldn't find the car after a movie, had managed to find my way down the east coast, get a place to live, enroll in college, all without help, on seven hundred dollars? My husband was many things, but he was not a fool.

I took a detour by the home of the Episcopal priest, the man I had trusted with the truth. Sitting in his study, I told him about Fred's finding out, hoping he might say something forgiving. He looked me over with disapproval. "You're getting a lot of sun. You'd better watch that."

I took it metaphorically. I was sullied.

After three days, I hated Jackson. Everywhere I went, people stared, eyes questioning while their mouths made polite conversation. "Why, Norma, good to see you. We heard you'd gone off somewhere. Where was it again?"

Nobody in Mississippi went to Miami. In their eyes, it was a place filled with Yankees, Jews, and Cubans.

"Back with us now, are you?"

"School? You don't say." Smile of polite disbelief. "Well, say hello to your mama for me."

On my last day, desperate for a friendly voice, I called Bruce from the pay phone next to the post office. I reversed the charges, almost weeping with relief when he answered.

"I hate it here. I can't wait to come back."

"Not long now." Bruce sounded excited. "I found us a new place to live, a house in the country. You're going to love it."

Somebody wanted me. And not just anybody, I consoled myself: a brilliant, handsome, progressive man, who saw me as more than a housewife. I still depended on a man for my identity, but I failed to see that.

Fred did not offer to take me to the airport. He brought the children on Monday after school to say goodbye. We milled around in front of my parents' house while he stood silent.

Clay cried. "I don't want you to go."

"I know, baby." I ran my hand over his silky brown hair and hugged him tight, my smart, brown-eyed son.

Allison stood back, arms folded, looking at me with furious blue eyes.

"Will you come visit me in Florida?" Fred would never let them come now.

Clay nodded, wiping his eyes.

I wiped mine.

Linden's looked serious. "Do you have a cat?"

I squeezed her. "Honeysuckle, remember? She needs a little girl to play with." I traced her face with my hand.

"Then I'll come."

When I bent to hug Allison, she pulled away. "I love you, sweetie."

"No, you don't." She twisted out of my arms and took Fred's hand. Blond like her father, and on his side now.

I couldn't breathe for the pain of leaving them.

Thomas let himself be hugged, and he giggled when I tickled his ribs. I kissed the top of his thick curls, smelling him. He didn't understand I was going.

I cried and waved as the station wagon pulled off.

My sister Mary Elizabeth drove me to the airport. "I don't know how you can do this to these children; I honestly don't."

I kept silent. I didn't have an answer for my proper sister, who, between being the world's most perfect wife and mother, periodically went crazy. Manic depression, we whispered to each other, but never to her. She'd written one of those letters I kept in the blue suitcase, telling me how my actions were killing our mother. I could tell by the twist of her mouth she took my escape personally. I had let her down. Everyone was needed if we were to maintain "our way of life," and I had broken the contract.

On the flight back, I went over the trip. I arrived in Jackson a proud graduate student and departed a craven adulteress, at least in Fred's eyes. He'd given me a last chance, and I'd walked away. Jackson looked the same as when I lived there; it even smelled the same—of pine sap and melting tar—but it was no longer home. My children were growing up without me. Tears came; I went and sat in the lavatory until they stopped.

19

Bruce had found a tiny cottage north of Homestead, on forty acres of lime and avocado groves. We rented three damp-walled rooms, built for in-laws who had since died. In the bigger house next door, the landlord was an accountant, and his wife ran the grove.

The house was small, but we were surrounded by abundance. It was like living inside the song from *South Pacific*: mangos and bananas could be picked right off the trees. If we wanted limes, we walked behind the house and took as many as we needed. If we wanted avocado salad, we went to the side yard, where ripe fruit fell to the ground. Driving past harvested tomato fields, we stopped and filled a basket with vine-ripened discards.

Bruce believed in frugality. He worked to help poor people, and we should live in the same way, which meant he did not believe in acquisition. As a part of the movement, I shouldn't be attached to stuff either. The house came with beds; a breakfast table which would serve as my desk; and two white, armless, vinyl loveseats. We made bookcases from the traditional student materials—concrete blocks and boards.

Except for a stove and refrigerator, the kitchen was empty. One afternoon, shopping, I had to list the dishes I would cook in a square cast iron skillet I coveted. I named cornbread, spaghetti sauce, stir-fried vegetables, tuna casserole, and pineapple upside down cake. Bruce relented. I added a saucepan, a sharp knife, two plates, cups, forks and spoons to the cart. With each addition, his frown deepened. "We don't need two of everything."

"There are two of us," I said.

"We can drink from the same cup and share a plate. We can take turns eating with the same fork."

I was pretty acquiescent, but enough was enough. I'd left behind twelve place settings of Francis I sterling flatware; I was not sharing a fork. I could imagine what my aunt Miss Hosford would say about us eating off one plate. Bruce gave in, and agreed we probably also needed sheets. I said nothing about towels; I knew better. We would dry ourselves with the ugly fuchsia ones that had traveled south with us. Our household was complete.

The landlords kept their distance. The husband worked for a big accounting firm in downtown Miami. Occasionally, Bruce asked him to give me a ride as far as the university. I dreaded these long drives. The man seemed angry before his day began. I tried desperately to think of something break the silence. "Why is the water in those lakes so blue?" I pointed out the window to a hole dug to mine phosphate.

"Suspended solids," he said.

And that was it. I spent the next ten minutes trying to think of another conversation starter.

They had an ancient cat named Sarah. The family thought so much of Sarah, a granddaughter had been named for her. She was fifteen years old, an emaciated, half-blind Siamese with matted fur. On warm days, she sat sunning herself between the roots of one of the avocado trees between our houses.

One day, Yossarian wandered over, picked the cat up by the nape of her neck, and shook her like a sack of floured chicken parts. By the time he stopped, Sarah was dead. Bruce heard the landlord's wife screaming and ran over, but he was too late to do anything.

The wife had one of those complexions that refused to tan in the Florida sun. When she got excited, she turned blotchy. She yelled at Bruce, saying she knew something like this would happen; they should never have rented to us; we weren't even married. She told Bruce he'd better keep that dog at home. If she ever saw him at their place again, she'd shoot him.

I considered myself fortunate to have been at school. Bruce dug a shallow grave in the grove for Sarah, and by the time I got home on the bus, he tried to turn the whole thing into a joke. "It was a mercy killing," he said.

I was horrified and scared by the woman's talk about our not being married. I hadn't forgotten the business about my committing a felony. For the next few weeks, I crept around the yard, keeping as many avocado trees as possible between me and next door. When Yossarian was outside, he was fastened to a long chain in the front yard.

20

Driving from Mississippi to Miami, I discovered Bruce wasn't a Yankee. He'd been born in Connecticut, but his family moved to Miami Beach when he was twelve. His dad was dead, but his mother still lived there. He seemed in no hurry to travel the fifty miles from Homestead to the beach for a visit. I found this odd. If I were in Jackson for a day and didn't go see my parents, there would be hell to pay. Bruce put his mom off, telling her he was busy opening the new office, getting started in the job. I didn't push it. I was already enmeshed in strangeness and not eager to add a mother-in-law to the mix. Plus I was nervous about meeting her. I was still married to another man, and, worse, I wasn't Jewish.

When we finally drove over for the official visit, I put on a nice linen outfit with heels. I planned on using my Mississippi manners to win her over.

I had seen postcards of Miami Beach and expected white sand with girls running hand-in-hand out of the waves. Reality looked more drab: two- and three-story apartment hotels with peeling paint. I failed to see the candy-colored art deco marvel South Beach would one day become. Miami Beach looked like one enormous nursing home, with ancients sitting outside doorways in aluminum chairs or clicking by on walkers, everyone keeping warm while they waited to die.

Bruce's mother did not live in one of these places. She had a condominium in a high rise facing Biscayne Bay. I had never seen a high-rise apartment building outside of New York City. I thought it odd that in Florida, with plenty of room, anyone would choose to live in a stack of cubes.

The lobby had slippery marble floors and enormous vases filled with artificial flowers. The hall smelled of other people's food. Every door had a mezuzah, an object I was unfamiliar with. Bruce explained that each one contained a tiny scroll with words from the Torah. The whole place felt foreign in a bad way, and I suffered another one of my what-am-I-doing-here qualms.

The door opened, and there stood Jeanne Rogow. I was blinded, not by the glare off the water, but by the peroxided cotton candy of her hair. She had tied it back with a bright blue chiffon scarf. These scarves, I discovered, were her trademark; she owned one in every color. She must have been in her mid-fifties, thin, with skin as brown and creased as a walnut. She greeted us in a short, sleeveless dress, white to show off her bronzed arms and legs. She wore a paste of dark foundation, rouge, blue eye shadow, and black mascara. Her crimson lipstick crept into tributaries around her mouth. She was not my idea of a mother.

With a shriek of joy, she grabbed her only son and turned a brief blue gaze on me. All conversation was directed to Bruce. "Why did you wait so long to come? You only care about poor people."

I was accustomed to getting by on charm, but smile and twinkle as I might, nothing I did charmed Jeanne Rogow. I was a *shiksa*, the *goy* who'd stolen her only son. He was a Jewish prince, and I did not deserve him. She looked me up and down with no sign of approval and told me not to put my purse on the furniture. She didn't, and I shouldn't. She said the floor would be fine.

We toured the apartment. I complimented her white and gold furniture, the matching carpet and draperies, and the view of Biscayne Bay out the window. I made agreeable noises over copies of European landscapes in gilded plaster frames. The couch and chairs were covered in plastic, the lampshades in cellophane. There was a plastic runner over the carpet in front of the couch and another down the hall.

At one point, she gave Bruce a poke and winked at me. "Nice body, huh?"

Were we talking about his nice naked body? Mothers where I came from pretended never to have seen their adult sons without clothing.

We sat down to dinner. The food seemed almost intentionally strange. Looking back, though, we were served this same menu each time we visited. It was Jeanne Rogow's celebratory meal. She did not cook; everything came from a store called Epicure. There was gray, jellied fish from a jar. I mashed my portion with a fork, pushed it around the plate, and tried to disguise the taste with beet horseradish.

She eyed the uneaten remains. "What's the matter? You don't like gefilte fish?"

Next came matzo ball soup. She watched as I chased a large, corn-bread-like lump around the liquid, trying to cut off a piece.

The brisket had been warming in the oven all afternoon, along with the potatoes.

While we ate, she told us stories from her day. The bus driver had been rude, but she put him in his place. A man got fresh with her in the shop, but she told him where to go with that mouth. In the hotel restaurant, the waitress made a smart remark about her taking the basket of rolls. Who paid for that bread, she wanted to know? I heard about an older man she was supposed to marry, a man with real money. He'd given her this apartment, but he wanted a pre-nuptial agreement, an insult to a decent woman. He'd turned out to be another person trying to cheat her, so the marriage was off. Life, like her day, had been filled with disappointments. I was but the latest.

She looked at my plate. "She doesn't eat."

"Everything is delicious." I tried to make it true with my widest smile.

Dessert arrived in an aluminum tin, a sweet noodle pudding called kugel. I liked this one, especially the crusty edges.

We helped clean up, and I got a look inside Jeanne Rogow's refrigerator. She was the one who didn't eat. There was cottage cheese, a can of peaches, and a bag of hard rolls, probably the ones she'd taken from the restaurant.

The rolls were part of a pattern. The butter at dinner came in individual, foil-wrapped squares. The sugar bowl was filled with single-serve packets. There was a plate of tiny creamers. The towels in the bathroom had hotel names. Everything from the toilet paper to the paper napkins had been pilfered.

Looking at her through the eyes of my aunt, Miss Hosford, Jeanne Rogow was no lady. She was loud and brassy, and back home they would have called her common. But those were words from my old life. She was a transplanted Yankee, Jewish, a single woman making do in a way no soft-spoken Southern woman of my acquaintance needed to. She supported herself by working in the handbag shop at the Fontainebleau Hotel. She called herself a widow, but as Bruce reminded her, she had been divorced when his father died.

"Always with the legal stuff," she said.

The bright chiffon scarves holding back the dyed hair or knotted around her sinewy neck were defiant flags flown in the face of a harsh reality.

I saw Bruce in a different light after meeting his mother. His unquenchable optimism must have come from overriding her mistrust. Unlike many of the civil rights lawyers arriving in Mississippi, he had not gone to Harvard or Yale. He might have been born in Connecticut, but he was raised in a small apartment on Miami Beach and graduated, not from Deerfield or Groton, but from Beach High. He had climbed above his circumstances and lifted himself in that same way above all of life's difficulties. He had the sunny, confident disposition of an only child who's been told since birth that he was perfect.

Having Jeanne Rogow for a mother made Bruce more sympathetic. I saw her as his burden, and I liked the way he carried it, lightly and with humor. She was his mother, and he loved her, but on the way home he laughed at the plastic-covered furniture, which, according to him, we could sell for new when she died.

My charm offensive failed. Jeanne Rogow gave me a new name. I was "that woman from Mississippi."

21

We didn't laugh about Auntie Helen and Uncle Louie. Louie Rogow was Bruce's rich and childless uncle from Connecticut, his late father's brother. He owned a company that made ball bearings for military jets, and his generosity made it possible for Bruce to go to college; Uncle Louie bought him his first car and helped with law school. One day, if Bruce continued in his uncle's good graces, there might be real money. And, if he didn't, the money would all go to Israel.

In town for a week, Louie and his wife wanted to come down, probably to take a look at the new *shiksa*. An impression must be made. This visit was not as scary for me as meeting Bruce's mother, because Auntie Helen was not Jewish either. We invited them for Sunday brunch, an important enough occasion to justify the purchase of more plates, forks, and knives. I made salade nicoise and Annie Carter's cheese straws. We bought a decent bottle of white wine.

After it happened, we wondered if Auntie Helen might have been drinking before they arrived. Yossarian hated the smell of alcohol on a stranger. Whatever it was, as Auntie Helen came up the front walk, without a sound, Yossarian lunged. Only the length of his chain prevented him from sinking his teeth in Auntie Helen's generous, white neck. She screamed and stumbled on the concrete walk in her little high heels.

"You ought to watch that dog," Uncle Louie said.

He helped Auntie Helen regain her balance. Bruce sat her down in the living room and went to chain Yossarian to a tree at the back of the house, safely out of reach of Helen's neck. I poured her a generous glass of wine and watched her face regain its natural pink. I said, "He's usually such a good dog."

We ate our salad and cheese straws. Uncle Louie complimented my cooking. Unlike Jeanne Rogow, he seemed to like me, and with three glasses of wine, Auntie Helen grew warm and talkative. Bruce seemed subdued around his uncle.

When they left, I mentioned his mood. He told me Uncle Louie's generosity always came with conditions.

That was it for Yossarian. Not right away. Bruce loved the dog that had been his protector during scary times in Mississippi, but he couldn't afford to throw away his best chance. When Uncle Louie announced a second visit, an ad went in the *Homestead News Leader*. "Trained watch dog, $50." The man who took Yossarian away looked like a thug, but Bruce didn't want to talk about it.

A lesson here for me: if you didn't mind your keeper, you could be gotten rid of. Without Bruce, would I be any more able to take care of myself than his mother, with her bright scarves and stolen sugar packets?

22

One way my present life differed radically from the old one was our nightly romp in bed. Fred had been a hasty lover. I didn't learn about premature ejaculation until years later, but I realize now his problem had a name, and we might have been able to do something about the terrible sex, if anybody, including doctors, had been willing to talk about such problems.

Bruce Rogow was the opposite. He enjoyed all of love-making, including the parts that came before penetration. He took his time. We savored each other. As far as I was concerned, he was a terrific and satisfying partner. I got enormously excited during sex, and lay afterwards feeling warm and happy. If anyone had asked, I would have claimed complete gratification.

The tiny bedroom of our cottage came with twin beds. We pushed them together, put the mattresses crossways on the metal frames, and bound the whole arrangement with a black fitted sheet. This gave us what appeared to be a king-size bed. Whenever we made love, the bed squealed along the terrazzo floor, working its way toward the door and threatening to become twin beds again.

One night we were at it, with Bruce moving and me feeling the usual nice way, when he turned us over and put me on top. He had never done this. I began to rock against him, back and forth, like riding a horse, only better. An entirely new feeling arose. At first it was merely a tickle of pleasure, but the feeling grew, carrying me somewhere I'd never been. Rocking away, I realized with a flash of surprise, I was totally out of control. As long as I moved like this against Bruce, desire ruled, and reason vanished. Where I was headed might be death; I didn't care. I rode pleasure to a place where our bodies were no longer separate; there was no bed under us and no color except black. From a long way off, someone screamed.

Gradually, I settled from that black place to a gray one, where my body, when I possessed a body once more, throbbed with what felt like aftershocks. I found myself in Bruce's arms, on our scattered bed, head resting on his chest.

He watched me, wide-eyed and frightened.

"That was it." I was laughing and crying. "That was an orgasm. I had an orgasm."

"You yelled so loud, I thought you were dying."

"I thought I was dying. I was dying. I have never felt anything like that in my entire life." I fell on my back beside him. "And never experienced anything as wonderful. I can't believe it."

"You never had an orgasm?"

"Now that I've had one, I can say absolutely, positively, I have never had an orgasm before in my entire life." I turned to face him. "You gave it to me. You are a wonderful man. I adore you." I kissed him all over his face. He looked pleased but nervous. In my excess of pleasure I had become a creature who frightened him.

"Didn't you ever masturbate?" he said.

"Women don't masturbate."

"Sure they do."

I sat up. "How?"

"The same way men do. By massaging that little place right there." He touched a spot so sensitive it made me jump.

"That can't be right."

"Of course women do. You never did it, not even accidentally?"

"We weren't allowed to touch ourselves down there. It never occurred to me." I shook my head in disgust. "I'm thirty years old. I feel like a complete idiot."

"It's not too late to learn. I'd love to watch."

"Are you kidding? I could never do that in front of you."

He turned sleepily toward his side of the bed. "Let me know if you change your mind."

"Sure." I couldn't imagine being that unself-conscious.

I lay awake in the dark, amazed at my orgasm. All those years I spent looking and waiting, reading dirty novels trying to figure out the secret of how it was done, watching men howl above me. I could see they were going off to a place I never managed to find. They had been, and it was truly, amazingly wonderful.

Considering Bruce's new information, I stayed quiet beside him and listened. Gradually he grew still, his breathing smoothed into sleep, and I slipped out of bed. Could what he said be true? Women masturbated like men? I remembered seeing a movie once in New York, an Ingmar Bergman film, where a woman stood in front of a mirror and did something with her hand below the camera's eye, while the face in the mirror went slack with passion. I hadn't understood and, not understanding, hadn't thought to ask what she might be doing.

I squatted on the cold tile of the bathroom floor feeling unutterably nasty. Gingerly, I touched myself there. It felt nice, startlingly nice. I licked my finger and did it again. Even better. I made small circles with my finger around the spot Bruce showed me, a tiny penis of my own. The pleasurable ache began, and, like ripples in a pond, spread in tingling waves out, up, and over me. I moved faster letting the feeling mount. This was fantastic. I couldn't get over it. All those years of frustration, and orgasms had been waiting at my fingertips. I stopped thinking and rode the feeling, letting it build to that place where it threw me over into the void. I rocked with my second-ever orgasm, trying not to make noise, holding onto the towel bar to keep from falling.

The pleasure subsided to shivers, and I squatted there in the dark, smiling and considering my discovery. If I could do this to myself whenever I wanted, I was free. I never had to love a bad man again or make love to anyone I didn't like. I was in control. I shook my head over my stupidity. Everyone else in the world probably knew this.

Women in the South were so repressed and so withholding. We battled to find the best man, stealing him from another woman if we had to, and we held on whatever his failings. Salvation through men: God the father, God the son, and God the holy husband. Salvation never came through other women.

I held my breath, listening to see if my muffled moans had awakened Bruce. The bedroom was silent. Sitting on the closed toilet seat, my head in my hands, I remembered those quiet sexual battles, quiet because women never admitted a war was being fought or that real casualties were being produced. The point was to win. The solace of being born female was to get a good man, rule him by guile, and be provided for. Our entire upbringing aimed us toward this parasitic, undercover work.

"Wouldn't you hate to be a man?" We used to say to each other at our bridge luncheons in Mississippi, looking around to see who might be getting fat, slipping from perfection, taking herself out of the race to be eternally young and darling.

"Can you imagine having to get up and go to work every morning whether you felt like it or not?"

"I couldn't stand the responsibility of supporting a family."

"Or going to war and getting shot at."

"I could never do it."

"Me neither. No wonder they die early."

We laughed with relief, never seeing the bars of our cells.

I recently read a book by a woman who advocated the abolishment of sexual intercourse. That sounded like an extreme solution, but if I could get back the decade I spent hunting for the right man and the second decade spent trying to find an orgasm, I would gain years to write and study. I could be published by now, or at least a professor.

Sexual satisfaction was better than giving up sex. Sexual satisfaction, I decided on that toilet seat, made me a more fully realized human. Women deserved bliss as much as equal pay, and not getting it was part of our repression. Bruce had handed me an incredible gift, one that might free me—even from the giver.

23

Love was good; school was good; but I missed my children. I was eager to hear their voices each week and terrified I would get Fred on the phone instead. When I called home, I stood at the pay phone in the Homestead pharmacy praying he wouldn't answer. By now I knew this phone booth like a prisoner knows his cell: the folding door that never quite shut out the drugstore chatter, the rounded seat I couldn't get comfortable on, the names and numbers scratched into the cream-colored paint. Did James still love Clara; did Juan heart Ana?

My relationship with Fred deteriorated after the first visit to Jackson. Before, he occasionally sounded friendly, the way I imagined formerly married people were. We'd discuss how the children were doing, and he'd ask how I was. During these calls, when he handed over the phone, my conversation with the children felt easier. Since the trip to Jackson, he didn't pretend.

On a Monday night in September, prayer didn't work, and Fred answered. "You are a selfish and evil woman." His voice was low and spiteful. "You are nothing but a whore, and you don't deserve to be these children's mother. You will never get them anywhere near that man."

I shifted from foot to foot to ease the cringing until he put Clay on. Had the children heard the names he called me?

Bruce drove me to the drugstore to make these calls. I waited until I hung up to cry. "Can he keep me from seeing the children? He says they will never come to Florida."

Bruce said, "Of course he can't."

"What about the adultery thing?"

"Judges are reluctant to separate a mother and her children. Don't take anything he says to heart. Anger is just his hurt coming out. He still loves you."

"It didn't sound like love." I felt bruised by the ugly words.

The next week Fred answered again, and I stiffened, waiting for the verbal blows.

"Norma?" In a happy-to-hear-you voice. "How are you doing?"

"Fine, I guess." Shocked, I sat.

"How's school going?"

I breathed in gratitude. The man who once liked me was back. Something must have happened. I was so relieved I didn't stop to ask myself what. Emboldened, I said, "We have to stay friends."

"Of course," he said.

"We have children together."

"We'll always have the children."

There was a pause.

Fred said, "I thought you might like to talk to someone."

"What do you mean?"

"You know, someone objective."

"You mean like a psychiatrist?"

"Something like that."

He wanted to help me. I could hardly believe it. "I have been feeling sad, but I can't afford a psychiatrist."

"A friend here recommended a guy. If you want to go, I'll pay."

"Why would you do that?"

"I'm just trying to help. I can tell you're upset."

"You'd be upset, too, if your husband said you were evil."

"I lose my temper."

"Would you really pay for it?"

"Your health is important to me; you're important to me, no matter what I say when I'm angry."

I felt myself melting under his kindness. This was the Fred I loved and married. We could be friends even if we weren't together. "That would be great."

Fred gave me a name and phone number. I hung up thinking he didn't hate me after all. He'd worked through his anger, and the relief of not having to face his wrath every week was enormous. I wanted to shout the good news.

There was hope for the future, not for our future together, but as civilized people and the parents of four children.

Bruce was not so sanguine. He didn't trust this sudden change of heart, but I wrote his words off as jealousy and felt pleased about that.

The doctor's office was within walking distance of the university. He was a short man with a deep monkey-like space between the bottom of his nose and his upper lip. I didn't often get a chance to look at him. He told me he was a Freudian and indicated the couch. There was a pillow at one end with a clinical-looking white towel on it. I lay down. On my first visit, I was tongue-tied, trying to tell my story to the green wall in front of me with not a peep of response from the chair behind. Into one long silence, I said, "Is this what you want to hear?"

He made a neutral sound.

I talked about Fred and our marriage. I talked about civil rights and how bad things were in Mississippi. I described Bruce and what he offered that no man in Mississippi could. I talked about my guilt over leaving the children and about my parents' unhappy marriage. I told several of my set pieces, my funny family stories. There was never so much as a snicker behind me, which made me realize, listening to myself, the stories weren't funny: they were terribly sad, and I made them humorous to hide the hurt.

After each visit, he said, "We will continue next week."

The silence felt critical. I kept twisting around to see his expression. He was always staring at his notebook, lips tight under that simian philtrum.

"How am I going to get better if you never say anything?"

"Trust the process," he said.

After two months, he suggested I go to Jackson Memorial Hospital and take a battery of tests. Fred had agreed to pay for them.

"Tests for what?"

"Routine personality tests."

I loved tests. I had been acing tests since the fourth grade. Why wouldn't I want to discover more about myself?

The testing took hours, pages of multiple-choice questions, the same things asked over and over in slightly different ways. My mind wandered away from the sheets I was bubbling. I needed to finish my paper on Marvell's

"To His Coy Mistress" by next week, and no matter how hard I struggled with it, Dr. Emery would hand it back to be rewritten.

My mind was the operative factor here. It never occurred to me this testing might be about my sanity. I was sad, yes, and I certainly felt guilty, but I never considered myself anything but sane. Did I really prefer reading to a party, the way I said those other four times? If I didn't concentrate, I would lose focus and answer wrong, if there were wrong answers.

I left feeling pretty good. I'd taken a test like this at the advertising agency where I worked as a secretary when Fred and I first married. They called in consultants, and we were given personality tests. I thought I'd make a fabulous score, they would realize the talent wasted behind an electric typewriter, and I'd be promoted. The results came back, were not shared with the staff, and nothing changed. Secretaries stayed secretaries, and bosses stayed bosses. Mine told me I was the most impulsive person the company had ever tested. By leaving home, I guess I proved their point. At the time, I was so dumb I thought it was a compliment.

When I returned to the doctor's office the next week, I asked about my results.

"Routine," he said.

He told me our sessions were ending. "Your husband has decided to stop financing your treatment."

"But I'm not finished." I didn't know what finished meant, but I expected to feel better about myself, which I didn't.

He shrugged. It was out of his hands.

I telephoned Fred.

"I didn't see the sense in paying for more treatment if you weren't coming home. You're not, are you?"

I took a breath, trapped by the black and white question, and gave my gray answer. "Not right now."

I discovered the truth years later when the same thing happened to my friend Marilyn. Paying for therapy wasn't a kindness on Fred's part; it was a ploy. When planning a divorce, husbands offered their wives psychiatric treatment. The therapist suggested testing, which sounded innocent enough, but was done to prove the wife unstable. In those days, with a sympathetic judge, a bad test result made it easier to permanently take away a woman's children or have her institutionalized. Realizing this decades later made me see how much cleverer Fred was than I imagined.

24

In November 1966, Fred reached me at the desk where I earned my fellowship by working as a counselor for the department of arts and sciences.

"I'm filing for divorce," he said.

When I was able to speak, I said, "Already?"

"I don't see any reason to postpone it, do you?"

I admitted that I didn't, except it sounded so final.

"You should get a lawyer."

I sat there in shock. Divorce was not supposed to happen to me. That's how crooked my thinking went—this was happening to me, as if I were not the cause. I wanted to find someone else to blame.

I telephoned my father. Could the law firm help?

"Is it true, what Fred claims? You left with that lawyer?"

Shame flooded through me. I kept the guilt buried—under Bruce's love, my new-found freedom, busyness at school—but now the man whose love and approval I had craved since I was old enough to think—*knew*.

"Yes." It came out in a croak.

"Don't even think about asking for custody," Daddy said. "No judge in his right mind would let you have those children after what you've done."

I sat there, gutted. "Okay."

"I'll have (He named the firm's only female litigator) call you."

I hung up and walked to the bathroom, head high, face stony. Safely inside a stall, I bawled. When someone came in, I lifted my feet and covered my mouth to prevent any sound escaping. In the terrible first year after I left, I acknowledged hurt when it arrived, but I never allowed myself to feel the entirety of the pain. Misery got stowed away, like the letters in the blue suitcase. I would deal with it later. Inside that stall, the full force of what I had done rocked me. I could not go back, and I could not control the consequences. When I was able to stop crying, I blew my nose on toilet paper and returned to my little office to meet the next student.

I got off the bus that afternoon and fell into Bruce's arms. "My father despises me. The children won't be coming, not ever."

He held me and spoke his comforting words. I was not comforted.

That's when I began thinking seriously about killing myself. I had failed at marriage and motherhood. I had brought pain to the people I loved most. If I died, the hurt would end, and I could cause no more damage.

I stared at the Lysol under the sink. I could drink it straight from the bottle. I saw myself writhing on the floor and decided Lysol would hurt too much. I studied the knives in the kitchen drawer. There was one long and sharp enough to reach my heart, but I didn't have the nerve. I kept thinking about my aunt Momae, who aimed a gun at her heart and hit her stomach by mistake. She died anyway, but not for a long time and in agony.

Riding home from school with Bruce in the evening, I considered opening the car door and falling out onto Dixie Highway. I didn't have the guts to do that either.

I went over and over my miseries. At school, I pretended to be normal, but with Bruce I talked about nothing but the pain. The children were lost forever. I was worthless. Everyone hated me. I didn't deserve to live, and the world would be a better place without me.

"I love you," Bruce kept saying. "Isn't that enough?"

It was not.

Poor man. If he heard me opening the knife drawer, he came running. One night I waited until he fell asleep and rattled the knife drawer just to hear his feet hit the floor.

He ran into the kitchen, his face twisted in fear. "Are you okay?"

"I'm fine. I couldn't sleep."

He took me in his arms. "I heard that drawer open and got scared."

I felt reassured. Someone cared enough to want me alive.

One evening (this was before we got rid of Yossarian), as we drove past the packing houses on South Dixie, Bruce stopped for a light. I jumped out of the car and ran. I ran past the darkened shed and into the night beyond. I didn't know where I was going. I wanted to run to the end of hurt. I scrambled through a stubbled field, tripped, fell, got up, and ran on. I heard panting behind me. I could run to the edge of the earth, but I couldn't outrun Yossarian. His tongue lolled, his tail wagged, the yellow eyes gleamed. He thought we were playing a wonderful game.

Bruce came gasping up. "What the hell do you think you're doing?"

I didn't have an answer.

He was furious and drove us home without speaking. When we were in bed, he said, "This is not getting any better. Maybe you should see someone."

A second man telling me to see a shrink. Was I crazy? If I were, I probably wouldn't know it. I was certainly miserable enough

I went to the school infirmary, and they assigned me to a psychologist. He was a shy young man with a head of pale, fuzzy hair. I liked him right away. Psychologists were different from psychiatrists. He sat across the desk and looked at me. He nodded when I talked and chuckled over my funny stories. I told him about Mississippi and civil rights. I told him about Fred and the four children, about getting married at nineteen and going back to college. I described teaching Sunday school and working for the Junior League while I sneaked around trying to find decent sex.

He said, "Sounds as if you had a choice: stay there and go crazy or leave."

Yes. I exulted. Someone understood. I could have stayed in Mississippi and become a drunk like my mother or gone crazy like my sister, or I could leave. It wasn't my fault; the South was toxic, and I had done what I needed to in order to survive. I closed that man's door after the first session feeling twenty pounds lighter. I could hardly wait to see him again. During the next seven days, I set aside choice tidbits to offer up at our session.

He spoke of the groups he ran, how much help people got out of telling their stories and hearing the stories of others. I loved telling stories. Group sounded fun, like a promotion. After three months, I felt almost well again. I asked if I might join one of his wonderful groups.

He looked at me for a moment without speaking. "Do you really want to tell that story in front of a group?"

I felt as if I'd been struck. What I had done must be worse than I knew if it was too terrible to tell in a group. I put on a pleasant face and buried the hurt. I would allow myself to feel it later where no one could see. Some people went through the world as exposed nerves; I was a padded cell.

I kept seeing the psychologist, chastened and less trusting. I didn't know how to stop going, and I don't think he noticed the change. I went until he told me he'd done everything he could.

The woman lawyer called from Daddy's office to discuss the divorce. I could hardly bear talking to her, imagining the disdain in her voice. We agreed on terms. I wouldn't ask for custody, and Fred wouldn't sue for adultery. I would get the children at Christmas, Easter, and for a month in the summer.

"Do you want to be present at the hearing?"

I felt a jolt of terror. "Do I have to?"

"It's your choice."

"No-fault" divorces didn't exist in 1966. I needed to be accused of something, and Fred was charging me with desertion.

I pictured going back to Jackson for the court appearance in the role of criminal wife and mother. Fred's angry, gloating face watching while my friend Jim Becker, his lawyer, took my children from me with a condescending smile. I imagined the frowning judge (In my mind he wore a wig.). I had enough courage to run away from Mississippi but not enough to return and face judgment.

I said, "I don't think so."

Daddy called. "We're asking $5,000 for your share of the house. I think that's fair considering what you've done."

I'd forgotten I owned half a house. Years before, Fred and I sat in Daddy's law office, signing the deed. When Daddy pointed at the line for me to sign, too, I asked why. In case anything happens, he said. I thought it rude of him to imply my marriage might fail. How stupid I'd been. He was looking out for me the way Southern men did. $5,000 for half of a $60,000 house sounded fair. I hadn't expected anything. I was still under the mistaken assumption that the less I asked for, the quicker I'd be forgiven.

The divorce papers were served at the dean's office. I opened them and read as far as the word "desertion." Blood rushed to my head. When I left with Bruce, I thought I was giving the children up temporarily. Now they were being taken from me by law and forever.

Someday I might be strong enough to read this indictment all the way through, but not now. I stuffed the envelope in my purse until I could get it inside the blue suitcase.

25

One of the courses I signed up for that fall was Renaissance literature. I'd taken world literature at Millsaps College and loved it. In the Renaissance course, we spent a semester reading *Paradise Lost*, *Paradise Found*, and *The Faerie Queen*. Our professor, chairman of the department, was a tall, austere man. He sat at one end of the seminar table observing the twelve of us with apparent disapproval.

"Can anyone give me the dates of the Renaissance?"

Eager to prove I deserved this fellowship, I parroted the dates I'd memorized in undergraduate school.

He gave me a pained look. "Wrong. The actual dates of the Renaissance are a matter of speculation and dispute."

I had waited with such anticipation to be a graduate student. My undergraduate years were amazing. Millsaps College, with its nine hundred students, was a real community of learning. We read *Mother Courage*, saw it performed, and talked openly about civil rights. Faculty treated the students as equals. Graduate school, I imagined, would be even better: more mingling with professors, more fervent discussions of great books and ideas.

The University of Miami appeared to operate from a deeply defensive position. If the rest of the country deemed us a party school, the professors in the English department would prove them wrong by making learning as unpleasant as possible. The students were dolts, and the faculty minor deities.

I discovered, to my dismay, what was meant by a research paper. Unlike my days at Millsaps, we were to express no personal opinion about the literature we read. Instead, we researched the research of others. If critics A, B, and C said such and such, and critics D, E, and F said so and so, we were to find a position G, some infinitely tiny point, and go on about it for twenty typed pages. I was not good at this kind of writing. My earlier academic success was based on a facility with the personal essay. No one gave a flying hoot what I thought about anything in graduate school, and I had little talent for writing that forbade my favorite personal pronoun.

In the second required semester of Old English, my struggle with the ancient language continued. The professor was a small, dapper Southerner. His chief pride was in having managed to grow a magnolia tree in Miami. He seemed pleased to have a fellow Southerner in his class. During the first term, I must have behaved as he expected, because he invited me home to have tea with his wife and admire the tree. During the second semester, he took me aside after class, his brow furrowed with disappointment. "You are not my idea of a Southern lady."

I nodded, knowing exactly what he meant. Growing up, my aunt Miss Hosford warned me of this failing. My voice wasn't soft enough; my sentences did not end in a questioning lilt. I argued instead of agreeing with the opinions of male authority. Unless I changed my ways, I would never be a Southern lady. I told the professor I was sorry.

Nor could I claim success as an object of sexual assault. Each year, according to rumor and tradition, one of our professors (a very married professor) chose a different female graduate student as his mistress. No one complained about sexual harassment. The word didn't exist, and who would have listened? The chosen one felt honored, and the rest of us gossiped about her and were oddly envious. Years later, a fellow student told me she, too, had failed to be selected as mistress of the year, but she had been kissed by the professor, and the doctor was a great kisser.

I was invited to join a study group, and Old English became bearable. Martin was dark-haired and intense, a young D.H. Lawrence with a photographic memory. He had memorized and could recite every poem he'd ever read. He recited until your head sank. Joanne was small, with soulful eyes and a capacious bosom. She and I became friends, she said, because we both lived in sin. Italian John DiMenna was from New York, where his father was a contractor, which must mean, we whispered, the mafia. This made him only more intriguing. Geoff Brown, trademark hair flopping over his forehead, was the baby of the group. We met to translate Old English assignments, each of us responsible for a couple of lines. Working together made the task light, and often hilarious.

My friends had teaching fellowships—they actually taught—while I, having arrived late, was made an academic counselor. I sat with undergraduate students and helped them plot a path through college. I was much more encouraging than my counselor at Ole Miss had been. I did not tell the girls they could become only secretaries or teachers. I told them majoring in English would give them a breadth of knowledge and the ability to think critically. They would learn how to write clear prose. With these skills, they could do anything.

After a few weeks, I was included in Friday night gatherings at Joanne's apartment in Coconut Grove. She lived with her boyfriend, David, on the top floor of a rundown mansion with a grand view of Biscayne Bay. We chipped in for the weekly meal: a huge pot of spaghetti, salad, and French bread. We spent the evening howling with laughter and drinking Chianti so cheap it turned our teeth purple. Nobody in this group found me old or odd. I was one of them, and I was so grateful for the camaraderie, I wanted to weep. I didn't, of course. Part of belonging meant never doubting my place or showing gratitude for it.

Bruce attended these Friday night gatherings. Every minute we were not working or in school, we spent together. We did the laundry as a couple and trekked together to the grocery store. I took it as an indication of his devotion, but discovered that with one car, I had far less freedom than I'd had in Mississippi: more freedom of thought, but little freedom of movement.

I wasn't sure what the group thought of Bruce. He left his suit jacket in the car but arrived in a starched shirt with a monogram in the spot where (as he'd told me in Mississippi) ordinary men had pockets. He rolled up his sleeves, loosened his tie, and slouched comfortably in one of David's sagging chairs. His legs, in perfectly creased trousers, were crossed; the light gleamed off his polished boots. We looked like hippies with our long hair, and he looked like a businessman.

We ranted against the escalating war in Vietnam, agreeing it placed an undue burden on the poor and minorities, as all wars did. We bitched about the Renaissance class, where everyone but Martin had their papers returned for revision.

Bruce said, "Aren't you wasting your time on Milton?" No one spoke, and he answered his own question. "Looking at the big picture," he said, "isn't it selfish to be playing in the academic sandbox while your peers are dying?"

Bruce was not fighting either, but he was in the Army Reserves.

John DiMenna said, "Personally, I'm grateful for the deferment."

"Believe me," Bruce said, "I'm happy not to be going overseas, too, but at some point you have to grapple with the real world."

His work with the poor was noble, my friends agreed, but privately, Joanne confided, they resented what felt like his condescension. I loved Bruce, and I loved my group. I wanted them to love each other. I found myself explaining him to my friends and them to him.

Graduate school was a world of its own. I had not seen one black student on campus. Compared with Mississippi, bigotry in Miami operated underground, but as far as I could see, except for foreigners, the university in 1966 was an all-white school.

I wasn't sure what had become of the movement I left Mississippi to become part of. Negroes made up only ten percent of Miami's population, not enough to inspire the fear and revulsion they aroused back home, where the sheer number of dark faces made insurrection a real possibility.

Bruce's mom called them *shvartzas*, with the disdain of someone who had never known a black person. Bruce laughed it off. That was just his mother. He never showed disappointment in his work. His clients came in all colors. He had cases about discrimination and migrant workers being denied rights, but there were no marches here and no civil rights murders either. The fight for change went on in a lower key. It didn't make the discrimination any less unjust, but the drama had been removed.

The country's attention was shifting from civil rights to the war in Vietnam. At night, hundreds of us marched, holding candles, down the medium dividing Dixie Highway. That was the sum of my militancy. I consoled myself. School was temporary, a time out. After I got my degree, I would do something that mattered.

Friday night supper gang

26

We had a fight. I don't remember what it was about, but in my fury over not winning the war of words, I slapped Bruce. I had grown up hitting boys who displeased me. Southern men almost never hit back. Bruce did. He punched me with his fist and punched me again. I fell on the bed and curled into a fetal position. I couldn't believe a man had hit me. He left the room, then came back—to apologize, I thought. He stood beside the bed looking down at me, and gave me a kick. "That will teach you. I'll bet you never hit me again."

He went to work, and I called my friend Joanne. I had never been hit like this by a man, or by anyone. I was furious.

She drove down, and we searched for bruises. Disappointingly, there didn't appear to be any. He was the perfect abuser, leaving no visible evidence.

Joanne made me feel better by being hugely on my side. "What are you going to do?"

"I don't know."

"You could get your own place." Joanne had a car, and though she'd lived with her mother before moving in with Dave, she bartended her way through college and was much more independent than I.

I'd never thought of having my own place, but the fact was, I'd gone straight from one man to another. For all my talk of women's rights, I had never lived by myself. "Can I afford a place?"

"I'll help you look," she said.

When he got home that night, Bruce and I made up with great sex. He told me that by hitting him, I caused him to hit me. That was his apology. I laughed at the absurdity of this defense but couldn't find words to fight the illogic.

Checking out at the grocery in Homestead the next Saturday, Bruce caught the cashier in a seven-cent error and barked her into tears.

Driving home, I said, "I think I ought to live on my own for a while. I've never done it, not once in my life."

I felt him tense. "You should do whatever you need to."

I took him at his word and watched the newspapers. I talked to my psychologist about moving, and he agreed it would be good to try living alone. The Friday night group thought it ridiculous to travel all the way from Homestead to school. One week in Rentals, I saw a garage apartment for rent in Coconut Grove for fifty dollars a month. Joanne took me by for a look. It was tiny, one room and a bath, but it would do. I told the owner I would take it and paid the first and last months' rent.

When I broke the news to Bruce, he said, "Fine."

I said, "I don't want anything to change. I just want to try it."

He said, "Fine."

Every time he said "fine," things felt less fine.

He took me to a dealer, and with my last $300, I bought a white motor scooter. I would have a place of my own and transportation.

The scooter became a metaphor for my unease. The thing terrified me. When I jumped the starter, I expected either no response (which I often got, being a little timid with my jumping), or for the machine to run out from under me. I practiced riding from school down to our house in the country. I took back roads and pulled over for faster traffic, but the wind from every passing car whipped me, and I felt fortunate to arrive alive.

My upstairs apartment had a single bed, a table, and a window over-grown with vines. When the day came to move in, I took a lamp from home, a suitcase full of clothes, and my books. Bruce drove me north without speak-ing. When we got to the apartment, he helped me carry everything inside.

He turned to leave. "I won't be able to see you as much in the future."

My heart bumped around like a beanbag. "Why not?"

"It's a long way from Homestead to here, and I'm busy at work. You're busy, too."

Logically, he was right, but I knew the words were meant to undermine me. I saw how controlling he was, but his was the only warmth I could count on. Why should he continue to see me? We'd made a bargain, and I was breaking it.

"You'll be fine." He opened the door to go.

I would not be fine without him. I thought I would, but I was wrong. I looked around the dark room at the single bed and the table where I had imagined studying. "Wait."

He stopped.

"Maybe I won't start tonight."

He didn't gloat; he didn't even talk about it. He drove us back to the country, his usual cheerful self.

I kept putting off the move, making excuses to the psychologist and to my friends. The next day didn't feel right; neither did the next. Bruce was being so kind. Before the end of that first month, I crept back to the little apartment, removed my things, and left a note for the owners, saying I wouldn't be needing the place after all. I never spent one night there, not a single night as an independent woman.

27

The Christmas holidays approached, and it was time to go home to Mississippi again. Fred offered to meet me at the airport with the children. I was surprised by the gesture and accepted. I loved finding the four of them waiting, jumping up and down when they saw me come off the plane.

Thomas grabbed hold of my skirt and wouldn't let go.

Fred seemed cheerful and pleased with himself, grinning like a twelve-year old. "Thought you'd like to know," he said, "I'm getting married."

I stood there stunned. I didn't want to be married to him, but I was astonished that he'd already chosen my replacement. "But the divorce isn't final yet," I said.

"As soon as it is. Probably next June."

"What is she like?"

"A really sweet girl. Her name is Helen, and she's crazy about the children."

My skin tingled with shock. I didn't feel replaced in the children's affections by Marie or their grandparents, but a new wife, a second mother? "How old is she?"

Fred hesitated. "Nineteen."

"Another nineteen-year-old?" I practically screeched. I couldn't help myself, I was that flabbergasted. "Isn't it a mistake to pick someone as young I was?"

His voice turned harsh. "Believe me, Norma, nobody is like you."

The glad greeting was over; I was back to being loathed.

Growing up, Mother gave the family Christmas Eve party, but Fred and I had taken it over. For the past six years, I showed off my festive house, my successful husband, our four darling children. My middle sister, Mary Elizabeth, now hosted. I was here as a visitor, the divorced woman.

I wore a new outfit Bruce helped me choose. The skirt was floor-length, red felted wool, with decorative scallops of heavy black braid. The blouse was white, long-sleeved and silk. I pulled my now-long hair back into a large knot and wore my Latimer grandmother's gold belt buckle at my throat as a brooch. I looked like a Victorian lady and hoped this made up for my circumstances.

I picked up the children, resplendent in their Christmas outfits. Fred stood silently in the doorway to see them off.

My sister and her small, tidy husband greeted us. They were cordial, giving me the kind of hug where only our cheeks touched. The children clung to me. Without their father, this was unknown territory.

I felt prickly as a hedgehog and stood in their parlor prepared to bristle. Bill Goodman, the tallest of my Watkins cousins, heir to my father's place as head of the law firm, came up with his daughter. "Pat," he said, "this is your cousin Norma. She's the black sheep of the Watkins family." Grinning at his joke.

I nodded: yes, I was. Humor made me feel more welcome than my other relatives' pretense that nothing had changed.

Privately, Bill Goodman whispered. "You can't do anything in this family that someone hasn't already done." Which made me want to know who had done what and how things turned out for them.

No one mentioned the word divorce or that Fred was not present. Like good Southerners, we pretended things had always been this way.

"Aren't you all just darling?" Hosford Fontaine, the aunt we called Miss Hosford, patted my children on their heads, speaking in the same distracted way she used with my sister and me when we lived at the family hotel.

"May I speak to you?" she said.

I bent to listen.

She murmured something.

"I'm sorry, what did you say?"

"Now that you're no longer living in the house, I'd like my painting back."

She meant the large oil that hung to the right of our fireplace, an elongated female figure by Andrew Bucci. He'd been a teacher at the art colony

Miss Hosford ran before the hotel burned. She gave us the painting when we married. It was one of my favorite possessions.

"You want the painting back?"

"I think I mentioned at the time that it was a loan."

She might have mentioned it, but after a decade, when I'd practically designed our living room around that piece, we owned it. Taking the painting back felt unfair and exactly the kind of thing my aunt would do. Wait until Fred heard. I looked down at her. "I'm afraid you'll have to take that up with Fred."

"I thought you might speak to him for me." She gave me a little pat and wandered off.

During the war, when we lived at Allison's Wells, this was the aunt who ruled my childhood, setting standards I never met, chiding me for my faults, turning meals into a litany of correction. After the hotel burned, she moved into a small apartment in Jackson's Belhaven district, where she painted, sculpted, and swam every day, the way she had at the hotel, but in other people's pools.

We laughed at her eccentricities. Inside her handbag, wrapped in a grubby handkerchief, she carried a demitasse cup and saucer. Whenever we went to a restaurant, she pulled it out and said to the waiter: "Be a dear and fill this for me." They were usually too astounded to refuse. When she was done with the coffee, she wiped the cup dry with the same handkerchief, rewrapped it, and returned it to her bag. Aunt Leigh, Uncle Doug's wife, the one who usually paid for these meals, called the cup, "that nasty thing," as in, "I can't believe you're bringing out that nasty thing."

We crowded around my sister's dining table, nibbling on the food Annie and Mother had spent days preparing: beaten biscuits with ham, cayenne-laced cheese straws, sausage balls, date rolls, and, my favorite, nut-filled butterball cookies dipped in powdered sugar. Mother made fudge and divinity and the same thick eggnog I once served. There was also plenty of hard liquor.

Uncle Doug bent to shake my children's hands. He said to Linden, "You're the smart one, aren't you?" Then to Allison, "And you're the pretty one." Doug Latimer had no children of his own, which didn't excuse this kind of ignorant remark. Linden was as pretty as Allison, but unconcerned with her looks. Allison was as smart as Linden, but found nothing to love about school. I didn't want Linden thinking she wasn't pretty, or Allison thinking pretty was enough. I smiled and steered Uncle Doug toward the Scotch.

My youngest sister, Sydney, stood with her new husband, the history teacher. He told us once at the dinner table that he had no use for Pax Romana, pronouncing it "packs". What he enjoyed teaching and re-enacting, he confided, was war.

Sydney had never lost what we once called her baby fat, but she was the most beautifully put together of any of us: blond hair perfectly colored and coifed, impeccable make up and manicured nails, a gorgeous, figure-hiding black outfit. She was also the least judgmental of my relatives. She nudged me now, wine glass in one hand, cigarette in the other. "How you doing, big bad sister?" She was the only member of my immediate family who did not have a letter hidden in the blue suitcase.

I looked around at my middle sister's heavy mahogany furniture and oriental rugs. Mary Elizabeth's tastes were traditional. She had Miss Hosford's soft way of speaking. Of the three of us, she was the most particular about Southern customs. When speaking of the help, she called them "the servants." When speaking to the help, she said things like, "Ora Dee, get Miss Norma a Coke-Cola."

After the hotel burned, Ora Dee Tucker moved to Jackson with her family and now spread herself among three households: my sister's, my mother's, and Miss Hosford's. Tonight, she moved quietly, clearing away plates, putting out more food, seemingly happy with her new life, and without a hint of resentment that her Christmas could begin only when we were done with ours.

I heard my cousin Babee say, "If people would only leave us alone."

This was the South's mantra: nothing wrong here except the trouble caused by outsiders.

"It's the fault of the Supreme Court," John Ray, a cousin-by-marriage, said.

"And the United Nations." Babee shook her head over the threat of global domination.

Ora Dee threaded through, collecting plates and glasses, pretending to be deaf. At least my relatives didn't use the "n" word in front of black people the way Fred's father did. Pop would say, "What do these niggers want?" while his gray-haired cook, Molly, offered a dish around the table. Molly also pretended to be deaf. Black people who wanted to keep their jobs spent a good deal of their lives pretending.

Standing among my relatives, laughing and drinking, I realized I still loved them, but the distance between our politics had grown too large to breach. They were content here in their closed world. In their minds, we had no race problem, and women had all the rights they needed or wanted. I smiled in what I hoped was a neutral way, no more able to argue than I had been when I lived here. The words I wanted to say stuck in my throat. If Bruce were here, he would set them straight and have them laughing while he did it. I knew better than to let anyone set eyes on Bruce unless we were married (an institution neither of us mentioned except to condemn).

People in the South were enormously courteous. That's what I thought watching the party. It was not necessarily genuine, but it got us by. We lived with the memory of old feuds, cheek by jowl with people we disliked or hadn't forgiven, and courtesy kept us from murdering each other—courtesy and the social grease of liquor.

On Christmas Day, in the afternoon, I drove to my old house to look at the children's gifts. Fred let me in and left me alone with them. The sight of the tree in the brick-floored entrance hall made my throat tighten at what I'd given up: I would never again share the joy of a Christmas morning with my children. I remembered the holidays we spent at Allison's Wells when I was a child. The world outside might be gray with war, but we were safe, tucked in next to a warm fire, surrounded by the people we loved. To be where you belonged and feel a part of the whole, this was the blessing I had relinquished. The hotel burned, and I left. Most of my sentimental memories depended on black people getting up early in the cold to build the fires and cook the quail we ate for breakfast. There had been no Christmas holiday for them. Knowing the past was unjust didn't cancel the longing.

I stayed a week to be with the children. They would not be coming to Florida until I either lived alone or became a decently married woman. That was part of the trade-off: I could visit them as often as I liked, but only in

Jackson. I didn't object to these rules; I felt grateful for not being put through a public trial, with the whole town privy to my messy life.

Two days after Christmas, Fred called. He wanted me to meet his fianceé. The three of us would get together in front of a counselor and discuss our relationship with the children.

I went to the meeting filled with optimism. If Fred was content, he need no longer hate me, and the bride-to-be had no reason to.

We met at the counselor's house in west Jackson. Helen, the fianceé, was tall, pretty, and very young. I wondered how she could take on a man with four children. When would she have her life? I said none of this. I smiled and congratulated them. She smiled back and clung to Fred's arm.

They sat on a couch. I sat in a chair next to the counselor, hands clasped to hide my nerves. I didn't notice the room, and I don't remember the mediator. Helen tilted toward Fred, who appeared to gain authority from her proximity. He spoke to me in a manner I'd grown accustomed to: the cold voice of a stranger.

The mediator went over the terms of my visits.

Helen detached herself from Fred and sat straighter. "Clay and Allison may continue to think of you as their mother, and perhaps Linden, but Thomas will be mine."

Fred looked puffed and proud. This had been rehearsed.

My skin felt hot. "What do you mean, Thomas will be yours?"

She looked certain in the way only a very young person can. "I intend to be the children's mother, a role you have relinquished. Thomas, being the youngest, will hardly remember you."

Was she insane? The night before, Thomas asked if he could marry me when he grew up. "I gave birth to them," I told her. "I will always be their mother." I heard the tremor in my voice.

Helen said, "We'll see about that."

Her eyes were not friendly. Not knowing me didn't mean she couldn't despise me for Fred's sake. Hating me might be a prerequisite.

I drove away, going over her words and letting the hurt sink in. A door shut here, another there, and pretty soon you were closed out. Back at my parents, I wept on the telephone with Bruce.

"Want to know my prediction?" he said. "That marriage will never last."

He sounded so certain, I felt better. If Fred was going to be this hateful, he deserved not to be happy.

"And don't worry," Bruce said. "She can't dictate how your children feel about you."

That evening I went to dinner at my friend Kay's house. Her husband was a lawyer and Fred's friend. I asked him why Fred still needed to hate me. "He's marrying someone else. Shouldn't we be friends for the sake of the children?"

Jim said, "You can't do what you did to the man and then tell him how to feel. You have to give him the freedom to hate you."

Helen couldn't dictate my children's feelings, and I couldn't dictate Fred's. The freedom to hate me: I'd never thought of that—I, who was so enamored by the idea of freedom. Actions had consequences, a late lesson to absorb at almost thirty-one. Fred must be allowed the freedom to hate me—forever, if he chose to.

I tried to process the concept of total animosity. We'd been married for ten years and had four children together. I left him, but could you turn off feelings so completely? Slam the door on the past as if it never happened: the joy at each birth, the terror over Clay's bad leg, the thousands of experiences we shared? In good times, we had been each other's best friend. All that was to be erased?

I didn't want to be his wife or lover, but I never hated the man. I admired his loyalty, humor, his business smarts, even his steadfast daily habits. What I couldn't stand was the back side of those qualities—the hard-headed, self-satisfied bigotry; the terrible sex with no desire to improve; his provincialism—Mississippi and the South trumped every other place; familiar ways were best; no need to look outside, where things were flawed, strange, and to be avoided.

This was harder to admit: I couldn't stand the thought of living the rest of my life with his frailty. Fred had inherited a partial deafness, complicated by Meniere's disease, a disorder of the inner ear that caused intense vertigo. When it overcame him, he couldn't tell up from down. Sick with dizziness, he was forced to literally crawl down the hall of the hospital.

In 1966, I was bursting with health, done with child-bearing, thrilled by learning, and tethered to a man who had already made his mind up about everything. Breakfast was to be served each morning at 7:30 and dinner on the table by 6:00. He was in bed with *Time* magazine at 8:30 (exactly like my father) and saw no reason why any of this should change. Last, but by no means least: blacks were servants; whites were superior; and the races should never mix.

Years later, I came to love regular habits. I mastered my mother's ability to give dinner parties and learned to appreciate my father's appetite for work, but that was later. At thirty, I wanted to spread my wings and fly. I wanted to go out into the world, discover my talents, and use them. I didn't want to be married to a man who had to crawl down the hall.

Perhaps I could have been Fred's wife at sixty, when I gained some measure of patience. I was seven years younger, and he was about to try a second marriage with someone seventeen years younger. What did the Irish say: live in hope, die in despair?

I returned to Miami feeling every bit the divorced woman. Being in Jackson, seeing the children in their new lives, and meeting Fred's future wife made our parting real. Divorce felt cleaner than lying had. I was not to be pitied. The children loved me; Bruce loved me; I was busy with school and had good friends. But I was divorced—from Fred, Mississippi, and the past.

Norma trying to look proper on a visit home to Mississippi

28

It hurt to pee. Nightly sex, for all its pleasures, had exacted a toll. After years of once-a-week sex (or once a month when I could get away with it), the nightly romps with Bruce produced unintended consequences. The school doctor diagnosed a bladder infection, the result, he said, of unusual sexual activity. I sat on his table in my inadequate gown and turned the color of a radish. I might be divorced, but I wore no ring. I was a woman living in sin. I figured the doctor could tell by looking, and any reference to sexual activity proved it. He prescribed medicine. I took it and got better.

A month later, my back ached and my pee ran red. This time it was a kidney infection: same cause. It happened a third time. Apparently, giving birth to four children in seven years had shifted my organs, and frequent sex rubbed everything the wrong way.

Bruce and I rode home from my latest trip to the university clinic. In two weeks, my first year of graduate school would be over for the summer.

"The doctor said I need surgery—he called it a front and rear repair."

"Sounds like something you'd do to a car," Bruce said.

We laughed, but mine was less than wholehearted. I hadn't had surgery since my tonsils were removed when I was four, and that had been a dreadful experience. "If I have to get an operation," I said, "I need to go home."

Bruce looked so alarmed he must have thought I meant for good. "Why?"

"So I can recuperate in my mother's house where Annie can take care of me."

"I can take care of you."

"I know, but you have to go to work."

I couldn't make him understand: if I were going to be cut open, I wanted to be home, in the place where I was born. I couldn't be operated on in a strange city. I needed to be in Jackson, Mississippi, with my people. This seems odd now: Miami was a larger city with better doctors, but I did not know those doctors, and they did not know me. The pull toward home felt instinctive. When in danger, head for the cave.

I looked at Bruce. "I want you with me in case I die."

"You're not going to die, but I'll definitely be there."

Over dinner, we tried to figure out how to make it work. I couldn't take Bruce home as my lover. I had health insurance through the university, but it didn't cover major surgery.

"I have insurance," Bruce said.

"How does that help?"

He grinned. "If we got married, you'd be covered."

My heart leapt, but I let nothing show on my face. "We don't believe in marriage."

"We don't believe in the institution of marriage. This is different."

We talked about it over ice cream, agreeing neither of us needed a piece of paper to prove our love, but I had been gone almost a year; my divorce was final, and there was no reason not to marry. The operation would be paid for. More crucially, we'd be legal. Bruce could come to Jackson, and I could bring the children to Florida. The truth was, I wanted to be married, or—to be accurate—I wanted Bruce to want to marry me. I spouted modern views about loving freely outside the shackles of the law, but I was a Southern girl. If a man really loved you, he married you. I kept this entirely to myself.

In bed, I turned to face him. "Are you sure?"

"Positive," Bruce said.

He loved me enough to marry me. I felt giddy with happiness. The children would be able to come for a whole month. It was almost enough to make me forget being cut open.

Bruce's boss offered his home for the wedding. He was a notary and would officiate; his wife gave us a party. It was a small wedding, as different as possible from the candlelit church where I married Fred Craig in a trailing white veil, flanked by nine bridesmaids in green velvet. We invited my friends from school and Bruce's colleagues from work. I wore a Mexican wedding dress made of cotton lace. Bruce wore a suit. He gave me a jade ring wrapped in gold wire.

We sent out announcements after the ceremony. Except for Uncle Louie and Auntie Helen, no family attended. There were few gifts, nothing like my first wedding, when the contents of a sizable china and silver shop were unwrapped on my mother's sun porch. Patt Derian sent a blanket cover, a fancy piece of linen to keep your skin from touching an itchy blanket. I had never owned one, but fifty years later, I still use it.

Bruce said his mom had not been nice to me and shouldn't be invited. She was furious. This slight confirmed the wrong-headedness of our relationship and made it unreal. She hadn't seen us get married, so maybe we weren't. She cajoled her ancient boyfriend out of a gift. He sent six Francis I steak knives, the most expensive present we received. Uncle Louie gave us money. Most of my relatives offered only congratulations, the minimum dictated by Southern courtesy.

I don't remember the wedding. I have photographs; I know it happened, but I can't remember being there. I look at the pictures and marvel at my youth—my face alight with anticipation. Age has stolen that light, narrowing the eyes, softening the jowls, settling me into a person I no longer recognize, but who looks suspiciously like Miss Hosford.

The first two years after leaving Jackson were like that wedding. I lived in a fugue state. Details emerge, but long stretches remain in fog. I blame it on the trauma of running away—that and the speed.

Each morning, I swallowed a twelve-hour, time-released capsule, provided by Patt Derian's doctor husband. At my request, he continued to renew the prescription from a distance. I've forgotten what excuse I gave, but the real reason was to stay skinny. With my daily go-pill, I raced through life, heart pounding, jittery with ideas. Taking an early morning Greyhound to the university, I spent the day in class, at work counseling, or in my carrel at the library. Home on the bus at 5:30, met by Bruce, I fixed supper, we ate, cleaned up, read, made love, fell asleep in each other's arms, and it was on to another fast-forward day.

I saw nothing wrong with making it through graduate school with the help of amphetamines. Sure, my hands shook, and I ground my teeth so hard my jaws ached, but if I stuck to one pill a day, the way I limited myself to half a pack of cigarettes, what harm could it do? I might not have been as casual about this as I pretended. I told no one. I don't think Bruce knew what the pill was. Women took pills; that's what we did. No one questioned it. We needed pills, and men didn't. I should have questioned that.

Safely covered by Bruce's insurance, I scheduled the operation. I chose June, when school was out and Bruce had vacation time before his two weeks of Army Reserve duty. We arrived in Jackson three days before the surgery, enough time for the introductions I dreaded.

Daddy looked Bruce in the eye and gave him a hearty handshake. Neither man mentioned being adversaries in the civil rights wars.

Bruce twinkled down on my mother. "What a pleasure to finally meet Big Norma." He took both her hands in his.

I watched her melt under the force of his charm. He called her Norma and addressed our cook Annie as Mrs. Carter. Mother pretended not to notice.

I went alone to pick up the children. Fred warned me he'd better not lay eyes on that man. The children appeared delighted by Bruce. It was hard not to be captivated when he put his mind to it.

Mother got me alone in her bedroom. "What kind of name is Rogow?"

"Russian."

"I mean, is it—is he—" She couldn't bring herself to say the word.

"Jewish?" I said.

The birthmark on her forehead bloomed red. She nodded.

"Yes, he is."

She never said another word to me about it, but the news must have spread around the family. When Uncle Doug met Bruce, he put a pudgy arm around his shoulders. "I've just finished reading a book about the history of the Jews," he said. "I never realized how much you people suffered."

Bruce loved being back in Mississippi. He got a kick out of meeting my relatives and found their bigoted comments hilarious. I enjoyed watching him operate. He was assured and positive and had an uncanny ability to turn my family's prejudice back on them and pretend it was a virtue. When Robert Kennedy announced his run for the presidency, Uncle Doug told Bruce he'd vote for Martin Luther King before he'd vote for Bobby Kennedy. Bruce clapped him on the back and said he would pass the message along to Dr. King, who would be pleased to know he had this kind of grass roots support.

Bruce was exactly the way I would be, if I hadn't been born here and wasn't too scared to speak up. The family was looking for a wild-eyed radical, and Bruce gave them courtly wit. The glory felt transferrable. Look, I wanted to say, marching around on his arm, this is how a right-thinking person behaves. This is what an honorable person believes. An honorable person might not choose to run off with a married woman with four children, but I did not consider that in my moment of glory.

For the operation, I went back to the doctor who first gave me birth control pills. I didn't know him nearly as well as the man who delivered my children and refused me birth control, but this doctor taught at the university hospital, which was recommendation enough.

I wasn't sure what a front and rear repair was except something to lift my organs. The doctor laughed, saying it would make my husband very happy. Except for a hymen, he told us, I would be a virgin again, as tight as any eighteen-year-old. Bruce laughed in response. I didn't think there was anything wrong with the old me, but I understood their cackles: a woman's body was there to please a man. After the operation, mine would please Bruce more.

I can't remember the operation any more than my wedding. I do remember waking up afterward. Bruce sat in a chair by the window. I had that floating feeling you get from morphine.

He said, "How are you, babe?"

"Could you look under the cover?" I said. "Everything feels wet."

Bruce lifted the sheet. Blood spread in a wide circle around me. He raced out of the room, shouting for help. Nurses came running, and I found myself being rolled down the hall on a gurney and anesthetized again. The doctor who operated had left for the weekend, so his partner substituted.

When I woke the next time, Bruce said they had left something untied inside me, and I could have bled to death. A blood transfusion ran into one arm. I felt very tired. All I wanted to do was sleep, and Bruce spent the night on a cot beside my bed.

The next morning, my father came to visit. Bruce left to get coffee. Daddy said, "I never saw a man so devoted. Refuses to leave your side. What does he think will happen?"

I might bleed to death. I didn't say that. I took the remark as a compliment and a vindication of my choice. This was what it meant to be truly loved, I wanted to tell him, not the fake living together and never touching he and Mother did. I felt protected. Bruce was strong enough to shield me from everything I feared about home.

By Saturday, I was back in my old bedroom, and Bruce had departed for Army Reserve camp. I was not allowed to fly until my post-surgery checkup. Mother and Daddy were at their separate bridge games. Annie finished her half-day and left me a jar of boiled custard in the refrigerator. When you were ill, boiled custard was the family treat. I was filled with a sadness custard couldn't reach.

Fred was getting married today, replicating the wedding we'd had ten years before, only fancier. At the Jackson Country Club, he was marrying another nineteen-year-old in white satin, with bridesmaids and a band. The children each had a part, and every friend I had was there. I sat in bed feeling sorry for myself. I didn't resent Fred's being happy, but I hated the role of Cinderella, everyone at the ball except me.

There was a knock on the porch door. I tottered out with my wounded walk. It was Ellen, a friend from Eudora's creative writing class.

"I thought you might like company," she said.

"I have never been so glad to see anybody in my life. Fred's getting married today."

"I know. That's why I came."

"I'm surprised you're not at the wedding."

I crept back to bed, and she climbed in alongside me. "Honey, I'm about as welcome at these Jackson shindigs as a loose pig."

I envied Ellen. She was redheaded and as brash as her hair. She never let being a Southern woman slow her down. She slept with any man she pleased. She called the act I thought I had to be in love to perform, "getting it out of the way." To cap the reversal, she then wrote stories about the men.

She pulled out a pack of Pall Malls and offered me one. "Marrying a nineteen-year-old. What is Fred Craig thinking?"

"My children are there, flower girls and ring bearers."

She made a face to show what she thought of Southern weddings.

The cigarette tasted foul. I squashed it in an ashtray next to the bed. "I have no desire to be married to Fred, but for some crazy reason, I don't want him marrying someone else."

Ellen laughed. "Every man we discard should take a vow of celibacy and go straight into a monastery."

I giggled, filled with that glee you get when you're deep into things with a sympathetic woman friend. We gossiped, laughed, commiserated, and by the time Ellen left, Fred's wedding was long over, and I was restored.

Bruce and I get married, June 1967. Uncle Louie on left.

29

I wanted the children's first visit to Miami to be perfect. For almost a year I'd written weekly letters describing the wonders of Florida: blue water, palms, alligators, and orange trees. They were ready to be amazed.

They would be with us for a month, and this was my once-a-year chance to be their mother again. I got them for a week after Christmas and another week at Easter, but these were short visits. Four weeks was long enough for routines, long enough to relax and be ordinary around one another, instead of over-excited and counting the days we had left. For one whole month I would be, simply and wonderfully, their mother. I was so thrilled I couldn't sleep.

I made lists in my head: places to go, dishes to cook, what I needed to buy. The first problem was finding space in our tiny cottage for the four of them. The bedroom was barely big enough for the pushed-together twin beds. We needed the living room for sitting around and the dining area for meals. That left the small porch in front, pale yellow stucco halfway up, screened on the top half.

Bruce and I measured. There was just enough space for four folding beds. I found a place that rented them. We needed four sets of sheets, and I knew Bruce would freak if I asked to buy them. I went to the local thrift store, but the sheets were faded and mismatched. I would not let my children sleep on thrift store discards. I found a linen supply place that rented sheets. They looked like the ones used in hospitals, stiff with starch, but they were sparkling white.

Lined up side by side, the beds took up the entire porch. The child sleeping in the fourth cot would have to climb over the other three. I took a last look around before Bruce drove me thirty miles north to the Miami airport. I was flying to Jackson to bring the children back. At nine, seven, five, and three, they were too young to fly alone.

Fred seemed especially quiet when he handed over the children at the Jackson airport. He was not the gloating bridegroom I expected. He scarcely said hello to me or goodbye to the children. He angled Clay's shoulders in my direction and muttered something that sounded like "Behave yourself."

After he walked away, Clay explained. "Daddy's mad at us."

Allison nodded. "For coming to see you."

Clay said, "He's been mad for five days."

They each carried a little suitcase and were practically vibrating with excitement over this adventure. None of them had been on a plane before, and the drama of the flight with a change of planes in Atlanta made them cling to me.

Bruce picked us up in the Volkswagen Bug. That's what we drove now. The blue Triumph convertible finally died. It quit one day in downtown Miami, making Bruce so angry he tried to push it into the Miami River. We bought a beige VW Bug, not as glamorous, but far more reliable.

All four children squeezed into the backseat, sitting forward, back, forward, back. They had met Bruce briefly when he came to Jackson for the operation, but they stared at him now as if at an alien.

Allison said, "Why do you have a mustache?"

"I like a mustache," Bruce said.

"Why?"

He reached around, pretending to grab her. "So I can tickle little girls when I kiss them." Allison screeched, and they all laughed. It was a beginning.

They couldn't believe how far away home was.

"How much longer?" Linden said.

I leaned around the seat and kissed her on the head. "I told you, we live in the country."

When we finally got to the house, they piled out of the car. Allison was first and fastest. She ran in the front door, through the living room, down the short hall, and bounced off the back wall.

"Is this it?"

I swallowed my hurt feelings. The cottage in the lime groves was tiny compared with their house in Jackson, but I had worked hard to cheer it up with yellow polka dot curtains and a colorful tablecloth.

"This is it. It will be like camp."

And it was. I assigned beds. We had a daily schedule: activities, rest time, cooking, eating, cleanup time, a story, and a set time for bed. Everyone had chores. Bruce and I took them on daily excursions. We visited Monkey Jungle, where the monkeys ran free and people walked inside caged paths. We went to Lion Country Safari and watched dusty lions sleep under small trees. I took a picture of the children under a sign that read, "Trespassers will be Eaten."

At Ocean World, Clay swam with Flipper, but Allison said the dolphin's skin felt icky, and she refused to try. Linden cried because she was too young, and they wouldn't let her in the pool. At dinner in Key Largo, Thomas threw a fit in the restaurant when his hamburger steak (the closest thing they had to a hamburger) arrived without a bun. He screamed so loud, I locked him outside in the car until he calmed down. The night wasn't hot, and I left the car windows open. Those were the days when you could do that to a misbehaving child without worrying about kidnapping or someone reporting you to family services.

We watched fish do tricks at Sea World and birds do tricks at Parrot Jungle. I was not fond of animals doing tricks, wearing miniature human clothes, riding tiny tricycles, carrying little parasols, but the children liked it.

By the time the month was up, there wasn't a tourist attraction within a hundred miles we hadn't visited. For an only child who'd never been around children, Bruce was wonderful. He thought up new adventures and made jokes to keep everyone in a good mood. He did all the driving. With the children lined up like sardines across the backseat, he sang to them in a funny falsetto: "Chantilly lace/And a pretty face..."

The children loved it. At night, back in the cottage, we waited, propped in bed, while they dressed in grown-up clothes and giggled in the hall outside our room. The bedroom door opened, and they performed short plays in the doorway. Thomas laughed helplessly and forgot his lines, which made Allison and Clay furious. He'd ruined everything. We clapped enthusiastically and told them their skits were brilliant, probably indications of genius.

Now that I didn't live with them, the children seemed much easier. I went a whole month without screaming once, and I cried when I had to give them back to their father in Jackson.

Fred was just as unfriendly. I wondered how many days he would punish them after the visit.

"Bye, Mama." Clay dragged his feet and waved until Fred said something and jerked him forward.

"I love you, Clay, Allison, Linden, and Thomas Craig." I shouted at their backs, and stood, crying and waving for as long as I could see them. People at the airport looked at me pityingly. What kind of mother watched her children being dragged away? I found my gate and flew home.

Back in Florida, I sobbed in Bruce's arms. "Fred hates me."

"He doesn't hate you."

"He despises me, and he's punishing the children for visiting us."

"Do you think you're a despicable person?"

"No." I sounded doubtful.

"Then it's his problem, isn't it?"

"He's going to turn them against me."

Bruce said, "In ten years they'll be grown. They will decide how they feel, and who they want to be with. Children have more sense than you think. They know what's going on. You'll see."

Ten years seemed like a long time.

The children come to Florida for a late Christmas; Linden gets a book

30

In Memphis, on Friday, April 4, 1968, Dr. Martin Luther King, Jr. leaned on a railing outside his second-floor room at the Lorraine Motel. From out of the darkness, shots. He died from a gaping wound to the neck. A white man was seen fleeing, and a high caliber rifle was found a block away.

On the morning of April 5, when I opened the newspaper, I was hit with the large black headline announcing King's assassination. The horrors I had left behind in Mississippi returned—Emmett Till's mutilated corpse in its open casket; Medgar Evers lying in a pool of blood in his driveway; the mud-covered bodies of the three young civil rights workers dug out of a landfill.

I was in my second year of graduate school and had been given a class to teach. I shared an office with Joanne and Martin in a shambling wooden barracks left over from WWII. I bought a large poster of Dr. King and hung it, draped with black crepe paper, outside our ground-floor window.

A group of young white men walking by spotted it. They ran screaming over, and one of them leapt and ripped the poster off the wall.

I couldn't believe my eyes. I yelled "Stop" out the window.

They yelled back. "Nigger lover, nigger lover," their eyes as filled with hatred as any racist crowd in Mississippi. They ran off, jeering and shredding my poster. I stood frozen at the window. Nothing had changed. What was the point in leaving home, when people here were just as cruel? Miami was growing more conservative with the arrival of the anti-Castro Cubans, but I never imagined this open hatred.

After Dr. King's death, riots, looting, and fires broke out in more than sixty cities. People died, and whole neighborhoods were left in ruins. We were told not to drive through Miami's black areas. A friend got pulled from his car in Coconut Grove and beaten almost to death.

It felt like the end of civil rights. The only bright spot Bruce and I could find was Robert Kennedy. The war in Vietnam was going badly. People were shocked at the Tet Offensive and revolted by the My Lai massacre. At night, the hawks brayed for war on our small television; Westmoreland wanted 200,000 more troops.

Lyndon Johnson announced he would not run for reelection. We jeered at his hound-dog image, telling him to get out and good riddance. Robert Kennedy decided to run. His words carried the same promise we'd first heard from his brother. We had a hero again, and we badly wanted a hero.

Two months later, another newspaper, the headline shouting: "R.F.K. shot." At the Ambassador Hotel the night before in Los Angeles, Kennedy had claimed victory in the California Democratic primary. As he left the ballroom by a back exit, Sirhan Sirhan, an anti-Zionist kitchen worker, fired multiple shots with a .22 revolver. The paper said Kennedy was hit three times. He was still alive, if barely. Twenty-six hours after it happened, he died.

We both cried. This was the death of hope, and we saw no way forward. Bruce went on fighting for the rights of the underprivileged, and I went on studying for my master's, but when the vile Richard Nixon won the presidential election in 1968, we sat in front of the television crushed into silence. Two people could do nothing against the evil of the world.

"We'll leave," Bruce said. "As soon as you're done with the degree, we'll get out of here for a while." Running sounded good to me.

31

I passed the graduate German exam on my third try. During my English department orals I didn't weep the way I had during my senior orals at Millsaps. I asked Patt Derian's husband for a tranquilizer. The one he sent worked so well, I lowered my head onto my arms, and observed my committee from a calm distance. My thesis was a two-act play: Dylan Thomas meets William Faulkner in Oxford; they get drunk and talk about writing, with all the dialogue taken from actual interviews. One member of my committee said my work reminded him of what Samuel Johnson said about women preachers: "It's like a dog's walking on his hind legs. It is not done well, but you are surprised to find it done at all." Until the tranquilizer wore off, I felt too serene to realize I had been insulted.

As promised, Bruce took a leave from his job. I withdrew the $5,000 I'd received for my half of the house. On Christmas Eve, 1968, we had tickets aboard the liner *Michelangelo*, sailing from New York to Naples. We gave away most of our belongings, found a home for the cat, and left.

We stopped in Mississippi to tell the children goodbye, another leave-taking, this time for six months, an eternity to a child.

"Where exactly are you going?" Clay wanted to see on the map, and I drew a line up the boot of Italy, into Austria, Germany, the Netherlands, Belgium, and across France to Spain.

Allison was suspicious, as she was of everything I did in those days. "Why do you need to go?"

"To see places I've read about. I'll send lots of letters."

Clay's face lighted. "With foreign stamps." Stamp collecting was his new hobby.

Thomas and Linden hugged me when I arrived and when I left. They had grown accustomed to these comings and goings. All the children had. I was like a Christmas stocking—fun but no longer part of their ordinary lives. Only I cried now when we parted. They were affectionate; they told me they loved me, but when their father honked for them in front of my parents' house, they flung on their coats and ran for the car.

Day after day, each of them laughed, cried, and learned without me, time I would never be able to reclaim. This empty feeling was what the priest meant by guilt—a sense of permanent loss. I tried to resign myself to playing a minor role in their lives. I would be like a favorite aunt. This was the trade-off I'd made for freedom. I had toughened, too; I didn't cry as much—to Bruce's relief.

On this visit to Jackson, we did the thing I promised myself years before, but never got up the nerve to do alone: Bruce and I took my mother's cook, Annie Carter, to register to vote. Driving Mother's big car, Annie sat in back in her white uniform. I was nervous, but she was her usual confident self. At the courthouse, the clerk looked her over.

"What your name?"

"Annie Carter."

"What do you do?"

"I cook for Mrs. Watkins."

He thumbed through the register. "We already have an Annie Carter."

Annie stood taller, staring at the man over an intimidating shelf of bosom. "Well, that ain't me."

He wanted to find a reason to turn her down, but there was Bruce on one side, waiting lawyer-like, and white me on the other. When we left, Annie snapped her first voter's registration card inside her pocketbook.

"Man trying to scare me," she said from the backseat.

"Didn't work, though, did it?" Bruce said.

"Nosirree." Her laughter was loud and satisfied.

In 1972, when segregationist Alabama Governor George Wallace ran for President, Annie told us that every time he showed his face on her television, she shot a stream of snuff at the screen.

This was my first trip to Europe. I had fantasies of Parisian cafes, a literary tour of the continent, with me as a female combination of Hemingway and Sartre.

Before we left, I decided to use my new surroundings to give up both smoking and speed. I had a persistent sore throat from my daily half pack of Salems, and the speed had begun producing hallucinations (I saw men who weren't there standing on the side of the highway). I quit cold-turkey on the ship, transforming myself from loving Norma into a snarling stranger.

We landed in northern Europe deep in January. I froze and whined my way through dark cathedrals and museums, finding comfort only as we approached the warmth of southern Spain. We rented a house on the Costa del Sol. I settled in and quit complaining. I grew plump on the fresh bread, rich butter, and cheese. The *International Herald Tribune* arrived two days late, which made the political news, however awful, feel muted and bearable.

During our fifth month in Europe, a telegram arrived. Clay had broken the bad leg again.

"We have to go home." It seemed perfectly clear to me—if your child was in trouble, you needed to be there.

I saw Bruce's disappointment. "There's nothing we can do."

"It doesn't matter. I have to be there."

Reluctantly, he booked passage back. He was right—there was nothing I could do once we got to Mississippi, but I was thrilled to see Clay and be able to reassure myself he was healing and not hurting. I was so glad to see them all, hugely changed in five months. I hugged them and cried, and hugged them again.

I had spent all my money on this dream trip, which, like many dreams, was not as perfect as I expected. No journey was worth the distance from my children. I thought I was tough enough be away for that long, but I wasn't.

32

We returned to better circumstances. Bruce was made head of Legal Services, a promotion we hadn't expected. He got a raise and an office in downtown Miami. It no longer made sense to live in the country. We found a furnished house for rent in Coconut Grove, with two bedrooms and an enormous backyard swimming pool.

We felt rich, but not so rich that, on our first night back in town, staying with the couple who had stored my books, Bruce didn't open the closet in our room, spot the sandals he'd given the husband when we left, and take them back.

"You can't do that," I said.

"Sure I can. See, they're dusty." Bruce wiped them off. "He doesn't even wear them. He'll never notice."

I shook my head in disbelief. He did things I would never dare, and I envied him the guts.

All we needed was a cat, and we adopted two adult Siamese whose owner had died. They were already named—large, placid Romeo and small, clever Juliet. We took the names as an omen: even our cats were lovers. We neglected to remember the doomed part.

The rented house was shaded by an enormous ficus tree. Casement windows opened into a jungle of ferns. I began sneezing. Each morning, I sat on the side of the bed with my feet on the tile floor and sneezed ten times.

Bruce said, "Good grief."

"I can't help it." My voice sounded nasal. I blew my nose into a tissue.

"Do you have to do it so loud?"

"Sorry." I padded out to get the morning paper and sneezed six more times. I kept extra tissues in the pockets of the loose cotton dresses I wore.

"You shouldn't put your bare feet on the cold floor." Bruce spoke from behind the newspaper. We sat in the dining room looking out on the blue rectangle of pool.

"I don't think it's the cold floor."

"The sun, then. That's what makes me sneeze. Looking at the sun in the morning."

I shook my head in denial and opened the paper to the comics. This sneezing irritated us both. "Maybe I'll go see an allergist."

The doctor said I was allergic to household dust, insect wings, live oaks, and cats.

I told him, "I can't live without cats."

"Then you'll always sneeze."

I didn't tell Bruce the cat part. He might make us get rid of Romeo and Juliet. I began taking weekly allergy shots, but they didn't appear to help. Every morning, I woke up, sneezed, blew my nose, and started the day. Every morning Bruce groaned at the noise.

I got the message: the man was not sympathetic, but neither was I. I had been raised to see ill health as a weakness. I didn't expect coddling—a little less blame maybe, but no coddling. My strategy was to try to do the sneezing and nose-blowing out of Bruce's sight and hearing. The sniffles dried up by mid-morning and, to my ears, my new, lower voice sounded sexy. After six months, I quit the shots and couldn't tell the difference. I stuck to the Southern strategy: things would get better by themselves.

In 1969, Coconut Grove was the center of Miami's hippie scene. On Sundays, young people of every color crowded into Peacock Park with their long hair and flowing garments, playing music, the air thick with marijuana smoke. They were nomads, against corporations, middle-class values, consumerism, and the Vietnam war. So were we. We couldn't claim to be hippies: we had jobs, or at least Bruce did, and lived in a house. When he married Helen, Fred bought her all new stuff and returned our wedding gifts—nine barrels of china and silver. I might wear long gauzy skirts and grow my hair down to my waist, but you couldn't be a hippie with twelve place settings of Francis 1st in your father's basement.

When my children arrived that summer, we took them to Peacock Park, laughing as their eyes grew large. I felt pleased to be expanding their horizons, showing them a world they would never see in Mississippi.

A high wooden fence surrounded our backyard pool. As part of the new freedom, Bruce and I swam naked. Old customs and restrictions were being cast aside, and we threw off the restraint of bathing suits. Naked bodies were nothing to be ashamed of. This went against everything I'd been taught growing up. My father darted from his closet to the bathroom to prevent us glimpsing his boxer shorts. But the times, they were a-changing, and I tried to let go of my prudery.

I remember being tanned all over, and how nice that felt. I also remember, when the children arrived that summer, they were uneasy with our nudity. Bruce fed them the new creed—bodies were nothing to be ashamed of—making them feel the shame lay in refusing to go along. I forgot my long-ago misery when Helen, Daddy's friend from Hawaii, tried to make me do the hula without a bathing suit top. I forgot the night when the man from Bruce's board at Legal Services tried to make me take off my clothes and run into the ocean. I joined Bruce in jollying the children into compliance. It would be fun—nobody could see us. Allison flatly refused, but the other three took off their clothes and seemed happy enough. I had doubts about them seeing hairy, not-their-father, Bruce, but I dismissed these as hangovers from my Mississippi past. Looking back, I was an idiot.

Summer was almost over, the children went home, and I had no job. Bruce expressed concern. He was all for equal rights for women, especially when those rights included two paychecks. I had my degree, and I needed to get to work. Isabel's husband taught at the local community college. He told me there might be an opening. It wasn't a position in the English department, and it wasn't full-time, but it was a start.

I was hired to teach in New Careers, part of Lyndon Johnson's poverty program. I would improve the English reading and writing skills of welfare mothers trying to come back into the workforce.

We met every day, seven comfortable-looking black ladies, one crazy white lady, and me. I decided to focus on black literature and share with them their proud heritage (a heritage I had been totally unaware of in Mississippi). These women had never been on a college campus, and going to the library felt terrifying. I went to the librarian and asked if I could borrow a few books by black authors to keep in my classroom. He refused, saying if he gave out books to every faculty member, there would be none left for the library.

I didn't to give up. I went to a bookstore and bought paperbacks by Frederick Douglass, Langston Hughes, Ralph Ellison, Richard Wright, and Malcolm X. Except for the white lady, who appeared to be in the middle of a breakdown, we were a happy bunch. We spent our hours together reading, writing, and talking. We couldn't do enough talking. They wrote about the books they read and about themselves. These were the first black people I'd gotten to know outside of servants in Mississippi, and I was filled with admiration, not only for their struggles, but for the values they held onto and their determination to educate themselves out of poverty.

At the end of the term, the class wrote a play together and performed it. Their English scores leapt upward, and, at long last, I had accomplished something worthwhile. On a tiny scale, admittedly, but my ladies went on to greater success: they started small businesses and got jobs at local colleges. I was finally part of a movement, which had by this time marched right by me and on to Black Power.

The college was impressed enough by my results to hire me full-time in the English department. My first job paid $8,999 for nine months of teaching. I considered this a fortune and did not ask what the men were paid. I taught five sections of English composition. My first class started at 7:30 in the morning. I came into a dark room, flipped on the lights, and was greeted by a chorus of groans.

I was not satisfied with teaching composition the way my colleagues did: teach, test, and grade. I devised elaborate point systems to make students responsible for their results. I took the new fashions to an extreme and wore nothing but long skirts to class. The students asked if I had legs, and I told them no, I rolled on casters.

I taught American literature and discovered I was not, after all, the gentle, lecturing professor I had admired as an undergraduate back at Millsaps. I was no good at standing up and regurgitating an hour's worth of notes. I wanted to be professor-as-colleague, not the all-knowing expert.

The college president invited me to be part of something called the Innovations committee. We were to look at where education was headed in the future. Two things happened on that committee to change the course of my career: I read *Teaching as a Subversive Activity*, and I met a man named Mc-Gregor Smith. Mac taught in the journalism department, but he was working on a PhD, using ideas from the *Subversive* book to design an innovative model of education.

The book said teachers shouldn't be experts, standing in the front of a room spouting facts. Students were not in college to memorize, be tested, and, in six months, forget much of what they learned. Learning was a lifelong activity, and the purpose of school was to learn how to learn, a skill most people could acquire given the right guidance. Everything students wanted to know was out there, in books or people. We learned best what we were passionate to know. Teachers should be guides, helping students identify their passion, plan a course of study, and follow it.

Mac was allowed to try his new model with three students and two courses. He called it Life Lab, life as a laboratory for learning. As the idea grew, he added students and courses. In Life Lab, a teacher's role was to help students design study plans and meet with them once a week in what Mac called peer groups.

I decided to try the model in my English classes. I remember discussing it with my chairman; I'm sure I did. One class, the control, I met with as usual, three times a week. The second class, I met with once a week to help them implement their study plans. The rest of the time, they got together on their own. I gave each class a pre- and post-test. At the end of the term, the independent class outscored the traditional one.

Word of this spread around the English department, and at the next faculty meeting, I was confronted. This experiment was not to be repeated. What would happen to professors if students were allowed to work on their own? It was an insult to the profession. Was I trying to say their knowledge, their very presence in front of the classroom, was of no value?

I stood my ground, doggedly arguing the virtues of *Teaching as a Subversive Activity*, determined not to cry. They wanted none of it. I must go back to teaching the proper way, and I did. I bowed to the status quo as I had to bigotry in Mississippi. I had the courage to stand up to power, but only to a point. I wasn't willing to quit my job over a principle.

33

Bruce turned out to be right about Fred's marriage. The nineteen-year-old gave birth to a son, Fred's fifth child, then left him. She tried to leave the baby behind, but Fred refused. He was now married to Clay and Allison's fourth grade teacher. They continued calling her Miss McClemore until she insisted on "Mama." When Linden wrote to me, she always put the word in quotation marks.

I had a new person to dread when I called Jackson each week. I gritted my teeth, waiting to see who answered the phone. No caller ID in those days, no way of knowing what dragon waited at the other end of the line.

Susan: "Hello."

Me: "Susan?"

Susan: "Yes, Norma." Voice dripping with disgust, hardly able to hold the phone to her offended ear. The third Mrs. Craig had fallen straight into the wifely task of hating me.

One week when I telephoned, she answered in her schoolteacher voice: "None of the children is available to speak to you."

Nobody is home, I told Bruce. My gut feared worse.

A week later the message was the same.

I said, "What do you mean they won't talk to me?"

"They are unavailable." She hung up.

On Monday, I found in the mailbox the letters I had written to the four of them the week before. I saw the envelopes marked "Return to Sender," and telephoned Fred at his office.

"We do not wish the two of you to have further contact with the children. You, and I mean you, singular, may visit them under supervision here in Jackson. There will be no more trips to Florida."

"But that's not our agreement."

"The agreement is no longer in effect."

"You can't do that."

"You forget, I have sole custody. This is for the children's own good."

"But, why?"

"I think you know why."

My stomach hurt. I was pretty sure I knew what had happened and hoped I was wrong. I alerted my friend, Patt Derian. The next time Clay spent the night with her son, Craig, she telephoned and put Clay on the line.

"Thomas told," Clay said.

"Told?"

"About us swimming with no clothes on. About going to the park with the hippies. Don't cry, Mama."

I didn't blame Thomas. He was only six years old and loved to talk. "And then we," he'd say, "and then we." Babbling through the details of his day. I could hear Fred: You did what? Was Bruce undressed? Except he refused to say Bruce's name: You saw him, too? You saw that man? I never told the children to keep what we did a secret, but through the years they had learned caution. Their father grew angry before they came to Miami and became angrier if, on their return, they talked about anything we'd done. Thomas was the only one who hadn't absorbed the rule, and why should he? I felt stupid for letting it happen, for putting any of them in the way of Fred's fury.

My emotions shifted from wretched to rage. I would not stand by and let him do this to me. "I'll sue for custody," I told Bruce. He was all for it; he loved litigation, though he probably hadn't thought through the consequences: victory meant life with four children.

I called my father in Mississippi. He had a firm filled with lawyers, and I asked for one. "I want to sue Fred for custody."

"Are you sure you want to do that?"

"He and Susan are preventing contact with the children. I would never do the same to Fred. If I had custody, they would always be able to see their father."

"I'll support you, baby," my father said, "but you'll have to come here and appear in court."

The clench of fear. Fred had been itching for this moment since I left town: a public confession in front of a judge. I avoided it once by not contesting the divorce, but I couldn't give up my children without a fight.

I had left Mississippi in 1966; it was now 1971. Patt Derian said I had until age thirty to find the courage of my convictions: I was thirty-five.

The dreaded day arrived. For court, I wore my most demure dress, cream silk, buttoned to the neck, with a white collar. Except for the drumbeat of my heart, the room was quiet.

Across the aisle, Fred sat in his poplin suit, staring straight ahead, refusing to meet my eye. He had been forced to live with the humiliation of a runaway wife, but his day had come: I would have to answer for my sins.

On the witness stand, stewing with fear, but outwardly placid, I answered the questions from Fred's lawyer.

"Did you leave your husband and children?"

"Yes."

"And did you leave with another man?"

"Yes."

"A man you were not married to?"

"Yes."

"And you slept with this man?"

"Yes."

"In the same room?"

"Yes."

"In the same bed?"

"Yes."

The questions were beginning to sound odd. What would come next—pajamas or nightgown? But Fred's lawyer stopped, perhaps out of respect for my father. Tom Watkins—managing partner of Watkins & Eager, personal lawyer to former Mississippi Governor Ross Barnett—sat on the first row, stern and supportive.

There was silence. Everything was out in the open, everything Fred wanted the world to hear me admit, and the sky hadn't fallen. I felt absolutely calm, as if another, better person inhabited my body.

In his summary, my lawyer explained: all this had happened years before and was not relevant to the matter before the court. I had been married for five years, completed graduate school, and was a professor. Though living at a distance, I maintained close ties with the children, calling, writing, and visiting regularly. I deserved custody because I could now support them, and I would never try to separate them from their father, as he had done to me.

I could tell the judge was impressed. I was a sensible, soft-spoken woman, a mother who regretted the past but loved her children and thought they deserved two parents. I was Tom Watkins' daughter.

Fred's lawyer asked for a recess. Outside the courtroom, we learned the other side wished to mediate. Was I willing? My lawyer said I might win custody if I continued the fight, but I might also lose. I was satisfied. The children didn't want to leave their father, and a part of me suspected, for all his help, Bruce Rogow did not want four children.

Back and forth we went. Would I give up my bid for custody if the children resumed their visits? Yes, but only if calls and letters were exchanged freely. Would I agree not to swim naked in front of them? Yes. When they visited, would I agree not to do anything that was "different" from their customary upbringing in Mississippi? I figured this meant hanging out in Peacock Park with the hippies. I said yes.

I walked out of that courtroom triumphant. Fred had gotten his wish. He'd hung me with a Scarlet A and, even in conservative, Jim Crow Mississippi, that wasn't enough. I wasn't condemned as an unfit mother, and the force of his hatred could not move the judge.

Fred left the courtroom with a new enemy. My father refused his request to testify against me and was added to the list of people Fred hated. It never occurred to me Fred would ask my father for such a thing, and I didn't discover it for years. When I did, my admiration for my father grew. He never agreed with my politics, but I was his daughter, and he loved me enough to help me stay close to my children. He loved me enough to stand up to Fred Craig.

I remember the feeling of achievement after that victory. I once wondered if I could atone for one bad act—leaving my children—by creating a good life. After that day in court, I felt whole again. Bruce and I might not be able to take the children to Peacock Park to watch the hippies dance, but there were a hundred other places to go. Fred couldn't keep us from talking or the children from listening. They would hear other opinions and learn to think for themselves. Meet black people who were not servants. I could show them women were not inferior and deserved careers as satisfying as men's.

I had also learned a lesson. By going into that courtroom, I faced my greatest fear and was not destroyed by it. I came out stronger. I no longer had to weep in frustration and take whatever Fred handed out. I was the children's mother, and I fought back.

34

I returned from work one day to find the front door ajar. The optimistic mind tries to make order of nonsense: Bruce must have come home early. When the stereo wasn't in its accustomed place, I thought he'd taken it to be repaired. Awareness arrived like a scene in a movie: camera pans the living room, where the television set is missing; the bedroom, with the dresser drawers pulled out, underwear dumped on the floor, jewelry in a heap on the dresser. Cue the crescendo: we'd been robbed.

My first thought was for Allison's bracelet. Aunt Leigh gave my daughter a rose diamond bracelet, which I asked to keep until she was old enough to wear it. I stirred frantically through the mess of costume necklaces. No bracelet. I started to cry. I didn't care about the TV or the stereo, but Allison was the least likely of my children to forgive the loss of a diamond bracelet.

Bruce rushed home when I called. He was furious. His handmade Spanish boots were gone, and the custom shirts with B.R. embroidered on the front.

Two weeks later, the police brought a young man by the house. He confessed to burglarizing thirty homes in the neighborhood.

Bruce went out to the car and returned with a report. "He's just a kid, and you won't believe what he's wearing—my boots. I said to him, 'Are those my boots?' He looked at his feet like he was as surprised to see them as I was. I'm going to find him another pair of shoes. Can't leave him barefooted. Can you imagine the nerve?"

I shook my head. I couldn't.

Bruce carried another pair of shoes out to the car and began spraying the inside of his recovered boots with Lysol disinfectant.

"What about my bracelet?"

"Gone. Sold the first day to buy drugs."

When the burglar went on trial, Bruce drove down to testify and returned with another tale. "I advised probation and a drug treatment program, and you won't believe what the kid wore to court—one of my shirts."

"He did not?"

"He did. Had my initials right on the front. I pointed it out, and he looked sheepish. I couldn't take the shirt off the guy's back. The judge and I both got a good laugh out of it."

Bruce didn't care about the lost shirts anymore. He'd already gone to the tailor and chosen fabric for new ones.

Allison was as angry as I feared about the loss of her bracelet. I promised to give her two thousand dollars to make up for it when she grew up. A promise I never kept. I didn't have two thousand dollars to spare until she no longer needed it.

I learned from that incident: Bruce's stuff—his boots and monogrammed shirts—was more important than my diamond bracelet (more important than I was?), and a good story outweighed a loss. As for me, not only had I failed to protect my children from successive stepmothers, I couldn't hold onto a bracelet.

35

Clay was almost nine when I left Jackson. He was thirteen now, rail-thin with hair to his shoulders, mature for his years from breaking the bad leg over and over and spending months in a body cast. He lay for weeks at a time, motionless from chest to ankle, reading. His father built him a platform bed. It hung from his bedroom ceiling on four heavy chains and swayed, giving stationary Clay the sensation of movement.

Fred came up with sweet ideas like the swinging bed, and I forgot the harsh words he threw at me. How could we not be friends, both caring so much for our wounded son? I would call home, filled with my toasty feelings, and run, once again, into the saw of my ex-husband's voice, cutting, cutting. Every time, I hung up the phone in tatters, trying to console myself with Jim Child's words: the man had the right to hate me.

I was home after school on the day Clay called. He was old enough to do that now—pick up the telephone and call whenever he liked.

"I want to come live with you."

My heart bumped with hope. "What does your father say?"

"He says I have to cut my hair."

I waited.

"I won't do it. I told him if he tries to make me, I'll come live with you."

"Of course you can come. All of you are welcome."

"Will you buy me a ticket?"

"Yes, but you have to talk to your father first."

I lit up inside. Clay wanted to come and live with us. In spite of Fred's hatred and the hatred of his wives, I had won, or at least I'd won Clay. Bruce was right: the children would grow up and decide for themselves. I called him at the office, triumphant. He sounded happy, too. He was good that way, optimistic about whatever life brought, even if it turned out to be a teenage son.

Fred phoned that night. "I'm against this. I've told Clay. I can't stop him, but he's leaving against my will. You may think you've won (How did he know?), but I want to warn you, nobody likes the kid. He gets along with adults because he's a cripple, and they feel sorry for him, but he doesn't have any friends."

I could not believe what I was hearing. What kind of father spoke this way about his son? I relayed the conversation to Bruce.

"It's the bitterness talking," Bruce said. "He can't stand losing to you."

We picked Clay up at the Miami airport. It was the start of a new chapter, and the three of us were excited. Clay moved into the second bedroom of the Coconut Grove house. He wanted a waterbed, so we bought one, painstakingly filling it from the outside hose, terrified of leaks. He went from a bed on chains in Mississippi, to the jelly wobble of a waterbed in Miami.

Another metaphor?

We didn't care how long his hair grew. He felt freed, and we doted like two people who had invented parenthood.

"You'll never get the others," Fred said.

Clay confirmed this. "Dad is really mad at me, and the others feel sorry for him."

I had one, and I was content.

Clay (right) comes to live with us. We cheer Bruce during a bicycle race.

36

Burglary spoiled the Coconut Grove house for me. I might call myself a liberated woman, but I was now a fearful one. I washed and rewashed my underclothes and still felt creepy wearing them. Everything the man touched felt polluted. When Bruce wasn't home, I sensed eyes watching through the casement windows. Each afternoon after work, I unlocked the front door expecting to see everything gone again. Even with Clay around, I didn't feel secure.

The neighbors added to our unease. A dean from the University of Miami lived with his wife on the north side. In their bedroom, they fought nightly battles ten feet from ours. Through a screen of palms, we heard curses and objects being flung against the walls. Their anger kept us awake and apprehensive.

We decided to buy a house and spent our Sunday afternoons looking. Clay usually went places with us, but he refused to march through empty houses. We looked at lavish, waterfront homes, pretending we had the money, and at the modest, boring houses we could afford. We searched for almost a year before I spotted a listing in the Sunday paper: "For sale by owner. Exotic wood house on two acres."

The man who answered the phone sounded less than welcoming. "It's a long way down here. A lot of people don't like the place."

I asked for directions.

He said we couldn't come that day. He wasn't ready.

On Tuesday after work, we drove down to the country where we had once lived, in the growing area south of Miami called the Redland. We found the address. From the road, through a forest of pines, we spotted the tip of a shingled roof and an unpainted wooden eave.

Bruce said, "This may be it."

I sat forward in the car, jittery with anticipation. We drove up a curving dirt road past thick clumps of ginger and guava trees. The house was small and built of cypress, with what I learned to call a scissor-truss roof, reaching the ground on one side and open to a jungle of guava and governor plums on the other. The upstairs bedroom was a slope-ceilinged loft. There were no screens on the windows. I watched mosquitoes buzz thickly around the owners' legs.

"Most people come in here and talk about how they'll put in sliding glass doors and air condition the place." The man I had spoken to on the phone looked us over. He was taller than Bruce with enormous hands and speculative blue eyes. His name, he told us, was Neal, just Neal. His wife, Mary, wore a long white sarong, pulled under her arms and tied in front. When she moved, it swung open, and I glimpsed a triangle of dark pubic hair. They had built the house themselves.

"We would never air condition," Bruce said.

"We'll need screens." I spoke hesitantly. They made me feel we didn't deserve their house.

"Mosquitoes don't bother us." Neal brushed a few off his arms.

I thought it was probably because of the smell. A powerful, musky odor of unwashed bodies moved in front of the pair like a separate presence. I held my breath and remembered the way we used to talk about colored people in Mississippi, as if body odor were a racial trait. These people built a house, living in a nearby shed with two children until it was finished. If you worked hard, and didn't bathe or use deodorant, you stank.

Neal frowned at Bruce's suit. "Most people from town don't like this place."

Bruce said, "We're different."

I was enchanted. Neal had made everything by hand. There were cunning kitchen cabinets and a thick teak counter fashioned from the deck of a sunken ship. In the bathroom, cabinets had been inserted between the studs. The door closed with a handmade latch. The ladder to the loft was the vertical trunk of a pine, peeled and sanded, inset with smooth, hand-carved footholds. I started to climb.

"Better take off your shoes," Mary said.

I did, but it was still scary. I was too awed by this couple to let my fear show. Coming down was worse.

"We'd have to have screens," I said.

Neal shrugged. If we insisted, screens could be managed.

We talked about when we could move in. How long would it take to make screens for the large, shuttered windows, as well as the smaller ones? Neal offered to build us a dining table with teak left from the sunken ship. We bargained over their furniture, a wicker couch and chair, which Mary said they had "liberated." That was how they talked. Except for the lumber and roofing shingles, everything in the house had been found at the dump, floated up on the tide, or been "liberated," which I took to mean stolen.

"You worked so hard building this place," I said. "Why do you want to sell?"

"I'm a sailor," Neal said.

I waited.

"Too many trees. I miss seeing the horizon." Neal didn't smile. He almost never smiled.

I felt the opposite. In this house, surrounded by towering Dade County pines, no one could see us, and no trouble would find its way in.

On the way home, we exulted. It was like a dream, exactly the house we wanted, simple, secret, and beautiful.

We raved about it to Clay. He was okay with moving to the country until he discovered he couldn't bring his waterbed. The raised floor of the new house wouldn't support the weight. He balked and sulked (odd having two male wills in the house) until I made him a deal. There was a small shed on the second acre, built by a man who helped Neal with the house. If Clay gave up his waterbed without a fuss, he could sleep there. At fifteen, he would have his own place.

A month later, with Clay, Romeo, Juliet, and a long-legged tiger kitten named Spider, we moved into our new house. Neal had built clever screens, mounted in teak grooves so they slid up. I could reach out to close the handmade windows when it rained.

I never lived in a place I loved so much. I hung a bird feeder in the guava tree on the open side and watched in wonder as birds changed with the seasons. In winter, the painted buntings came, the females pale lime green, the males a brilliant blue and red. An oriole gave a piercing five-note cry from the top of the schefflera tree. Blue jays, cardinals, and doves fought over the seed. When winter ended, the red-winged blackbirds flew in and bickered in the plum trees. Every day at twilight, I heard a catbird's plaintive cry.

Clay reveled in his shed an acre away from the grownups. He turned his bunk bed into a nest of discarded candy wrappers, broken-spined books, and (this was a horrible surprise) cigarette butts. I discovered he smoked when I went one day to wash his sheets. I threw a fit. He claimed he didn't do it much, and he would quit, both of which turned out to be untrue. It wasn't as seamless bringing him into our lives as I'd imagined, and I found myself making excuses to Bruce, explaining Clay, asking forgiveness in advance. My health got worse. I hoped it wasn't the glorious green outdoors the house let inside, along with humidity, mold, and bugs.

I still sneezed; my nose ran, and now a cough appeared. A quiet cough, I chose to believe, a poignant cough. It happened when I went to bed. A tickle began, low in my throat, and then the cough, which I tried to muffle.

Bruce shifted beside me, burying his head in the pillow. The cough grew worse and became part of my days. At work, I tried to cough into the pauses. People said, "What do you get out of being sick?" Or, "When you decide you're ready to be well, you'll quit that business." This was 1973, and illness was the victim's fault, an indulgence to be given up. I read somewhere that people who repress anger get hives, and people who repress tears get allergies. Maybe this was my body's way of punishing me for leaving home.

The sniffles lasted all day, and I kept tissues in every room. I pasted a photograph in our album, taken of me in New York, nose in a Kleenex, essence trapped in a gesture. Making love, I had to stop and blow my nose. The liquid running out of me all day was clear, watery, and slightly salty. I licked it off my upper lip rather than let it fall into whatever I happened to be cooking. Clay laughed; Bruce got disgusted. He called it snot, one of my least favorite words. His disdain made me resentful. Would he rather have it in the soup? Besides, it was more like tears.

One night, with Clay tucked in his shed, Bruce and I stood outside look-ing in through the big front windows at Neal's teak dining table, the iron wagon wheel chandelier hanging over it, filled with candles, and the liberated furniture reupholstered in dark blue velvet. The house was softly lit. As part of our new and simpler life—I can't believe this now—no bulb was over forty watts, and we used only yellow bug lights. From outside, the place looked magical, like a cottage in a fairy tale. I held Bruce's hand, wiping my nose with the other, and admitted contentment. Life with a teenager was not as easy as I'd hoped; the runny nose might drive Bruce off, but on this night, all was right with my world.

I remembered, but did not mention, another night, when I stood and looked through the glass wall of the house Fred built us, admiring the cher-ry dining table, the soft brick wall, our pumpkin-colored carpet. I felt this same warm glow of satisfaction, a kind of house-proud happiness that en-compassed the man who built it. That was short-lived. I almost wrote "a false happiness," but it wasn't. There were whole years when a successful husband, handsome children, and my house were enough. Or maybe that's what false happiness is, satisfaction based on external circumstances.

I stood with Bruce outside our magic house in the woods, convinced that this time the feeling of warmth would not end.

Exterior of our cabin

37

Life goes on, even in a magic house. We dropped Clay off at school each day, a much longer drive from the country. Bruce left me at the college and drove downtown to Legal Services. At night, we reversed the trek. Bruce listened to my stories of teaching, praised my growing skills, and bemoaned my troubles with administration. College administrators had taken over the role professors played in graduate school—authority figures I tried to find my way around.

The English department forgave my experiment in independent learning. I moved on and was asked to teach black literature. We had an African American faculty member, but he didn't want to take it on. I couldn't wait to use the literature I had read with the welfare ladies, excited to be doing something to make up for doing nothing in Mississippi.

Twenty-five students signed up for the course. I walked into the classroom on the first day and spotted Jacob Alexander, a tall, broad figure in fatigues and combat boots, his dark face half-hidden by a full beard. During introductions, he told the class he had retired from the Air Force after twenty years. He looked like an Old Testament prophet, come to smote me for daring to teach black literature with my white face.

Nervousness crept into my voice. "You probably wonder why somebody with my skin color and a Southern accent is teaching this course." Their eyes said, yes, they did wonder, and they weren't sure they were going to put up with it. I told my story: how I'd run away from the bigotry of the South, too frightened to stay and help, not realizing that the fear was part of my own oppression as a woman. I told them reading and talking about black literature had opened a door into the lives of people I knew only as servants. "We wear the mask that grins and lies," Paul Dunbar wrote. I had seen only the masks.

Reading literature by people like those I lived with every day of my life, but never knew, made me ashamed for my years of ignorance.

Decades later, one of those students confided that they met after class to vote on whether to give me a chance. Jacob said they should and became my chief ally—or, as he put it, "I saved your ass." When the term ended, I sent him to Mac Smith at Life Lab. Jake had a wealth of experience and was eager to learn, a perfect candidate for alternative education. He charged through the two-year degree and went on for his bachelor's and master's degrees. In what felt like a short time, he was teaching alongside me, my friend.

Feminism was in the air. I decided to do my part by teaching a course in women's literature with a colleague, Fran. This gave me a chance to study oppression from a different perspective. In Mississippi, blacks had been held down, but women were right behind them, claiming our white purity, oblivious to our bondage. In the name of Southern womanhood, we perched on our pedestals, out of the way. It was our responsibility to keep alive the South's lost and romantic past. Doing so meant we weren't to have jobs; working would make our men feel bad about themselves. We were also taught to fear anyone of color who didn't work for us. Black people were not quite human, which was why they must be kept down. Women needed to do the same: stay home, raise the children, and let the men run things. Inside our big houses, voting for the men our husbands told us to vote for, supervising the black help, we were supposed to feel privileged and protected.

I watched Bruce's face when I tried to explain the importance of women's rights. He wasn't unsympathetic, but he'd been raised in Miami by a mother who went to work every day. What was the big deal? He acted as if the whole movement were a storm in a teacup, the way he had treated my fury at being stomped out of that law school library. Odd, the way he grasped the indignities of segregation, but not the bias against gender. Odder still, the way I overlooked and excused it.

During that women's lit class, one of the female students fell in love with Fran, and I watched as the complications of a same-sex romance unfolded. It looked a lot like the regular kind: the young woman pleaded for Fran's affection, while Fran remained kind but unresponsive. Heartsick notes were left on our desk: "Check one if you'll never love me. Check two if you might."

I remembered the guidance counselor at Ole Miss telling me only two careers available to a female English major: secretary and teacher. I had disdained both and gotten married instead—the only option I knew for escape. I ended up a secretary at the advertising agency and now, during my first years at Miami-Dade, I discovered how wrong I'd been at eighteen—I loved teaching.

In the spirit of the early 1970s, I divided my composition classes into groups by their birth signs, earth with earth, fire with fire. Students kept journals and shared their writings. I was flattered one day when a young man asked if he could visit one of my classes. I was so good at this, strangers wanted to come and watch. The minute class was over, he leapt across the circle, screaming, "Don't be looking at my woman," and began punching one of my students. I broke up the fight the way any good Southern female would, by bursting into tears. "Stop it," I said. "I can't stand violence." Much to my surprise, they stopped, but this incident cured my swollen ego.

In another section of English composition, a skinny black kid who wasn't doing well sidled up to me before class. "Look what I got?" He pulled a small black pistol from his backpack, not exactly pointing it at me, not exactly threatening to blast me full of bloody holes.

In a flash, I turned into my aunt Hosford Fontaine. "Put that away this instant." He obeyed and slunk to his seat. I went on with the class, not admitting to the pounding heart and fever of dread brought on by the sight of that gun. I've tried to remember if I reported the incident to my chairman. Maybe I did, making light of it: "You won't believe what happened." The young man quit coming to class. I was hugely relieved, spared having to fail him, spared another visit with that gun.

I shared these stories around the dinner table with Bruce and Clay, feeling like Wonder Woman. Bruce had his tales of the law; Clay described his adventures at school (He had already been advanced two grades). I sat with my little family in the golden light of our cabin, feeling giddy with success. I had recreated the best dinners of my childhood, when Daddy kept us enthralled, before the arguments over civil rights made me cry through meals, before Mother came to the table each evening wobbly with bourbon.

The dining table at the cabin

38

The students voted me Best Teacher at the end of that year. Fran told me I'd won the day before, and I was dumbfounded. Not since being chosen pinup girl of a Cub Scout troop in the fourth grade had I been hit with such an unanticipated prize. On Honors Day, with Bruce beaming from the audience, I got up to accept my plaque and made what now feels like an embarrassingly feminist speech: thanking my husband for ironing my long skirt, calling the God I no longer believed in "She."

My glow of self-satisfaction was short-lived. In fact, this may be a life rule: beware the smug glow. I had been teaching full time for three years. If all went on the way it should, especially with this new honor, I would receive what was called a continuing contract: I would have tenure.

Instead, I got a notice in our country mailbox to come to the post office and sign for a registered letter from the college. Rumors flew around campus. Student enrollment was down, and everyone without a continuing contract was being fired. "To fire" was not a verb administrators liked to use. They called it a reduction in force: we were being riffed.

I never realized how much I depended on this job for my self-esteem. I felt completely squashed, crawling through my days like a worm. I had left my children, my home, everything—for Bruce, of course, but also to become an independent woman, and that was being taken away. I would be a parasite like my mother, accepting whatever allowance Bruce was willing to hand over. Clay was sympathetic, or as sympathetic as a teenage boy can be to adult troubles. Bruce was, too, but I was not sure he would love me as much without an income. I thought of Yosserian, discarded when he got in the way of prospects. Earning my keep was part of our deal.

My colleagues said the registered letters required you to make an appointment with the campus vice president. You went to his office and he riffed you. My solution, as it had been for other disasters, was avoidance. I refused to claim the registered letter. Summer arrived, school let out, the post office kept delivering notices, and I kept ignoring them. One morning the phone rang. It was the vice president. He began a smooth speech about needing to see me, and for one fleeting second, I had a flash of hope: I was different; he was firing everyone except me.

I interrupted. "You want me to come in and be fired, right? I don't want to drive sixteen miles to get fired. You can do it on the telephone."

He did.

The loss of my job was like a permanent storm, and I rained unhappiness on Bruce and Clay. The children were due for a summer visit. I looked forward to having them. The commotion might help me forget my misery. I noticed Bruce seemed less thrilled to be gaining three additional children this year.

I waited until Clay wasn't around. "What's wrong?"

"Everything has to focus on them when they're here."

"They're my children. It's only for a month."

"A month out of my life."

"You said you were willing to have all four of them come and live with us," I howled with rage. "Now you can't put up with them for a month?"

Bruce said Clay took all his energy.

I told him where he could take his churlish self if this visit was too much for him.

We made up, and he was kind when the children arrived. Clay loved showing his siblings around like a native. After they left, I tried to talk to Bruce about the way he acted before they arrived. Was this going to be a pattern?

"Don't make it into a big deal," Bruce said. "Why don't you use the energy to find another job?"

I hated it when he put me off by refusing to talk—but he was right, and I did try. The paper published a story titled "Best Teacher Fired," and I got a feeler from the Catholic college fifty miles north, but nothing came of it. I was worthless: bringing in no money, plus I had added Clay to our expenses.

In August, the academic dean called me in. The college wanted to rehire me, not in the English department, but as a team leader in a new program called the "I" Division. "I" stood for interdisciplinary learning. I would be the leader of a team of four professors: English, psychology, social science, and natural science. I exulted over being rehired, and especially the team leader part. My favorite thing when we lived at the hotel was bossing other children around.

The program was similar to Mac Smith's Life Lab, but not as free. We met with students for three hours a day, four days each week, using classroom activities that combined the four basic general education courses.

The storm had lifted, and I tried to look at the experience. My suffering—buckets of self- loathing, moping, and tears—was self-inflicted. I could have picked up the registered letter, gone for a meeting with the dean, and enjoyed a three-month vacation. That's what Bruce would have done. Or I could have done what my friend Isabel did: use the time to take graduate courses, switch from English to social science, and never grade another terrible five-hundred-word essay.

Bruce would never have spent three months sulking. Except I didn't know I'd be rehired until I was. I was a sufferer, and he wasn't. For him, this was always the best of all possible worlds, and in his world he liked me better employed.

The head of the I Division was black. I looked forward to my first black boss, payback for those years of ordering the help around in Mississippi. He was a former math instructor and turned out to be tall, dark, and angry. He wrote Black Power poetry and liked to recite it at faculty meetings, poems about injustice and taking revenge on the honkies. He did rap before rap was born, slam poetry before the word existed. As it happened, my black boss did not like women, or at least he didn't like me. I was too opinionated, too strong-willed, too talkative—all my best qualities.

I went to his office to ask for more pay for a woman team member who had done hours of extra work. His face closed as I spoke. My voice got higher; I was begging now, talking about how unfair the situation was. I felt tears coming, and there I was, crying once again in the face of male authority. Daddy all over again, but black daddy this time.

He watched until I ran out of words and said, "No."

I left hating him, realizing the tears were anger, and had always been anger, not sadness, fury at being female and powerless.

My boss never forgot it. Whenever my name came up, people told me he sneered, "She cries."

After my day at school, I moonlighted, running an evening peer group for Life Lab down at Homestead Air Force Base. One group grew into two, and then three. I told Mac Smith I was carrying almost a full load of classes for his program and asked if he would get me a transfer. Magically, he did, and when the year ended, I escaped I Division and began working full time for Mac.

Life Lab was college for adults who had been forced to delay their education. Students wrote study contracts for each course, outlining what they planned to accomplish and what grade they wanted to earn. For an A, they did a project of excellence. One of my students, for her nutrition project, started a catering business, delivering hot, vegetarian meals to the homebound. Students could register for up to fifteen credits a semester, while physically meeting with a peer group for only three hours a week.

The group meetings were invigorating: students talked about what they had accomplished and shared resources. It was learning the way I remembered from Millsaps, a community of equals inspiring one another. As peer group leader, I was there, not to be the expert, but for guidance and support. Students documented life experience for credit and combined course work—getting credit in English composition for writing a paper for psychology. Everyone kept journals, and insights were exchanged among peer groups through what we called links. The program acquired a huge collection of audiotapes, talks by famous names in every field. These substituted for the usual classroom lectures and could be checked out or ordered by mail.

Students who couldn't otherwise go to college because of jobs or children signed up in droves. We brought on a full-time faculty member for every major field. Each of us ran four peer groups and served as teacher of record for the courses in our discipline. We had twenty part-time faculty leading groups all over Dade County. After Jacob Alexander got his master's degree, he ran peer groups in the prisons.

At the end of the term, students handed in fat portfolios of their work. We kept these as a record of contracts fulfilled. Policemen and veterans loved Life Lab. They could get an associate's degree while working, and veterans got V.A. benefits.

During Life Lab's heyday, the Southern Association of Colleges did its ten-year accreditation of Miami-Dade. The program passed with high marks. The V.A. investigated us, questioning why so many veterans signed up. Our students packed the meeting, and the V.A. gave us their blessing.

Life Lab was the perfect program for mature students. We got a few immature ones trying to game the system, but for most, it was an incredible way to go to school while working a full-time job or raising children, and to have previous achievements recognized.

Most of my peer groups met at night. I came home late, too revved up by the experience to go to bed. Bruce and I sat at the teak dining table, while I told him of the day's small victories. He was that rare thing, the engaged male listener. I never felt closer to him.

In those days, the early '70s, everybody joined some kind of consciousness-raising group. A bunch of us faculty, led by a counselor, sat in a circle once a week and talked about our goals. I said my five-year goal was to be head of Life Lab and to work two days a week from home so I could write. Still intimidated by Eudora Welty's telling me I didn't have a voice, I wasn't thinking of creative writing. I thought I might do articles on education. In *One Writer's Beginnings*, Welty wrote, "You can have your first choice in life, but probably not your second." She was talking about work and love. What she didn't say, and I discovered: you may achieve the goals you so blithely set at a weekly group meeting, but you cannot imagine what you will sacrifice in exchange.

I was thrilled with my handsome husband, my smart son, and my all-encompassing job. Life was good.

One night, as we prepared for bed in our loft, Bruce looked at the softly lighted room and at me, waiting under the covers. "How long do I have to be this happy?"

I laughed, taking it as a compliment. "Forever, of course."

Norma at cottage in woods, early '70s

39

Daddy called to say Mother was back in the hospital. She'd been in twice before for an intestinal blockage. Each time, the surgeon removed the blocked portion, got things working, and sent her home. Each time, she collapsed internally again, and now, after a third surgery, she was very weak. I flew to Jackson.

Bruce would bring Clay, if— We thought "when," but we said "if."

At Baptist Hospital, my sister Mary Elizabeth and I stood in the hall with the doctor. Adhesions, he told us. Bands of fibrous scar tissue from her hysterectomy caused the blockages. He shook his head. There was nothing more they could do.

I thought about Mother's long-ago operation, the one my father said made him stop loving her. She had the hysterectomy while he was away in the Navy, when doctors said her heart couldn't take another pregnancy. Daddy blamed her for giving birth to three daughters instead of the son he wanted. He blamed her for being operated on before she could try again. She was dying from the operation she got to keep from dying.

I needed someone to blame and, as usual, I blamed her. The illness had been caused by her lifestyle. From the smug security of my happy marriage, I saw a woman who chose to stay in a loveless marriage, with a man who didn't want her.

When I was fourteen, Daddy left home. I remember filling out papers at Central High, and writing in the space next to my parents' names the humiliating word, "Separated." I remember how empty and awful the house felt without him. After a few months, family pressure and community expectation forced him home. I didn't care why he'd returned, or whether he wanted to be there. I didn't stop to ask why he no longer loved our mother. Parents were supposed to stay together, and he was back. That was all that mattered. (I managed to block all of this when I left my children.)

Mother accepted not being loved as the price for remaining Mrs. Tom Watkins. The privilege and security of being my father's wife was worth any sacrifice. When I asked once why she didn't leave him, she claimed she stayed for us. I believe she stayed because she still loved him, had always loved him, and never gave up hoping he might wake one morning and love her again. This did not happen; my father was politely distant and never, in our presence, physically affectionate. She assuaged her disappointment with afternoons of cards and liquor, which led to slurred-voice dinners. Daddy chewed at the other end of the table with his eyes shut, pretending to be somewhere else. I believed the absence of love could kill you—helped along by bad habits. Mother's evenings ended with bourbon and a cigarette, and her mornings began with black coffee, Bufferin, and another cigarette.

She lay in the hospital bed, tiny under the white covers. The operations had reduced her to a size she'd always longed to be. I went to Francis Pepper, Jackson's finest women's store, and brought back a dress to fit her tiny new self, black silk with a white ruff. She smiled at the sight of it, and we hung it from the door of the hospital room's closet. "I can't wait to wear it." Her voice was a murmur. "When I'm better."

Heavily drugged, she dropped in and out of sleep. I stood on one side of the bed patting her hand, wishing I'd been kinder, wishing we'd been better friends.

My sister Mary Elizabeth hissed. "Stop patting her like that. She's not a pet."

I snatched my hand away. My sister's blue eyes were filled with rage. "Sorry," I said. Apologizing as if I were patting her. The look told me that she and Mother were in this business of dying together. I had taken myself away, and was now an intruder.

Mother's eyes opened. I bent to kiss her.

"Don't come too close," she whispered. "I smell bad."

My feelings about my mother were a mixture of love and exasperation, but this broke my heart. I took the hand without tubes and kissed her on the forehead. The birthmark, shaped like a map of South America, the one that flared when she got angry, was barely visible against her white skin. I said, "No, you don't."

She wore an "Archie Manning" button pinned to her hospital gown. Manning was the starting quarterback for Ole Miss, and Mother was a rabid Rebels fan. She attended every game played in Jackson and watched the rest of the season on television, sitting on the edge of the living room couch, cigarette in one hand, drink in the other, criticizing the choice of plays and cussing the coaches.

I said, "I see you have your hero pinned over your heart."

She grinned with a hint of her old spirit and gave my hand a squeeze.

Daddy came after work and sat next to her bed. He hated hospitals and sick people, but he bent close and held her hand. "I love you, Norma," he whispered. She gave him the sweetest smile, as if it were worth dying to hear those words.

Did he love her? He sounded as if he meant it. Maybe he'd loved her all along in some hands-off way, or maybe he loved her now for leaving and setting him free.

No one mentioned the word death. It wasn't done. Mother was going to get up and dance in that new dress. Until the last breath, there was always a chance for improvement.

She died in the early morning when none of us was there. The Methodist minister said she had spoken with him often about death. When I burst into tears, he tried to comfort me. "She wasn't afraid." I wasn't crying because I thought she was afraid. I was crying over the lie, the way we tried to fool each other with our bright talk, sparing her feelings while she spared ours, no one willing to be truthful, not even at the end. A reminder of the way we lived our entire lives in that town.

In death, Mother looked like a small white-wrapped package, as fragile as porcelain. I was relieved she didn't have to hurt any more and sad that we hadn't been closer. Perhaps she forgave me for leaving, but she never actually liked me. I didn't praise her enough for her very real talents. I blamed her for the drinking and the double chin and for not being able to hold onto my father's love. She blamed me for leaving, casting aside every lesson she'd taught me about being a good Southern wife.

In the local paper, her obituary appeared opposite the comics. She was "Wife of Prominent Attorney." Even in death, a woman got no name of her own.

After the ceremony at the church and the burial in the Watkins plot at Greenwood Cemetery, we gathered at the house. Relatives and friends crowded in to enjoy the ham, fried chicken, cakes, and pies they had brought by earlier. The women began eying my father speculatively, measuring him for a new wife. Everyone said how smart and darling Mother had been, and what a shame it was for her to go so soon. She was fifty-nine.

You left in the South; you departed for a better place. Nobody died.

All signs of this gathering had vanished by late afternoon, when Daddy called the three of us together in the living room. Clay was with his dad; Bruce had gone to look up old civil rights buddies.

My father sat on the couch, Mother's will in front of him on the glass-topped table. He slid on his black-framed reading glasses. He was vain about his looks and wore them only when he had to.

My two sisters and I sat in a semi-circle around him, showing no signs of expectation or greed. The will was not long. Our mother had little of her own.

Daddy began in his courtroom voice. "I leave my emerald dinner ring to my daughter, Mary Elizabeth." My middle sister sat with a little close-lipped smile. She was the good daughter, the debutante and Junior League volunteer, still married to her first husband. At regular intervals, she had a breakdown and had to be hospitalized. Being Southern, we didn't talk about that either.

"I leave the dining table, chairs, and buffet, a gift to me from my family, to my daughter, Sydney." Sydney was the youngest, our baby, Daddy's final chance for a son. Everyone loved her the best. The words "a gift from my family" were in there, I guessed, to remind Daddy that the furniture he took for granted, including the table where we ate dinner every night, had never been his.

I wondered if my sister would carry away an entire roomful of furniture, leaving Daddy to eat supper in the kitchen with Annie. He didn't appear to mind. Mother was gone, and he was free to live and love as he chose. We could take all the furniture.

A share of an oil well went to Mary Elizabeth, and another to Sydney. A diamond stickpin for Sydney and a silver tea service for Mary Elizabeth. I began to get the picture. The silver flatware went to one of my children, the mahogany secretary in the corner to another.

"That's it." Daddy shuffled the pages.

I had been disinherited.

I identified the pressure in my chest as hurt. My sisters stared at their laps, embarrassed for me.

Daddy cleared his throat. "Your mother loved you, baby. She made this will seven years ago and must have forgotten to change it."

I didn't believe it, and neither did he.

Seven years ago I ran away from the life Mother groomed me for—the lovely house, successful husband, darling children, the days filled with tennis, bridge, and volunteer work. I must have seemed like Esau to her, selling my birthright for a mess of pottage.

But that was a long time ago. I thought the past had been forgiven. I married a lawyer and become a college professor. I might not look like a Jackson matron with my straight hair and long skirts, but I lived a good life. Mother was charmed by Bruce and seemed to get over my desertion. When I flew home for each of her operations, she acted genuinely glad to see me and grateful that I'd come.

But I realized—sitting there trying not to cry, telling myself it didn't matter—there were deeds that could never be forgiven. People pretended to your face; the uncles and cousins smiled. They gave me hugs and teased me the way they always had. But under the façade of Southern courtesy, they remembered, and they minded. I had torn the fabric of the family. Whatever satisfactions I managed to find out there in the world with strangers, I was welcome to them. I could not have the one thing I longed for when I re-turned: to be accepted and loved as I had once been.

In the kitchen, Annie wiped her eyes on her apron. Mother had over-worked and underpaid her. She had scolded, flattered, condescended, and confided in her, but in that house during the long hours Daddy spent at the office, Annie Carter was often Mother's only company. She had not been left anything either, but she loved my mother, and her grief came from a place of pure loss.

In Mother's room, my sisters and I stood with our hands in her jewelry box.

"You pick first." Mary Elizabeth meant because I didn't get left anything.

I fingered the strand of pearls.

She said, "You already have pearls."

I dropped them. "I don't want anything." My only desire was to be a thousand miles from here, in our cabin in the woods, back in my other life. I had chosen that life, and if, at times like this, the choice hurt, so be it. I lived with people I could speak to without lying, and I was no longer afraid. I talked about civil rights and women's rights and railed against the Vietnam war without being called a Communist.

Sydney said, "Mother did love you." Her blue eyes filled with tears. She wanted everyone to get along. She wanted this to be over so she could pour herself a big glass of wine.

I felt my eyes sting. Pity was almost worse than being disinherited.

"Why don't you take the gold beads?" Sydney said.

I picked up the necklace, the beads cool in my hand. I could not let myself cry. Crying would make them think I cared, that I was sorry I left and missed being part of what once felt like a circle of unbreakable love.

40

Bruce, Clay, and I drove back to Florida in my mother's Oldsmobile 88, a white-topped, aqua monster, with a steel body and a gas-eating engine. We didn't want an old car, but Daddy said to take it, and Clay was almost sixteen, eager to drive. It felt odd riding south in that heavy car, a gift my mother never offered.

The idea of Clay's driving made me nervous. In many ways, he was still the dreamy kid he'd been at five. He lived in his head and often stumbled through the physical world. I had sent him to a progressive private school, where he starred academically, but faltered in other ways. The principal took me aside one day and told me my son was president of the flying club. When I looked confused, he said he didn't mean planes.

I was not totally surprised. Once we left Clay with a babysitter for the weekend and returned to find our small stash of marijuana missing, the jar re-filled with leaves and twigs from the yard. Clay denied everything, saying the babysitter must have done it. After the principal approached me, I became watchful. Clay was too smart for his own good, book-smart and life-stupid. I found his marijuana and confiscated it, but he always managed to get more. He tried every drug he could lay his hands on. He took a horse tranquilizer and couldn't get out of bed for two days. I picked him up one afternoon after school; he was red-eyed from smoking pot. He slumped dopily in the backseat. When I yelled, he stared malevolently at the space between my eyes, precisely where I used to look during my mother's lectures. Seeing my bad habits reproduced in my first-born increased my rage.

"We let you come here," I said. "We've given you privileges you would never be allowed in Mississippi, and this is how you repay us?" I even sounded like my mother.

He sat in the backseat with his red eyeballs, saying nothing, grinning maniacally. An acre away in his shed, he smoked forbidden cigarettes. One morning he accidentally set the woods on fire. Thank God the next-door neighbor was a fireman and off duty that day. He spotted the smoke and came running with a hose.

Clay had morphed from my darling boy into a teenage problem. None of this was winning him points with Bruce, who had been focused on what he called The Big Picture since he was sixteen. He tried to talk to Clay about the future. It wasn't enough to be smart, he said. You had to have goals. Clay stared at him the same way he did at me. I went from one to the other, telling Clay how lucky he was to have a model like Bruce, asking Bruce to be patient, torn between the two of them.

Clay grew bored with high school, and I got permission from the dean for him to begin taking classes at Miami-Dade where I could keep a better eye on him. He tested out of a year's worth of credits, took a year of classes, and graduated with an associate of arts degree at fifteen. The local paper published a story about the boy genius.

In the fall he would begin classes at the University of Miami. He wanted to learn how to drive, and Bruce offered to teach him. I didn't have the patience. They drove Mother's Oldsmobile up and down the traffic-free street in front of our house. When Bruce felt Clay was ready, he took him for his driver's test, and Clay passed.

Bruce and I traveled thirty miles to downtown Miami each day for work. I was caught up in the expansion of Life Lab; Bruce was working on a case that would eventually go to the Supreme Court. In spite of our apprehensions, we were relieved to have Clay get around on his own.

He was sixteen years old and a junior in college with a driver's license and a car.

41

The call came while I cooked supper, one of those phone calls you imagine when your lizard brain wakes you at 3:00 a.m.

It was a highway patrolman. "You have a son, Frederick Craig, Junior?"

My body went cold. Clutching the receiver, I said, "Yes."

"There's been an accident."

"Is he—?"

"It's bad. You better get down here." Terror filled me as the facts arrived—where the car was, where Clay was.

He'd been driving Mother's car for three weeks.

Bruce said, "I knew it."

He was wonderful driving me to the scene, telling me to stay calm, that everything would be fine, while I huddled in the passenger seat, shaking and holding my aching gut.

Approaching Dixie Highway, we saw the lights and heard the wail of sirens. I spotted the other car first, a small, red Japanese model, crushed almost in half. I saw what was left of Mother's Oldsmobile, beached like a dead whale on the side of the road.

I clutched Bruce's arm. "Clay's dead. No one could come out of that car alive. They didn't want to tell me on the phone."

"It'll be okay." Bruce patted my hand and tried to get our Volkswagen through the crowd. Blue lights flashed, a clutch of people had gathered, an ambulance screamed away. Bruce parked, and an officer directed us to a low green building.

Inside, the fluorescent light was blinding, and at first I saw nothing. I spotted Clay, sitting on a couch, his head in his hands, sobbing. I went weak with relief. He was alive, and nothing else mattered. I'd never heard him cry this way. I sat down and took him in my arms. "What's wrong? Are you hurt?"

"My knee," he said.

I looked. His jeans were torn and the knee was cut a bit, nothing serious. Miraculously, the bad leg had not broken.

A highway patrolman called Bruce aside, and I watched Bruce's face harden as he listened.

"What? What did he say?"

Bruce looked at Clay with something close to loathing. "There's been a death. He's killed someone."

"Oh, God." I was filled with anguish for my careless, dreaming son, followed by anger. "What happened?" I shook Clay's shoulder.

He sobbed louder. "The other car ran a light, and I hit them. The light was green, and I turned to speak to the guy in the backseat, and this other car drove into the intersection, and when I turned back, it was too late."

I was bewildered. "What guy in the backseat?"

"A hitchhiker. I picked up a hitchhiker."

Stupidity piled on carelessness. Weariness washed over me.

The highway patrolman shook his head. "He had two hitchhikers in the car, ma'am." He turned to Clay. "And the light was red, son. We have witnesses. You ran a red light and hit that car."

"Two hitchhikers?" I said.

"Yes, ma'am. One was a runaway girl, twelve years old. She was hurt. The ambulance just took her to the hospital."

Anger filled my stomach with fire. "What do we do now, officer?"

"Let me speak to the captain." He left and came back with a larger man, a man I recognized. He had been a student in my Life Lab group at the air base. "Bill." I ran to him, crying. "What do we do?"

He took off his hat, his face sad. "Mrs. Rogow, I'm real sorry, but there's no doubt your son was at fault. One child died at the scene, and it looks bad for the other one. The mother's hurt, too. They were in one of those Jap cars. Didn't stand a chance."

I wept, wiping at the tears with my hand. We had laughed, calling Mother's Oldsmobile the Tank, a car built so solid even my daydreaming son couldn't kill himself in it.

The captain shifted uncomfortably. "You can take him home now, ma'am. There'll be a hearing. I'll charge him with careless driving and take his license. The court will get in touch with you. Whose car is it?"

"Mine." We had put the car in my name.

"You'd better call your insurance company. We'll have the car towed." He turned to go. "I sure enjoyed that class. I'm real sorry about this."

Anger turned into numbness. During the ride home, with Bruce stiff and furious beside me and Clay snuffling in the backseat, I went over the night in my mind. I had been at the stove, stirring the rice and laughing. In an instant everything changed. Except things had already changed. While I laughed, a child died. While I laughed, my son killed someone. So many lives ruined by one careless moment. Clay had many careless moments, but this was the worst. He was now entangled with death, police, judges, and he was only sixteen. I thought of all the warnings we'd given him: "Watch where you're going." "Don't smoke in bed." "Wake up, Clay. This is your only life."

Bruce spoke, low and angry. "He killed a black child. He hurt poor black people, the same people I work to help every day, and your son kills them." The snuffling stopped in the backseat. "Do you know what they found on the dashboard?" Bruce spoke in a harsh whisper. "A hash pipe."

"Clay." I turned to him. He hunched over, his head in his hands. "Look at me." He wouldn't.

"If that man hadn't been your student," Bruce said, "Clay Craig would be in jail this minute, charged with vehicular homicide, not careless driving."

I dreaded calling Clay's father. A terrible thing had happened on my watch. Fred hadn't wanted Clay to come to Miami, and he'd been proven right. I was a bad mother.

In the midst of crisis, though, Fred was sympathetic. He was concerned about Clay, sorry for the human damage, and understanding of my anger. Clay got on the phone with his dad and spoke in a voice too low for us to make out.

In the days and weeks after the accident, while we waited for the hearing, our lives went on inside a bubble of apprehension. Clay hardly spoke. He wasn't allowed to go anywhere. I got him a tutoring job in the English lab at the college. We moved him from his shed to the small downstairs bedroom in the house. Without a license, he couldn't drive.

The second child died. The paper said there was no money for their funerals. I wanted to call the family and send money, but the insurance company warned me not to contact them.

There were lawsuits. The family sued me; the mother of the young female hitchhiker sued me. I got calls late at night from strange lawyers, threatening me with suits. I hated to hear the phone ring. I answered every call the way Bruce instructed: "You will have to contact my insurance company." My savings went to pre-pay the mortgage. Bruce said they could take my money, but not our house.

In the weeks before the hearing, Clay refused to talk about the accident. I wonder now why we didn't take him to a counselor. He said he was sorry, then nothing. When we tried to make him talk, asked him how he felt, asked him if he realized what he'd done, killing two children, the woman's entire family, he nodded his head and said nothing. He must have felt something, something horrible, but nothing he wanted to share with us.

Bruce, on the other hand, talked about nothing else. In bed at night, he railed. "I can't forgive your son." Clay no longer had a name; he'd become my son. "I've spent my whole life trying to make things better for black people, and your son murders them." When he was really angry, he called Clay "that little fucker."

"I didn't kill them," I finally said, trying to make him stop. "Stop blaming me. If you need to say these things, say them to Clay." I put on a tough voice, but I was crushed. His words broke something inside me. If there was an accident on the evening news, Bruce turned to me with a look that said, see: this is what we're part of because of your son. I learned not to look at him. No matter how hard his eyes bored into the side of my head, I kept staring at the television screen. I felt anger at these times, not hurt, anger that I was being blamed. If I said so, Bruce screamed. "You don't understand. I can't look at my friends. I'm ashamed at the office."

I felt trapped between his anger and Clay's sullen silence. My son, in a moment of carelessness, had done a terrible thing, but I never doubted his essential goodness. Inside his silence, I knew he suffered. Bruce wanted a final judgment—he was a bad kid and would always be a bad kid. The baleful looks he sent my way asked me to choose, and I couldn't; I wouldn't.

At the hearing, Clay wore his long hair pulled back into a ponytail and tucked under his shirt collar. The room was filled with dark faces, friends of the woman's family. They muttered as Clay passed: "Son of a bitch." "Put him in jail." I flinched for my son. The judge hammered the room into silence. Bruce acted as Clay's lawyer. For that day, he appeared to remember the good feelings he'd once had. He admitted blame but spoke movingly of the boy's good mind, his future, the uselessness of jail. His voice broke with emotion. The high school principal spoke for Clay, saying what a bright boy he was, an example for the other students. Clay was the son of a professor and an attorney. The mother of the two dead children was black and so poor her church had to come up with the money for their burial.

"Put him in jail," the crowd yelled. Clay stood quiet, head down. The judge hammered. I could hardly hear over the noise of my heart.

The judge spoke. "Do you realize the enormity of what you have done? Through your negligence, you have destroyed a family. You caused the deaths of this woman's only children." The room was silent.

Clay said, "Yes, sir."

"It is the decision of this court that you shall be fined one hundred and fifty dollars, and deprived of the privilege of driving for three years, or until you post a cash bond with the state of Florida in the amount of $20,000."

The gavel fell. We were free. Around us, the black people shifted, muttering. "Bastards," a voice said. I met no one's eye on the way out.

I had $300,000 in liability on my policy. The insurance company settled the law suits within those limits. The telephone calls ceased. It was over.

Except it wasn't. Bruce was still angry, and Clay wasn't sorry enough. If my son tried to say something funny, Bruce frowned. I'm not sure what he wanted—switches and ashes, weeping admissions of failure, gratitude for being saved from his stupidity. Whatever it was, Clay didn't provide it, and the atmosphere in our house was thick with resentment and harsh, unspoken words. I wanted peace. I wanted things back the way they had been before that horrible night.

Clay had a girlfriend named Kim. She lived in South Miami with her divorced mother, and they invited him to come and stay in their house. Kim would drive Clay to his classes at the university. Her mother said it would be good to have a man around. We waved him off, relieved not to have to look at his sullen face and be reminded of the cracks in our marriage. I recognize those cracks now. At the time, I thought, by sending Clay away, we had smoothed things over.

42

I owned a birthday book where I kept a record of family births and deaths. Next to my birthday, the fortune read, "You have been blessed with a strong constitution. If you do not mistreat it, it will serve you well." Except for one broken arm, a humiliating siege of boils in first grade, and the operation to repair me after having four children, this had so far proved true. I never considered myself sickly.

Gradually, my cough grew into something worse, a sinister tightening in my chest, as if I were being squeezed by a giant boa constrictor.

I had tried allergists; now I tried a chiropractor, the husband of a friend. He pressed and pulled; he prescribed relaxation and breathing exercises, and when I did not improve, he dismissed me. I got the same reaction from each doctor I visited during those years. If they couldn't repair me, they became irritated, as if the illness were my fault and my failure to respond a sign of stubbornness.

I found an over-the-counter bronchial dilator that worked for a while. When I ran out of the stuff, I gasped my way to the drugstore counter, with hardly enough breath left to ask for the medicine when I got there. I searched for air to carry the vapor to my lungs, all with a pleasant look on my face, so no one in the store would say, "Anything wrong, miss?" I waited for the medicine to take effect, heart pounding, skin prickling in a way that meant I might pass out. As it took hold, there was an almost sensual joy in the gradual, miraculous loosening, the cool air flowing in and out unhindered. The snake around my chest loosened its hold. Five minutes later, back on the road, I forgot my fright, forgot I had ever been sick.

I could stand it during the day, but the nights were awful. As soon as my head hit the pillow, deep, choking coughs began. Sometimes they wakened me, or Bruce shook me awake: "You're coughing again."

"I'll go downstairs." I stumbled down the loft ladder and settled in the bedroom below, trying the medicines various doctors had given me, one after another, hoping to find a mixture that let me sleep. Some nights the medication worked; I read for an hour and fell asleep again. On other nights, a steel band fastened around my chest until the world blacked out at the corners of my eyes, and I prayed to live. At those times, I sucked futilely at the dilator, concentrating on getting the next breath in and out.

I never thought of my illness as anything but that: a bunch of symptoms I needed to get under control. I was suffocating; it was a physical condition, not a sign.

I tried anything people recommended: vegetarianism, other allergists, pulmonary specialists. Everyone suggested remedies, and I gave them all a go. A few actually worked for a time, especially the prescription drugs. I could smell chemicals on my breath from the pills I took.

One night, when he woke me from a drugged, coughing sleep, Bruce said, "I could use a respite from this." He had left Legal Services and begun teaching at Nova Law School in Fort Lauderdale. This meant a doubled driving time. Climbing groggily down from the loft, I felt the same way: I could use a respite, too.

Living with Kim, Clay saw us for an occasional dinner, but he never had to put up with my nightly bouts. I doubt he knew I was sick. I made a point of ignoring the symptoms when I could.

An Indian doctor came to Miami from London, a man with many letters after his name, none of them M.D. He was famous for his healing powers and notorious for the cruel regimens he demanded of his patients. A friend at Life Lab told me I should call him. Bruce thought he sounded like a quack and advised me not to. I thought I might anyway.

I went on one of my bad days. I was putting in long hours at school and had begun work on a doctorate. Bruce was in a funk, complaining that when he left in the morning, I was too busy to say a proper goodbye and too tired at night to be a good companion.

The visiting doctor used borrowed space in a chiropractor's office. I was led to a small, cold room and told to remove my clothes, including jewelry, and to cover myself with the blanket provided. I lay on the table feeling chilly and apprehensive. The doctor entered, a pale Indian with piercing brown eyes and long wavy hair.

He pulled the blanket away and studied my naked body impassively, ignoring my embarrassment. When I described my symptoms, he nodded, impatient, as if he knew all this without my saying. He didn't examine me in the usual way, but sniffed instead, smelling me thoughtfully and with increasing disapproval, from feet to head. I felt unclean.

"You must stop all medication," he said. "All. You will go through hell."

"If I stop taking the medicine, I'll die."

"You will not die." He paused. "And if you do, next time God will give you a better body." The intensity of his eyes was frightening.

I laughed uncertainly, but he didn't smile.

"Asthma is a symptom," he said. "We are not going to treat the symptom. We will treat the whole body and let the symptoms take care of themselves." He pressed with his hands, putting intense pressure on my chest and on each leg, beginning at the ankles. He showed me a new way to breathe, deeply through the nose, filling the abdomen first, then a forceful exhale, pushing the air out through the mouth.

"In asthma, the problem is getting the air out, not in."

I started to have an attack.

"Do not be afraid." He took out long, silver acupuncture needles and placed them, swiftly and with surprisingly little pain, up and down my legs, in the center of my chest and along my arms. I grew relaxed, almost sleepy. The attack subsided.

He turned out the light and left me glowing in the dark like a silver pincushion. I was in a trance, my breathing slowed, and time seemed to stop. He returned, looked at me, and touched me kindly, stroking the hair back from my forehead. The gesture of kindness made me cry, which made me ashamed, and I tried to stop.

"Don't control. Don't control." He touched my chin. "There is no mortification in crying. Let it out."

I wept as if for years I had suppressed sorrow, and his touch released it. I kept trying to make myself stop.

"I said, don't control." He took my mouth and stretched it open, wide, wider, until the muscles that held my jaw released. He put his fingers on my jaws and squeezed until I cried out in pain. Roughly, he sat me up.

"You have much stress in your life and in your body. Give me your head." He took my head in both his hands and turned it until my neck gave a series of pops, which felt strangely good. He bent me over, pressed the weight of his body on my back, and my spine cracked with a weird sensation. I felt better, loosened from some invisible restraint.

"For forty-eight hours," he said, "eat only yogurt, lettuce, and bran. Come back Friday. And, remember, no medicine."

I left feeling lighter on my feet and breathing easy. On the way home, I bought two bunches of romaine, a large container of plain yogurt, and a package of bran. I hated yogurt and never ate lettuce without salt. Bruce laughed, watching me dip the leaves of lettuce in yogurt and chew them. "That is the most ridiculous thing I've ever seen."

"It tastes terrible."

"You've been sick for years. Do you actually expect yogurt to change that?"

"I don't know." I continued watching the evening news, chewing morosely. "I have to try."

"The man is a fraud. He's not even a real doctor. How much money did he charge you?"

"Fifty dollars."

"That's fifty dollars down the tube, babe."

"Maybe." I didn't want to talk about it.

Bruce went up to bed, and I waited downstairs. The asthma attack arrived on schedule. A steel band tightened around my chest, cutting off the air. The pills and sprays were in my purse across the room calling to me: Come on, take us; it's easy, but I did not relent. I practiced breathing in and out to the count of four, concentrating on my index finger. I held the finger in front of my face as if it were a candle, and, with each breath, I tried to extinguish an imaginary flame. The band tightened, and my skin prickled. I would not panic. I squeezed the breaths in and forced them out, my finger the only object in the universe. Gradually, my breathing eased, the band loosened and set me free. The attack was over. I was wet with sweat. When I looked at the clock, three hours had passed.

The next morning I ate more lettuce, yogurt, and bran and listened to Bruce laugh.

"I lived through the night," I said. "I actually lived through the night without medicine. It's a miracle."

He shook his head in exasperation.

The second night I had no attack. I stayed downstairs waiting, fell asleep at nine and slept like a child for the first time in months. When the alarm went off at six, I lay there smiling. After forty-eight hours, the tension had drained out of me, leaving me grateful and at peace.

On Friday I went back to the Indian doctor. I told him about the miracle and thanked him.

He nodded, as unsmiling as ever. "For twenty-eight days, eat anything you want as long as it is raw: nuts, fruits, vegetables, even eggs or fish, but all must be raw. Drink only spring water. At the end of this time, call me in London, and I will tell you what to do next."

Bruce was incredulous. "Raw? I'm not going to eat raw food. It's the middle of winter."

"I'll make you other things."

"I can't believe you're falling for this guy. Did he charge you another fifty dollars?"

I hummed, cutting raw carrots into little sticks, pretending I hadn't heard him.

For thirty days I ate only raw food: fruit with yogurt in the morning, a salad at lunch, another salad at supper, and fruit and yogurt for dessert. I stopped sniffling; I quit coughing; the wheezing went away. The raw diet made me lose weight. During the years with Bruce, I had grown plumper. We liked to share a pecan Danish on Sunday mornings, devouring a twelve-inch round of the sticky stuff while we read the paper in bed. Now, the pounds fell away, and I admired my new bottom in the bathroom mirror.

"Have you noticed?" I spoke happily as I crawled into the loft bed one night. "I'm getting skinny."

He turned away. "It's not being skinny that makes me love you."

He assumed everything I did was done for him. I had a discomforting thought. Was it? Did I need to make him love me?

Norma in sleeping loft at the house in the woods

43

When I tried to figure out later what went wrong, I blamed Bruce for taking a teaching job so far away. I blamed myself for being unwilling to give up the cottage in the woods and my position at the college to move to Fort Lauderdale. I blamed my asthma. I even blamed the PhD.

We had been together nine years, and one Sunday morning after satisfying sex, the kind I had grown to expect, lying in comfortable warmth together, I stared happily up at the knotholes in the loft ceiling.

"Isn't it weird," I said. "You can have so much and still want more? I keep wanting someone to fall in love with me. Somebody new, I mean. I yearn for a man to be goofy over me, even though I don't need it." I was experiencing a pang of guilt. I had fantasized during lovemaking that Bruce was a bearish, red-bearded man from work. In my happiness, I made my husband the gift of a weakness, confessing to keep the gods from getting jealous.

Bruce had introduced me to the great freedom of bad thoughts. "You don't have to act on them," he told me, "but it's okay to think them. Everyone does." This was a revelation. In Bible-belt Mississippi, I'd been brought up to believe the thought was as evil as the deed. I interpreted this to mean if I fantasized about something, I might as well go ahead and do it, since I'd already committed the sin.

Lying in the loft on that Sunday morning, next to the man I loved, with the sun piercing the leaves of the guava trees outside, watching painted buntings flutter from branch to branch, I took a happy breath. "I know it's only my ego grasping for reassurance."

Bruce made a noise of agreement from his pillow. "I've also been feeling the need lately to give more of myself."

I turned to look at him. "Give yourself how?"

"To become close, warm friends with a few people."

I felt a prickle of alarm. "What kind of people?"

"All kinds of people."

"Including women?" Why did I ask questions I didn't want the answers to? In fact, why had I opened this whole can of worms, me and my gift to the gods?

He chuckled. "Including women."

My heart hiccupped in fear. "How close? Do you mean sexual friends?"

"Including the possibility of sexual relations, yes."

The chasm yawned. Two minutes before I had been skinny and beloved. Now I was old and rejected. My throat closed. I couldn't swallow or speak. I held my breath trying not to cough. "You always said you'd be faithful because you'd be disappointed in yourself if you weren't."

He gave a grunt of impatience and got up, stooping to avoid the low beams. "It's no longer a problem. I have such a secure self-image now that being unfaithful would not mar it. I am a much more unselfish person than I was before I met you. Then I had women for pleasure. Now I can do it for the woman. And I know so much more about lovemaking. I know how to be unselfish."

I climbed out of bed after him, holding the sheet around me, not wanting him to see me naked. "Do you know how disgusting you sound?"

He shrugged, sliding his feet into sandals. "I can't stand the thought of sleeping with only one person for the rest of my life."

I took a long, loose dress off a wooden peg next to the closet, slid it over my head, and followed Bruce down the ladder to the kitchen. I felt numb. Everywhere I looked was dark, as if the world—the morning light on the leaves outside, the birds at the feeder—had disappeared while we talked. "But you promised, we promised, to be faithful to each other." A wheedling in my voice.

He didn't look at me. He opened the refrigerator and undid the tie on the coffee bag, as if this were every other morning of our marriage. He wore the same pair of loose trousers he pulled on each morning, black and white stripes with colored birds embroidered around the knees. We'd found them in a market in the mountains of Guatemala. His thinning hair was rumpled, his face, with its eagle nose and hooded eyes, impassive, sweetly busy making our breakfast. "As long as I love you and treat you well," He paused to pour ground coffee into the top of the Chemex, "what I do in the large private sector of my own life, an area every person deserves, is my own affair."

I snarled. "That is a really bad pun." He laughed. My face twisted as if he had hit me. Tears flowed, and behind the tears came rage, a red curtain of rage. "We agreed. You promised." I was sobbing now, my voice rising in frustration. I knew how ugly I looked and how much he hated crying. I wanted to murder him.

"If you were unfaithful," Another pause as he poured the boiling water, "I wouldn't throw at you some commitment you made ten years ago." He watched with satisfaction as the dark brown liquid dripped through the filter into the pot.

This was his morning ritual, brewed coffee and freshly-squeezed orange juice. I straightened the bed while he made breakfast, and we sat together, reading the paper and looking out the screened wall into the jungle until time to leave for work. This was our favorite time, and Sunday with its fat newspaper, our favorite day. The bed remained unmade, and I could not see the words in the paper. No national disaster matched my own.

"Well, I haven't been unfaithful," I said.

He was silent.

"This is the death of trust." I spoke to the back of Bruce's newspaper.

He didn't answer.

I tried reason, making my voice calm, wiping tears away. "Fidelity is a harder path, but it's worth it. The end is worth it. I know. I tried the other way in my first marriage."

He smiled philosophically over the top of the local news. "The end of it all is the grave."

The tears started again, shameful hot tears. "I'll leave. In fact, we might as well split up now."

He remained unperturbed. "I'm committed to spending the rest of my life with you. This wouldn't threaten that."

"You are not the person I married." Sobbing again. "Your values have changed. Mine haven't."

All through Sunday, whenever I thought of another argument, I prodded Bruce with it. I worked fidelity like a bone. I got tired of hearing myself, but I couldn't stop. Bruce stayed maddeningly calm, showing impatience, but never getting angry and never relenting. Nothing I said moved him.

I shoved him twice that day, trying to make him hear me. He looked at me with pity, which was better and worse than that first year, when he cared enough to hit back. When he didn't hit me, I knew the trouble was serious. At midnight, I finally let him sleep, too tired to argue any longer. I lay awake in the dark loft, listening to the tree frogs whistle. It had been a mistake all these years to threaten him, even in jest, with castration, saying if I ever caught him screwing another woman, I would cut his pecker off. I should never have made those scissor motions with my fingers.

At the office on Monday, red-eyed and exhausted, I confided to my friend Esther. Esther was one of Mac's first Life Lab students and now helped run the program. She was plump and cheerful, a good listener. Through the whole story, she watched me above her glasses with a bird-like intensity. When I finished, she said, "Sounds like he's already done something and is trying to get your reaction."

I raised my eyebrows in surprise, swallowed the pain of those words, and left her office. I couldn't stand hearing that. I went to talk with Tim, Life Lab's psychology faculty member, the man I'd imagined having sex with. I did not share that part of the story.

He said I should trust the process and be totally accepting. What hogwash. I hated that new-age stuff about giving up attachments and living without desires. It sounded plausible, but what good did it do when you were boiling with despair? I couldn't accept Bruce's being unfaithful. I had given up everything for this man. I canceled this thought. I had not done it only for Bruce. That sounded awful. I gave up everything for my principles, too, and to escape to a place where I could go to school and live by the values I cherished. I had a lot of other reasons for leaving, or that's what I tried to make myself believe on this black day.

People back in Mississippi, the ones who didn't know about Bruce, when they found out I was gone, said they'd never heard of anyone wanting to go to school that badly. I liked having people think I left for an education instead of a man, but I knew the truth. I could lie to them but not to myself: I loved Bruce, and I might never have left without him. He was the ship I sailed on, and I loved him more than my life. I would drown without him.

Carefully, over nine years, I tried to build a life as respectable as the one I pretended to live in Jackson. Better. Any Baptist in Mississippi could lift the roof off our Florida house and find a life of probity. I went to school; I worked hard; I taught oppressed people; I lived in a modest house in the woods. We drove Volkswagens and didn't eat meat; I recycled my newspapers and composted my scraps. After a year of living in sin, we had married. I wrote letters to my children and called them every week. I visited them in Jackson and flew them to Miami. We sent Clay to an expensive private school and on to college. I had never been unfaithful. Look (I carried on my running dialogue with the Baptists), I did one bad thing, but everything since has been good.

It was Thursday, and I stood at the stove making a supper of brown rice and vegetables. From London, the Indian doctor had added these to my menu. "We've been happy." I spoke to the back of Bruce's head. "You know we have. You said so yourself. You said you were so happy you didn't know what to do with rest of your life."

Bruce sat at the dining room table and refused to look at me. "I'm bored. Dr. Goldberg says I'm deeply bored."

At my insistence, he had gone to see a psychologist. I grasped at that visit like a lifeline. Wouldn't any sensible psychologist tell a man to stay where he was, not to jeopardize ten years of marriage? Evidently not.

"What else did she say?"

He thumped the table. "I'm really tired of talking about this. I can't stand the questions anymore. This has been the worst four days of my life. You want me to say I want only you, that I will tell you every detail of my day, every person I have so much as a cup of coffee with, that I have nothing to hide. You want me to say I can be completely honest because no one else means one tenth as much to me as you do. I know what you want. I can't do it. You're driving me crazy."

I persisted, my heart hanging like lead in my chest. "What does the doctor say about that?"

"She says I act out of a need for discovery."

"You act? This is not something you're considering? It's something you've already done?" I pushed the skillet to a back burner and wiped my eyes with both hands. The world grew still. Even the tree frogs stopped to listen.

Bruce sighed hugely, as if his life poured out in that exhalation. I looked at him and saw the dark circles under his eyes and the exhaustion. I also saw guilt.

"I didn't want to tell you," he said. "I hoped you'd understand and leave me alone, give me space enough to get through it, but you won't, will you? You won't give me an inch or a second to myself. You won't give me room to breathe. You are driving me insane with your insecurity and jealousy. Yes, in answer to your question. Yes, I've done it."

"Done it?" There was a clanging in my ears, the sound of blood pounding.

"Done it, done it, damn you. Do you think you own me? Do you think you can tell me how to spend every minute, command my every thought? You drove me to it. I sometimes think I did it to prove, to myself at least, that I'm free."

I felt very tired, as if all the days since Sunday had been a journey, a long, dark trip on foot, and I had finally reached the destination, a terrible place I never wanted to come but recognized as the home of my dread. I wrapped both arms around myself. "Who is it?"

"I don't think that matters."

"It matters."

"It's none of your concern. She's there. She's a person I met and got to know."

"Do you love her?"

"What kind of question is that? I love you, or I try to. This is something I have to do. I never asked for it, it just happened, and now I want to see it through."

"How old is she?"

"What difference does that make?"

"It makes a difference."

"She's twenty-five."

He said the words flatly, and they penetrated like nails. She was young.

His mistress, his new lover, did not have loose flesh on her belly from four pregnancies, or a stretched navel. She was taut and unmarred in a way I could never be again. I couldn't fight youth with brains or humor, any more than I could overcome being a girl for my father. I put my head in my hands and sobbed. "Twenty-five."

"God, not again." Bruce slammed out the screen door.

I sat, unseeing, at the dining room table. Rice congealed in the skillet, forgotten. What would I do with my life; what would become of me? I went and got my journal and read the words I'd copied from Faust. Tears dripped onto the page.

> *Who made the room so mean and bare—*
> *Where are the chairs, the tables where?*
> *It was lent for a moment only—*

On the night I told Fred I wanted to leave, he cried out. "No one has ever loved me." I pitied him then, but I ached for him now, hating myself for what I'd done. I didn't realize he suffered like this. If Bruce left me, I would have nothing but myself. What could I do with a self without a backbone, a self that could not stand alone?

I was still sitting there when Bruce returned. He closed the screen door quietly, leaned down, and kissed my neck where my long hair was pinned up into a clasp. "I love you," he said. "I keep trying to tell you that. I don't know what's happening to me. Maybe I'm going crazy, but I know it's you I love, and you I want to spend my life with. If you could just understand and let me get through this thing."

I turned and clasped him around the neck, burying my face in his warmth, feeling the anger dissolve. This would work. It had to. I would be strong and accepting the way Tim advised. I would ask no questions and expect nothing. No thought of being an independent woman now. Bruce wouldn't be able to resist my compliance. I wiped away the last of my tears and lit the flame under the rice. "Are you hungry?"

44

Acceptance worked best at night. I came home tired and was glad to see Bruce when he got there. I felt softer toward him and didn't have the energy to ask questions. In the morning, though, I woke with a sharp tongue, moving from sleep to grief.

"What's her name?" I spoke to the ceiling.

"What are you going to do, call her up?"

"I just want to know her name."

"Jacque. Jacque Steinberg."

"She's Jewish?"

"Her father is."

"I thought you didn't like Jewish women." (A sample of the betrayed woman's craziness—This must be a mistake; he doesn't like Jewish women.)

"Her mother's not Jewish, so she's not Jewish."

"If her father's Jewish, and her name is Steinberg—she's Jewish."

"Okay, if it makes you happy, she's Jewish, but she wasn't raised as a Jew."

"When do you meet her?" This was later. We were at the breakfast table.

"In the late afternoons, early evenings."

"When?" My voice got sharp. "We're always together."

His mouth twisted with embarrassment. "On the nights you teach."

"Where?"

"At the Holiday Inn by the race track."

I felt a jolt of rage and humiliation, remembering the nights I'd come home, filled with my stories about class and how things had gone, happily chatting, while Bruce listened, pretending to care, still warm from this woman's arms. He spent money for hotel rooms on her, the man who questioned every dollar. Our whole life together was a lie. Resilience, I reminded myself, calm in the face of adversity, but inside I stewed, and I wonder now what cost my body paid for this repressed fury.

We were driving home from a weekend in Jupiter, where I had remembered my vow and remained collected. In the car, from my numb center, I asked one more question. "How did you meet her?'

"She's a law student," Bruce said. "I don't know why you want to know this. It doesn't change anything."

I waited.

"She started coming by my office after class, just to talk. I liked her. She was friendly. All of a sudden one day we were kissing."

"In your office?" I thought of the hours I spent hanging his framed autographs of Supreme Court justices, arranging the books and his leather desk set, choosing the right coffee cups.

"See, I knew we shouldn't talk about it. I never intended any of it. It's just something that happened."

The tall feathery shapes of Australian pines went by in a blur. Bruce was enjoying this. He liked telling the adventure of his unintended romance. He considered himself blameless, as if infidelity were a germ he'd picked up.

His voice rose. "She needs someone older, a teacher who can be a friend. She's never had a good relationship, never had an orgasm before—" He stopped, looking at me nervously.

I swallowed what I wanted to scream: Bruce, the woman's Messiah, great giver of first orgasms. Instead, I said, "And you helped her."

He nodded eagerly. "I did help her, but then she fell in love with me, and I guess I became infatuated. Something happened that's not finished. I never meant for it to happen, but I have to see it through."

"How long has it been going on?"

"Six or seven months, I guess."

I reached back in my mind. That meant he was sleeping with Jacque the last time we went to Mississippi. The vision of happiness I paraded before my family had been a lie. What hurt the most was counting up those lies. He had let me go on, stupidly philosophizing about fidelity, when he was already sleeping with the woman. Letting me believe I was on the edge of convincing him to stay faithful. I was trying to argue him out of an abstract affair, while every Thursday night he writhed on a motel bed with another woman. In our bed, he whispered he loved me while thinking about Jacque. He made love to me and fantasized about her body.

"Are you having trouble breathing?" Bruce sounded solicitous.

"No."

"I love talking to you like this. When we can talk without you getting angry, I know you're the one I want to be with. Everything gets clear in my mind."

I looked silently out the window into the dark, dead to the core. This eerie calm was surely temporary, and probably a defense, but there was power in it.

"I mean it," Bruce said.

"I'm glad I can help." How easy it was, after all, to lie.

45

A Supreme Court trip was coming up in February, the fifth for us. These trips had become special rituals. It was an honor for Bruce to have a case accepted for review, and a great occasion for us both. He rehearsed his argument for weeks, in the shower and in front of the mirror. Several times a day, I heard him begin in a booming voice, "Mr. Chief Justice, and may it please the Court." It made me giggle.

Over meals, I picked at his argument the way the justices would, and we tried to find holes in his reasoning. The case was always a winner, we agreed, a perfect argument. Three of the four had been winners. I was proud to be of help, even in an indirect way.

During those past arguments, I sat in the audience. The velvet curtains twitched, the nine justices appearing as if by magic, in robes black as crows' wings, stern-faced and implacable as God's judgment. I trembled in my seat for Bruce, answering with him in my mind, marveling that he was able to remember his argument with the constant barked interruptions. Afterwards, we celebrated with long, expensive dinners and lots of wine, picking apart the opposition's case, deciding which justices would vote with us and which against. Bruce always had regrets: he should have answered differently or said this instead of that. I told him he was a champion, and I meant it.

Supreme Court appearances had become major signposts in our life together. I thought this one might give us the space to find ourselves again. Lovemaking had been terrible the last few months. I lay there angry and resentful; Bruce was impotent.

I remembered Mother telling me years ago, "Don't ever marry for sex. When that's gone, you'll have nothing."

"Too much pressure," Bruce told me. "Too much jealousy." "Never mind," he said, when he failed. "I can satisfy you." He would work avidly between my legs, watching with one eye to see how he was doing. When I came and opened my eyes, I saw him, still watching, eyes glittering beneath the hooded lids, pleased with himself. The old cow had been serviced once again. The whole business left me sad and angry. His real love life happened elsewhere. Maybe a trip to Washington would change things.

Bruce cleared his throat at the dinner table. "Jacque wants to come to Washington for the argument." He looked at me, eyes wary.

"What?"

"She helped me research the case. It's only natural she would want to hear it."

"She can't come."

"We can't keep her from coming," Bruce said.

I choked back the rage and went running the next day to Tim, my long-suffering friend at the office.

"Don't go," Tim said. "It's a no-win situation. Don't do it. Going will only make you feel bad."

I looked at him, so kind and thoughtful, a red-bearded Santa. What he said made sense, but it was sense for someone else in another, more perfect world. "I have to go. I always go."

On the plane to D.C., I decided to be calm and polite no matter what happened. If I got the chance, I would invite Jacque to tea and find out what she wanted.

"We may not even see her," Bruce said.

"You got her a pass for the argument, didn't you?"

"Yes, but she'll just be another person in the audience. It's not like she's staying with us."

We ran into her that first afternoon in the National Gallery. I realized later this could not have been a coincidence. I took her aside. Bruce watched from a distance, pretending to study a painting. I was cool and polite. "After the argument tomorrow, I'd like you to meet me for tea in the court cafeteria."

She looked frightened. "All right."

She was petite, a doll of a woman, with a mass of dark curly hair and a pert nose. I gave her a nod of dismissal, took Bruce by the arm, and left.

"We're having a talk tomorrow," I said.

"That's good." He sounded nervous.

After another successful argument, which I barely heard, Jacque and I sat across from one another at a small marble table, our tea bags floating in paper cups of tepid water. I had on my best suit, black wool with a white satin blouse. My hair was pulled smoothly back and tied with a black bow. I felt thoroughly in control. Bruce sat at a table across the room, studiously ignoring us.

I said, "What do you want?"

"I only want to be able to see him until graduation." She sounded apologetic. "Just until May."

I spoke sternly. "He has no intention of divorcing me. I guess you know that."

"I know. Just three more months, that's all I ask. Then I'll go away."

On the plane home, I felt relieved. I had faced the enemy, I had not been unkind, and I had not broken down.

"I made some decisions on this trip," Bruce said.

I waited, holding my breath. He was going to tell me it was over with Jacque; he wanted life back the way it was, with just the two of us. He'd been wrong.

"I'm going to find an apartment in Fort Lauderdale," he said. "I need to see this thing through, and I want to spend more time up there."

"With her?" My throat was so tight I could hardly get the words out.

"Jacque has her own apartment."

"But you'll be with her."

"We'll spend time together, of course. I need to see what's there for me."

I let the tears come.

Bruce sighed and turned away.

"When did you decide this?"

"While you two were talking in the cafeteria. She's so vulnerable."

"Talking? You were happy for us to talk."

"You're strong, Norma. Jacque's not."

"Christ, I can't believe this." I pounded my fists on the armrests and stared out the plane window, wiping at tears as they ran down my face, ignoring the flight attendant's polite inquiries.

Bruce spoke for me. "She's fine."

"Why?" I tried to be calm, but my words came out in a near shout. "Just tell me why." People in nearby seats turned to look.

"Try and keep it down, okay?"

This man, so thrilled with his new life plan that he has to blurt it out in an airplane, wanted me to be quiet.

"I don't understand." I sobbed in a whisper. "Why do you need to do this? I said you could see her. I resigned myself to that. Why this?"

"Stop asking me that. Stop trying to make me explain. I can't handle it. Stop begging me all the time, pleading with me. You never leave it alone."

I stared out the window. We flew through clouds the same steel gray as my heart. This was it: I had been miserable before, but this was the worst, the unhappiest moment of my life. I tried to do the meditation Tim taught me, to feel the misery and say, this is misery; this is how it feels. Go inside and experience it. I couldn't do it. My chest had filled with stones, and I could hardly breathe. Outside, tiny drops of water ran down the darkening window. Tears slipped off my chin. I mopped them with a sodden tissue.

46

Neal, the same silent man who built our house, built us a cypress platform, high enough off the ground to see the horizon, supported by cables bolted around three big pines. Twenty feet up, our floating deck swung in the breeze. We named it Sky Lab for the first space station. On Tuesday after work, I climbed up. I was afraid of heights and held my breath on the swaying ladder. From the platform, you could see almost to the Everglades. I sat contemplating my future.

Bruce had left Monday morning, taking some of his clothes, saying he would see me Thursday night. This was how our new life would be: Monday through Thursday, he would spend in Fort Lauderdale, and Thursday night until Monday morning, he would come home to me. A jay flew by my ear, giving a territorial squawk. Squawk, yourself, I thought. I'll show you squawk. I screamed, a single wail flung into the surrounding trees. The sound came out embarrassingly loud, and I didn't repeat it.

Tim had suggested that, too: "Take one time during the day and give yourself permission to be miserable. One hour. Cry, scream, say everything you can think of to make yourself unhappy. When the hour is over, stop. After that, don't let yourself think miserable thoughts. If they come, push them away. Tell yourself, 'I have an hour to be miserable tomorrow.'"

I hadn't been very successful with this technique. I tried. I thought about work, about my children, about supper, and what to do in the garden, but in the midst of the most ordinary notion, I pictured Bruce making love to Jacque. I saw him rising on his strong arms above her, pumping up and down. I heard the sounds he made in bed. At those times, I moaned and held my ears to keep out the noise of the scene in my head.

Clay was back in Mississippi, doing a year of college there. I was glad. I didn't want any witnesses. No one in my family knew about my troubles. I was too ashamed to tell them.

Tim was patient. I sat in his office after returning from D.C., spilling my guts while staring unseeingly at his posters of chakras and acupressure points, the rows of books on the Tao and Buddhism.

He said, "The mind is a drunken monkey."

"What's that supposed to mean?"

"The mind is a drunken monkey. You have to chain it, not let it make you crazy. Do you actually know what Bruce is doing right now?"

I paused to think. "No."

"Anything you imagine him doing is just that, your imagination. You have no way of knowing, so you make things up. Stop doing that. Do you enjoy these movies?"

"Movies?" I must have missed something.

"The movies you run in your head. Seeing Bruce making love to that woman?"

"God, no."

"Then stop it. Don't run them. You're doing it to yourself. When a movie like that starts, speak to it sternly. Tell it to get out of your head."

I smiled. "Does that work?"

Tim nodded. He really was a kind man. Why couldn't I have fallen in love with someone like this instead of Bruce? Why couldn't I love a friendly, bearded man with twinkling blue eyes?

Tim said, "Stay in the here and now. Here, now, in this room, you're okay. Nothing bad is happening. Everything else is illusion. When you get caught up in illusion, chain the monkey. Throw him out of your head."

I practiced driving home. I wondered where Bruce was at that moment. I pictured him having dinner with Jacque. He told me she was a good cook, and that her apartment was filled with light and ferns. Stop, I ordered myself; stop the movie. In the present, I saw a barn ahead, or maybe it was a packing plant. Grass grew around it, tall and golden. A water tower rose over it in a comforting way, and the sky was filled with clouds.

On the third Thursday of the new plan, I felt tension building before Bruce arrived in the evening. I tried hard to be easy around him, relaxed, as if he'd been away on a trip, but I seldom succeeded.

We ate supper. I made brown rice with sautéed scallops, and we watched television together. On Friday morning, he tried to make love to me, couldn't, and I pretended not to mind. I wonder now how I could have let him touch me, but I was in love with the man and desperate to keep him.

I went through Saturday and a movie Saturday night without exploding. We were polite, nice to each other, like houseguests getting through a week-end. On Sunday morning, I felt him slip out of bed and down the loft ladder. I heard him pick up the kitchen phone, dial, and whisper into the receiver. "I'll meet you—"

I exploded with rage, pounded across the loft, and down the ladder, hitting the kitchen floor with a thump as Bruce hung up the receiver. He looked frightened.

"How could you?" I screamed into his face. "How could you call her in my house?"

He backed toward the stove.

I socked him in the mouth with my fist, as hard as I could, knocking him against the cold burners. He covered the place where I hit him, and when he took his hand away, he had blood on his lips. My anger melted. I led him to the sofa and got a cold cloth.

He wept. "I don't know what to do. You are my roots. I know that. I can feel myself being ripped away from you, and I can't stop it."

I patted him on the back, comforting him like a mother. "It's all right. We'll figure something out. Shhh, don't cry." Inside, I felt triumphant: I was his roots. I was the person he belonged with. We slept that night wrapped in each other's arms, his head against my breast; but he left early Monday morning, looking sad, but leaving me anyway, going back to Jacque and the whispered appointment.

47

That week I decided to cut my hair. For ten years I'd let it grow because Bruce liked long hair. It hung in a thick brown mass inches below my waist. Because of the Florida heat, I pulled it back into one of the large, ornate clips I'd collected over the years. Recently, I'd seen a photograph of myself taken at a law school dance. I looked plain as rice with my hair draped like curtains around my face. No wonder Bruce chose Jacque. My hair was my own now, and I would cut it. With my heart in my mouth, I watched the beautician snip and trim, leaving me with shoulder-length waves. I felt young and lightheaded when I walked out of that shop.

"It's not going to make me come back," Bruce said when he saw it.

"I didn't do it for you." I sounded defensive instead of empowered.

He said, "None of these things you do has any effect on my decision. Cutting your hair, losing weight, going to strange doctors. None of that changes anything." He was sharp this weekend, angry, as if the quietly sobbing man from the week before never existed.

I sharpened in response. Paying the bills, I found one from Saks. Bruce had bought several hundred dollars' worth of something. I asked him about it.

"Jacque needed a few things."

"You're buying her clothes now?"

"She paid me back." He called down from the loft where he lay in bed reading. "We were out shopping, and she didn't have any money."

My fury felt almost like joy. I could see the two of them, Jacque coming out of the dressing room, turning in front of Bruce for approval, their pleasure in the joint purchases, carrying packages out of the store like a couple. Bruce loved to shop, and he had a good eye. My favorite clothes were gifts from him.

I opened the refrigerator and grabbed the first thing I saw: a carton of eggs. "You cretin," I shouted. "You're disgusting." I heaved eggs over the railing of the loft, aiming at Bruce, invisible above me on our mattress. "How can you talk about loving me when you sleep with her and buy her clothes?" I threw more eggs. My aim was not good, and they hit the loft ceiling instead of Bruce, dripping yolk down the walls, onto the floor, and onto a line of dress shirts Bruce had starched and ironed.

"Norma." Bruce spoke my name sadly, as if I were a demented child. I thought I heard him laugh. He left early that afternoon, and I spent hours cleaning up the sticky goo, hating myself for throwing something so messy, hating that I'd missed his head, hating him the most.

I lay in bed, tired from the fight and the scrubbing, but pleased with my newly light head. I'd done it for me, not him. I had done it entirely for me. Rapunzel cut off her hair.

48

Three weeks later, I left town for a weekend workshop.

Bruce asked if he could bring Jacque down to the house. "I just want her to see it."

"You want to sleep with her in our bed?"

"What difference would it make?"

I felt tired beyond caring. What difference did it make? He would be with Jacque while I was gone anyway. This was why people stayed in abusive relationships: the numbness, the surrender to crazy demands, anything to hold the pieces together. For all my swearing never to let it happen, I had turned into my mother, willing to make any bargain to keep the man. I wondered how she stood it all those years, feeling this bad. No wonder she drank.

I thought I was beyond outrage, but when I got back late Sunday, the same sheets were on the bed, stained and rumpled. A strange bottle of bath oil had been left on the shelf above the tub, and a tiny yellow dress hung in my closet. I tried to remember Tim's advice, to cultivate patience and detachment, but Bruce and I were attached.

That Thursday, I heaped the dress and bath oil outside the front door and attacked Bruce before he was out of the car. "You could have changed the sheets."

He shrugged, making me angrier.

"Her stuff was all over the house. Couldn't you clean up so we can pretend when you're here it's just us?"

He shrugged again. "I'm sorry. I didn't know it mattered so much." He turned to take his shaving kit out of the car.

I cracked. "I can't stand it. I can't stand it for another second." I climbed up the loft ladder and began tossing his shirts over the balcony rail. "Take your stuff. Take everything. I can't bear the sight of you. You are making me crazy." I threw two-dozen carefully ironed shirts onto the living floor. They floated down on their hangers and landed like flat, legless men. I grabbed the suits.

"Wait a minute." Bruce hollered up. "Just hold on a minute."

I ignored him, hurling the suits over the rail on their heavy wooden hangers. I started on his neat stacks of underwear and socks.

"You're the one who's crazy, you know." He ducked the falling clothes, trying to retrieve the shirts. "You're destroying this relationship with your jealousy."

"Hah." I began throwing ties, slinging them one by one, tangling some in the blades of the ceiling fan. I hurled the shoes, each with its heavy wooden tree, every pair brilliantly polished, standing together in his closet like soldiers. I tried to hit him with the shoes. (I had truly become my mother now, flinging shoes.)

"Ouch, damn it, Norma. Cut the fuck out."

The closet was bare. The energy I had spent emptying it had somehow used up my anger. Or maybe it was the sight of the barren closet and what that meant. Bruce loaded everything into the car. The reality of being left frightened me. He was going; I couldn't let him do that. He would never come back. I started crying. "Wait." I climbed down the ladder. "Don't go."

He rubbed his head where I'd landed an oxblood wingtip. "You're crazy, Norma. I can't stay here. You might kill me in my sleep."

"Stay." I tried to stop crying. "If I haven't killed you already, I'm not going to kill you now."

That night, as we lay in bed, peaceful at last, Bruce outlined his new fantasy: "What I really want is both of you."

I groaned. No matter how far I bent, he found a way to push.

"No, listen. Doesn't this sound nice? I'd be here in bed like this, and you'd be on one side and Jacque on the other. I'd have one arm around each of you—like one big happy family. Wouldn't that be perfect?"

"Sure, Bruce. Sure." The man was truly insane. I moved as far away from him as I could, stiff on my side of the bed. Long after he fell asleep, I lay awake, staring out the window, watching Orion blink in the western sky.

49

More tears Monday as I told Tim what Bruce wanted. It had been six months since the trip to Washington, six months of Bruce's divided life. I weighed one hundred and twelve pounds, the thinnest I had been since junior high. In the mirror, I could see the cords in my neck. They looked like beef jerky. Purple circles ringed my eyes. I worked as efficiently as ever, and except for the weight loss, no one at school noticed anything wrong. It made life seem like a mirage, to suffer so intensely and still teach, read papers, and talk to students. In truth, I forgot my misery only when I was with them. During the hours I taught, I was able to escape my own head. The stone lifted from my chest.

I stopped talking. Tim said, "Why don't you go see someone?"

"Are you giving up on me?" I tried to laugh, but the sound emerged like a sob.

"I'm your friend." He looked at me with great kindness. "You need to talk to someone more objective." He wrote a name and number on a scrap of paper. "Go see this guy. He's a buddy of mine, and he's good."

I looked at the name. He didn't sound like anyone who would understand the mess I was in. Maybe I would call him, and maybe I wouldn't. I didn't know what to do anymore.

I dialed the number and made an appointment with little confidence in the outcome.

Sitting across the desk, I studied the man. He had a nice, plain face. He was younger than I expected, but he acted as if he liked me and wanted to hear what I had to say.

"What seems to be wrong?"

"I've come to be cured of jealousy."

"Are you jealous?"

I nodded.

"Tell me about it."

"My husband has a mistress. She's fifteen years younger than I am, and he doesn't want to give her up. He says she can have five orgasms in a row, and, if I love him, I should wait and see him through this. He says I can have affairs, too. He won't care. He stays with her four days a week and with me three. When he comes home, I'm so angry for the first twenty-four hours, I tear at him with words. The last twenty-four, I'm too mad at him for going back to her to act normal. In between, I get falsely sweet, trying to convince him I'm wonderful and he doesn't need her. But it's not working. I hear him whispering to her on the telephone, and I slam him in the mouth with my fist. I find charges for money he's spent on her, and I throw eggs at him or dump his clothes on the floor."

The man smiled.

It did sound funny, and I got embarrassed. "Anyway, he says my jealousy is destroying our marriage, so I want to learn how not to be jealous."

There was a long pause. I held my breath waiting.

"Is this the kind of relationship you want?"

"Of course not."

"Then you don't have to put up with it, do you?"

With those words, the world cracked open. Truth arrived like light in a dark cave. I didn't have to do this. Nobody was making me. What craziness had I agreed to? Sure, honey, spend as much time as you need to with Jacque up there in Fort Lauderdale. Bring her on down here to our bed. We'll be one big happy family. I didn't have to do any of it. I wanted to lean over the desk and kiss the guy.

When Bruce came home that Thursday, I told him before he got his stuff out of the car. "We're not doing this anymore."

He looked surprised. "What do you mean?"

"I mean, I don't want a relationship like this. You can leave. From now on, spend all your time with her."

"Surely, you're not serious."

"Absolutely." I held onto a small knot of certainty, and I didn't feel the least bit like crying.

"Be patient with me. I'm sure this will work out." He was actually pleading.

"You go ahead and work it out, but apart from me. Decide what you want."

"You could have at least have called me." He slammed the car door. "I wouldn't have driven all this way."

I heard the anger in that slam. This was a man who did not like to be crossed, but what struck me were the words: I should have been thoughtful enough to save him the drive.

I said, "You can stay the night. I don't care."

He left the next morning after breakfast, taking the last of his clothes and the embroidered pants he pulled on each day. "I'll call you," he said.

"Fine." Watching his car disappear down the drive, that was exactly how I felt.

AFTER

50

I was forty years old and alone for the first time in my life. During the first weeks and months, I kept taking my mental temperature. Working, I was okay. I went to the office, taught, and scratched away at the first draft of my dissertation. I could go a whole day without thinking about Bruce, but when the sun sank behind the pines, at the hour he had once come home, loneliness dropped around me like a gray cloak. I kept reminding myself: if he were here, I'd be screaming at him.

When I made room in my heart for Bruce, I forgot one obvious truth. A man willing to carry off a married woman with four children wasn't likely to be the most steadfast partner. I'd read about the cowbird, laying its egg in a stranger's nest, leaving another bird do the work of raising chicks. And not in just one nest, but in up to thirty. Bruce was a cowbird of a man—spreading his seed, but not willing to stay around for the hard part.

On a Saturday morning, a few months into my solitude, I baked bread. Esther was hosting a Life Lab staff dinner. I had learned, being single, to over-plan my time. This was an idea I found in an article about getting over a bad relationship: over-plan your time. (Did men need magazines to tell them how to get over women? I suspected not.) I made sure I had something to do on Friday and Saturday nights. If no one invited me out, I asked people for dinner or organized a movie with Bob from the library, the same man who once refused to lend me the black literature books. We had become great friends.

Weekends were dangerous: self-pity could drop in along with the loneliness, but I enjoyed my days being home, messing around in the kitchen with the gray tiger cat circling my ankles like a fur chain.

"Lonely women make good lovers," the country station sang. I wiped my hands on my skirt and turned the song off. I was looking at men again. There were more of them out there than I remembered. Walking down Flagler Street, I caught myself picking out the nice ones, examining their bodies, meeting their eyes. I never used to do that. With Bruce, I seldom noticed other men. Now they were everywhere.

In peer groups, students became temptations. I would never sleep with a student. I erased that thought: never say never. Everything I'd sworn never to do, I'd done, like being unfaithful and getting a divorce.

Four months after Bruce left, I walked into my new peer groups and found myself searching the room for a sensitive male eye, a waking glance. When male students came to my office for help with English, I stared at their tanned forearms instead of their compositions, watching the way the blood rushed to their ears when they got embarrassed. The young men bent over my red pen while I stroked their necks with my eyes. They all hated English.

"I hope you can help me." A particularly toothsome young man sat in my office, eyes pleading.

I could give you something else, young man, I did not say, but the words sounded so loud in my head, I was afraid I might have. I said, "I'll try," and continued to mark "awk" next to the bad passages.

We'd laughed in graduate school about male professors and their lust for younger women, and here I was—lusting.

Occasionally, an older or wiser student gazed at me with a knowing eye. I grew cold and distant.

At home, after a day of reading diaries and journals for my doctorate, I relaxed with Barbara Pym novels. Pym was a good writer to take through celibacy. Her characters rarely acted impulsively. Even when the women felt deeply, they were never rash. Their lives were filled with other matters. I fell asleep with the book in my hands, dreaming of jumble sales and Anglican priests in the mists of far off England.

Waking in the morning, I learned to savor the silence. At tree level where I lay in the loft, the sun slanted across the wood floor in front of my bed. I climbed down the ladder and had coffee with hot milk and buttered toast. Mornings were not lonely. I walked out to the road for the paper, and though I missed having Bruce to talk to about current events, I enjoyed that freshly folded paper, all mine. In December, when Bruce first left, the air was chilly.

Each morning I started a fire in the wood stove. Now it was May, and the air had turned warm. I splashed cold water on my face and put on my summer uniform, a long, shapeless dress made of Indian cotton with straps over the shoulder.

This Saturday, as I did every weekend, I worked at the dining room table in front of the big window. A bromeliad bloomed in a clay pot, fleshy green leaves surrounding a pink ball of flower. The table was covered with my books, all long overdue. The library mailed me computerized threats but did nothing more to reclaim them. With Bruce not coming home, I didn't have to clear up my mess at night. When I got hungry, or my legs stiffened from sitting folded on the bench like a mendicant, I stopped and ate outside on the porch under the corn plant or inside on the blue velvet sofa, with the ceiling fan turning slowly overhead.

Sunday morning I lay in bed and thought about last night's party. Now that I was skinny, I enjoyed dressing up. I wore tight white pants and a turquoise Indian tunic bordered in gold. Tim flirted with me. He was thoroughly married, so it didn't count, but I felt appreciated. Since Bruce left, I'd gotten closer to my women friends. When he was here, he always came first—was he happy; was he bored? Now, it was as if the reach of my caring had lengthened. Esther, Pam, and I sat barefoot together on the floor after last night's dinner, swapping stories about men and laughing. They were strong, funny women, and I felt blessed to have them as friends.

My doctorate was a study of the journals and diaries of women writers. Dutifully, I read and took notes all Sunday morning. I ate lunch and went out to the garden, pinning my hair up and putting on an old straw hat. The jungle was noisy with cardinals, blue jays, woodpeckers, and the last of the red-winged blackbirds. An enormous tulip tree grew against one corner, lifting the porch and tilting the house back on its heels. I glanced at it, thinking for the hundredth time that I needed to do something about that tree.

In a small cleared space on the south side, we had made a garden. Here, the sun rested on my head like a warm hand, leaching out the morning of words. I squatted, sifting the soft earth and thinking how much I'd hated weeding as a child at the family hotel, when our aunt Miss Hosford forced my sister and me to do it. Life turned, and I now valued what I once found unworthy of my time: a warm, well-kept house, a garden, the pleasure of making a good meal.

Over the years, I had built a foot of soil on top of the coral rock under our land. From mulch, compost and manure, I'd made a mixture as brown and rich as chocolate cake. Digging now, I tried not to disturb the earthworms. Around the edge of the garden, I grew prickly Mysore raspberries. Behind those were plantains and bananas. I loved the banana flowers. Hanging on their long stalks, they looked like giant penises with heavy, plum-colored heads. I bumped them as I walked by and set them swaying. Martin, my poetry-quoting friend from graduate school, now raised orchids a mile east of here and knew everything about plants. He claimed there was a dish you could make from banana flowers. I needed to ask him for the recipe. They were too lovely not to eat.

The peacock came by while I knelt there, seeking the peanuts I kept in my pocket. I shelled them, and he ate from my hand, watching me coldly as he snatched each one. When they were gone, he swayed off, sweeping the ground with green and purple iridescence. "Remember, I raised you," I called after him. He did not look back. At night, in my high bed, I heard him scream from the neighbor's roof, with a shriek that sounded like murder. I liked hearing it, and sometimes I cried back, but not so loud the neighbor could hear. "I hear you crying, peacock; is it a cry against the night?" That was Wallace Stevens, but unlike Martin, I probably didn't get it right.

Humming, I transplanted lettuce seedlings. It was late in the year for lettuce. In the hot May sun, the plants would bolt and turn bitter before I could eat them, but I'd found the seed packet, forgotten between two pots in the shed. Next year, they wouldn't germinate, so I'd scattered them in the garden. Rows made gardening too much like ledger-keeping. The seeds sprouted like a crowd standing in one corner of a party. I broke them up, taking each by its tender neck, and scooping a small space in the dirt. I pressed the brown earth around them. They hung limply, and I watered, hoping they would revive.

Pineapples grew along the path back to the house. The tops I planted had become a thicket of spiny leaves. Here and there were pinecones of new fruit, bulging like red navels. It took eighteen months to make a pineapple.

Lunch was a salad of the lettuce thinnings and a can of soup. I enjoyed cooking for company. Putting a meal together for others felt like foreplay, an offering, love on a plate. With Bruce gone, I too often made do with scrambled egg sandwiches or opened cans. My friend Patti told me the measure of living well alone was to set a lovely table for one, with flowers, good silver, and a beautiful little meal. Dressing nicely and sitting down to enjoy it. I walked into her house one night and found her with just such a meal: dressed all in white, she sat before one perfectly set place, her blond hair tied up in a ribbon, eating like a princess.

When I'd washed my supper dish, I walked out to get the mail I forgot to pick up on Saturday. Night had come, and a faint mist hung like gauze in the governor plums. The road to the street was long and curved, two silver tracks with un-mown weeds in the middle. A clump of shell ginger by the gate grew dense and black as a wall, the flowers heavy with fragrance. There was no mail worth keeping. Walking back, I admired my house, glowing through the woods like a Chinese lantern. Branches of unripe plums tapped me on the forehead.

It was a larger house without Bruce, and a more peaceful one. I reminded myself of that when loneliness made my chest heavy. How much more room there was when two wills weren't crowded into one space.

I sat under the ceiling fan and read Pym's *Some Tame Gazelle*. On Sunday nights I felt cut off from the world. We lived in the middle of two wooded acres, and the house became the only lighted spot in a dark night. Music helped; I turned on the classical station, letting the sound wrap around my thoughts. When my eyes grew heavy, I climbed the ladder to the loft. The night filled with the hum of wind. A storm was blowing in. I wondered if I would dream of the panther again. I called it my Jungian dream: a black panther wearing a golden chain swam in a dark blue sea. It was beautiful to watch, but I had no idea what it meant.

Turning on the floor fan, I slipped under the sheet, whispering a fervent prayer against visits from roaches or night animals. Once, when I was almost asleep, an enormous Palmetto bug scuttled across my face, disappearing under the pillow while I screamed and fumbled for the lamp. Another night, I waked to the sound of heavy footsteps outside. Heart thudding, holding the sheet against me like armor, I flipped a switch on the wall next to the mattress. It turned on the outside floodlights. Below, on the ground, a possum paced, its long nose and bald tail swaying, its steps as solid as the man's who once lived here.

Norma on front porch of the house in the woods

51

More than a year had passed since Bruce left. I missed him, but I no longer mourned. He was still with Jacque. We spoke on the telephone occasionally, like old and slightly wary friends. He asked about the house; I asked about his cases.

On a Saturday morning in late June, I lay in the loft bed on my stomach looking out the window. In the grove behind our acreage, the lime trees were in bloom. The smell arrived, faint and sweet, like a wedding bouquet. If I breathed deeper, trying to get more, the scent vanished. Downstairs, the cats clustered around the bottom of the ladder and whined.

"When do you want breakfast?" I called. All three answered, and it sounded like "Neooowww."

After breakfast, I sat at the dining table, head buried in Virginia Woolf's journal. When the phone rang, I answered from another world.

"It's Bruce," the voice said.

Did he think I'd forgotten? "How are you?" I said.

"I miss you."

What was this? "And I miss you."

"I'd like us to try again."

Everything got quiet. I did not say a word.

"I'm saying, let's try and work things out." He spoke precisely, as if I were hard of hearing. "I want to come back."

"You can't just come back."

"I know, but next week is the Fourth of July. I thought maybe we could spend time together?"

"You mean like the weekend?" My heart hammered.

"A long weekend. We could meet somewhere."

"Not the house," I said. I didn't want him here.

"Somewhere neutral where we could just be with each other and talk?"

"What about Jacque?"

"I've told her if we can make it work, I'm coming back to you."

"How did she feel about that?"

"Naturally, she feels terrible. She says she won't wait."

"She'll wait."

"I wish you wouldn't be sarcastic about her."

"How should I be?"

"She doesn't hate you."

"Why should she? I didn't steal her husband."

There was silence on the line. I hoped he was choking on my words. "I've already invited Clay and Bob for dinner on the Fourth," I said.

Clay had returned from a year at my old college in Mississippi. In the fall, he would be a senior at the University of Miami and was back living with Kim.

Bruce said, "That's fine—that's great."

He must really want to see me. He hated having company when it wasn't his idea, and often when it was. "Let me think about it and get back to you," I said.

"Sure." He sounded disappointed, as if he'd expected me to leap into his arms.

I stretched after I hung up, trying to release the tension. Imagine his wanting me after those months of awful begging, and finally letting him go. Did I want him was the question. Doubt crept around the edges of this triumph. I shook it away. I said I would think about it, and I would.

The next morning I woke feeling inexplicably happy. I lay in the loft bed remembering the call: Bruce wanted me. He wanted me instead of Jacque. I wasn't sure if this feeling was joy or gloating. I hollered down to the cats, tickled at my mood. If one call made me feel this splendid, shouldn't I give him a chance?

At nine, I called Esther.

"How are you doing with the dissertation?" she said.

"I haven't thought about it today. Something's come up." I took a breath.

"If you guys aren't going to be using the Key Biscayne place over the Fourth, I wondered if I could borrow it." Esther and her husband owned a wonderful condominium, a weekend home on the water.

"We're having the kids here at the house for a barbeque. What's going on?" Esther enjoyed hearing stories from my sporadic love life: the dark, curly professor, a blond sailor in the Keys.

"It's Bruce. He wants to get back together."

"Ah." Esther hummed. "The worm turns."

"Something like that. Should I try it?"

"You spent a year getting over the guy. Are you ready to jump back in?"

I felt the doubt again, scratching at the back of my mind. "He's still my husband, but I want to meet him somewhere neutral, not here, and I thought of your place."

"You're welcome to use it, but be careful, not of the place—of yourself."

"I will." Did those two words belong together, Bruce and careful? Uncertainty niggled at me. I had worked hard for this peace. "Do you think I'm making a mistake?"

"Not for me to say, sweetie. If you want the place, it's yours. I'll leave a key at the front desk. You can pay me back in stories."

I thought all week about Bruce's offer. I thought about it until I wore thin the reasons for and against seeing him. We had been married for ten years. The children had visited since Bruce left. I took them to the Keys for a week, and they were fine with his absence. I admitted the breakup to my father, who told me he was sorry and said no more.

I'd found tranquility in being alone, but Bruce was the man I had given up my children for, the man I had loved and lost. The thought of his wanting me back was a powerful draw. When things were good between us, I was as happy as I'd ever been in my life. Here was a chance to return to those days. If I didn't try, I would never know.

I called Bruce back and told him the plan.

"You took your time." His voice teased, but I heard truth behind the joking tone: he was not accustomed to letting other people decide.

I reminded him. "Clay and Bob are still coming to dinner on the Fourth. We'll do it at Esther's instead of here." I wasn't sure whether I kept the dinner plan because I didn't want to disappoint my son and best friend or to show off: look who's back.

"It will be good to see them."

I hung up feeling very much in charge.

52

On Friday morning, I left for Key Biscayne. A hum of anticipation had powered the days since Bruce's call. Ten years ago, on the first Friday in July, I rode out of Mississippi with him and out of my life. This was an anniversary. How strange life was, the way it brought you around. We had three nights to figure things out. I looked forward to hearing Bruce admit his errors.

The Volkswagen sounded sick. The engine had a cough, which could mean bad gas or something worse. Owning an old car was the worst part of living alone and being half poor. The Bug was generally reliable, chugging along like a valiant lawnmower, but it was seven years old and given to strange and sudden afflictions. One part after another gave out: the transmission, the starter, and, two months ago, the valves. I was buying a new car piece by piece, except I couldn't seem to get all the pieces working at the same time. I looked out over the dusty green hood, wondering which part would die next, wondering if my apprehension weren't as much about Bruce as the car.

I paid the toll and climbed the high bridge to Key Biscayne. The bay opened in front of me, flat and still, pale green today, darker under the clouds. The sight of the water lifted my mood. I felt buoyant with possibility. This was going to work. I took a deep breath and tried to relax. The thought of seeing Bruce in a few hours made my stomach hurt.

At the gate to Esther's condominium, the grimy VW Bug was allowed past the guard with only the faintest of sneers. Carrying a large straw basket of clothes and another of groceries, I accepted the key from the man at the desk. Esther's apartment was on the eleventh floor. I let myself in. The rooms felt still. I had been here once before for a meeting, but the place was crowded, and I hadn't seen it properly. Out the glass doors on the east, the

Atlantic spread before me. We would be able to watch the sun rise. Out the bedroom window, I saw sailboats anchored down in Honeymoon Harbor, an auspicious name. I felt a glow of ownership. For four days I was resident in the beach cottage of my Florida fantasy all those years ago. Ten floors higher than I imagined (and ten floors higher than I cared to be above solid ground), but I was here.

I put my baskets down and investigated. Esther and her husband had fallen in love with the French countryside. With much effort, these rooms, once as white and square as other units, had been transformed into a cottage in Provence. Ancient, hand-carved beams crossed the ceilings. In the kitchen, wrought iron bakery shelves held painted crockery. There were butcher-block counters. Red geraniums bloomed on the balcony, and when I opened the French doors to air the place, their spicy scent floated inside. In the bedroom, a high-backed French bed with a lace coverlet and clouds of white pillows. A carved, mirrored armoire stood against the opposite wall. Bowls of potpourri filled the air with the scent of rose petals.

The bathroom made me laugh: piles of soft towels and dishes filled with fragrant soaps, an enormous white marble tub. I could live in this place. I sang while unpacking my clothes, hung them in the armoire, and stacked my books on a table by the bed. I slipped off my shoes and lay back against the pillows. I wanted to close my eyes for one minute.

I woke, heart pounding. The bedside clock said four. Bruce would be here in an hour. My shiver felt like apprehension. We had not been together in a year. He came to the house twice after he moved out, once for books, and once for what he called "my things." I remembered my outrage: "You can't have that chair. It goes with the desk we brought back from Spain. The bookshelves were built around that desk. I'm surprised you would even ask." His voice, dry with sarcasm: "Do you think I could I have the lamp you gave me for my birthday?" With every piece he carried off, he disassembled our life.

I turned in Esther's bed and stared down at the boats. I hated running these old movies. If I kept pushing the wheel of resentment, we wouldn't have a chance. The mind was a drunken monkey, as Tim said. Chain it up.

I ran water in the bath, an oval big enough for a family of four. It was built into a mirrored alcove, two slippery steps above a matching marble floor.

I poured lavender bath salts into the hot stream, pinned up my hair, and sank into the scented heat. Reflections of me disappeared as the mirrors fogged. My body, yellowish green under the water, vanished last from the ceiling. I lay there daydreaming, lavender fumes filling my head. On the mirrors, steam condensed into wet drops. Each drop held a tiny image of me, woman in a fly's eye. My chin bobbed above the water, which had started to cool. With one foot, I turned on a dribble of hot.

Did I love Bruce or hate him? Remembering the bad times, I hated him so intensely, all the hot water in the world couldn't soothe the ache. I wondered if anger hadn't eaten through my heart and burned away the place he held there. I loved him more than any man I'd ever known, more than staying with my own children. I had never met a person I could talk to so well. The simplest things, like reading the newspaper together in the morning, turned into an adventure. He was a sharpening stone for my mind, and I missed that. I missed the ten—no, nine years we had together before we tore each other apart. That final year had been hell.

I stepped out of the tub, scrubbed myself dry with an enormous bath towel, and made liberal use of Esther's powder—something called Orange-rie. It smelled like the lime blossoms behind our house. I dressed in white, a long skirt and a shirt with full sleeves. I knotted a yellow Indian scarf under the collar and let the ends hang loosely to my waist. Combing my shoulder-length hair, I wished for the long hair again. I wanted everything back the way it had been.

The gate called, then the front desk. I okayed Bruce's entrance. Only a few minutes more. Three quick taps at the door and Bruce's voice. My heart jumped. I opened the door, and there he stood, in jeans and a polo shirt, thinner than I remembered, but with the same intense face and lidded eyes. He'd grown a beard in our last years together. It made him fiercer looking, but his face creased in the familiar way when he laughed. He held out his arms.

I wrapped mine around his neck, feeling the length of his body, familiar and strange. "Wait until you see this place."

"Let me look at you first." He put his hands on either side of my face. "You look wonderful, but you're too thin."

I smiled. "Misery is the best diet."

He shook his head to stop me. "That's over now."

The words, which once would have made my heart glad, reverberated against a wall somewhere inside me. I stepped away from him. "You look thin, too."

"I've been sick, from stress I think. The doctor said it was mononucleosis. I was wiped out until I found the remedy you left inside the green dictionary."

He meant his school dictionary, a book so old we covered the tattered binding with flocked acid-green shelf paper. I used that dictionary all the way through graduate school and resented Bruce's reclaiming it when he left.

"Remember?" he said. "You wrote out Adele Davis's remedy for infections and put a copy in the dictionary—vitamins and a protein drink four times a day? Saved my life. I felt better after twenty-four hours."

"I'm glad." I was glad. I loved being able to help. The man was so self-sufficient and all knowing, it was hard to find a chink to fill.

The French clock chimed. I had bought shrimp for dinner, and brown rice, shopping for Bruce without anger or any feeling—as if my heart, like the aisles of the store, had been swept clean. "What time would you like to eat?"

"Let me look at this place first." He walked from room to room, shaking his head in amazement. The bathroom made him stop and laugh. "They've done an incredible job, but I can't imagine living here. I'd feel smothered having to go through that protective custody every day."

The complex was guarded by uniformed men. They watched the entrance, grounds, parking garage, and elevators. "Esther says they've never had a crime here."

"I'm not surprised." Bruce stood at the bedroom windows, looking down at the sailboats. His voice was sarcastic. "Everyone is safely locked inside, and the world is locked out."

I saw the incongruities better from my new distance. Bruce had been resolutely against possessions when we met. He made more money now, doubling his professor's salary with appeal cases. Esther's apartment was too much because he hadn't chosen it, but he bragged of driving here in his newest acquisition, a forest-green Jaguar. Bought second-hand, he claimed, but a Jaguar, nonetheless.

I put a pot of rice on to cook, and Bruce opened the bottle of wine. The setting sun reflected flag red on the water.

"Let's sit on the balcony," Bruce said.

I would have preferred not to, which I did not admit. It made me dizzy being up this high. I edged my chair against the French doors.

"You won't fall off, you know," Bruce said.

"I know."

"You'd have to throw yourself over."

The thought made my stomach lurch. Exactly what I feared. I concentrated on the view. The sunset behind us reflected flag red on the water. "This reminds me of the sunsets we saw from the deck of the *Michelangelo*, remember?"

Bruce nodded.

"I never felt as free as I did the day we sailed for Europe. Leaving everything behind, school finished. It was like starting life over on a fresh page."

"Seven years ago," he said.

"It was the greatest adventure of my life so far." Like most adventures, it hadn't been entirely pleasant. I studied his shadowed profile. "What do you remember best?"

He thought for a minute. "The food on the ship, those ornate menus they gave us each night at dinner with prints of old masters on the covers. What happened to those?"

"They're packed away somewhere."

"I'd like to have a few."

"Maybe you'll be back there with them."

"That's what I meant."

I said, "Remember Deidre?" Deidre was a young girl sailing with her mother. She'd flirted outrageously with Bruce, flinging herself onto his lap, peppering his cheeks with kisses.

"You acted awful," Bruce said.

"I was jealous."

"You were always jealous. I couldn't speak to another woman. Sometimes I think the reason I went off with Jacque was to prove I could."

The perversity of this tasted like gall. I let go of his hand and turned away. The sun was gone. A lavender border of light still edged the horizon, but the sky above us was midnight blue. I kept my voice quiet to hide my annoyance. "I guarded our love because I couldn't let it fail. You were my white knight, the reason I left everything I cared about in the world."

"Love is a child of freedom." Bruce repeated the words he'd used when he began the affair.

"So you said." My words had almost nothing to do with the emotion I felt. When I repressed anger, I said something innocuous like, "so you said" instead of hitting him over the head with a chair. Soft voice again. "If our love didn't work, it meant I'd given everything up for nothing."

"It wasn't for nothing; it doesn't have to be." Bruce's voice rose. "You are the person I want to be with."

I listened and marveled once again at how he separated words from actions. During that horrible year before he left, he kept telling me he loved me, but nothing he did made me feel loved. Words meant nothing. "Are you ready to eat?"

"Almost." Bruce poured himself more wine and held the bottle toward me. I shook my head. "In Europe," he said, "you refused to speak." He laughed thinking of it. "I had to do all the talking."

"You're much better at languages than I am. I get nervous about pronouncing things wrong and can't open my mouth. But it got lonely not talking to anyone else. When I couldn't communicate, I started to feel I didn't exist."

Not existing was at the heart of my relationship with Bruce, and not only in a foreign country. When we were together, he absorbed me. In the house alone, in that solitary air, I had re-formed myself. Speaking now, I spoke for me.

Bruce said, "We communicated all the time."

"But I only had you to talk to, so I couldn't verify things. I'd say, 'Look at that red hair,' and you'd say, 'That's not red,' and there was no one I could turn to and say, 'Has that woman got red hair or not?' It got where I wasn't sure what I thought anymore."

"You always did worry too much."

"Except about money. You worried about that for both of us."

He chuckled.

"You laugh, but it wasn't funny. Every time I found something I liked, you said, 'It'll be cheaper in the next country;' or 'We could never ship that home.' I wouldn't buy whatever it was, and then, of course, we never found it in the next country."

Bruce sipped his wine, and I saw his face reflected in the light from the glass door, a face of dark stone, lips curled in certainty. "Tell the truth," he said, "do you miss any of that stuff now?"

"Yes." I laughed at myself. "I miss the copper tea kettle with the blue and white ceramic handle you wouldn't let me buy in Amsterdam."

"I can't believe you still remember that."

"I'm hungry." I went into the kitchen, relieved to get off the balcony. I sautéed the shrimp, checked on the rice, poured dressing over the green salad, and put a loaf of French bread in the oven. Bruce sat with his feet on the railing, staring out to sea.

I called to him. "Dinner's ready. I have mint chocolate chip ice cream and those chocolate cookies you like for dessert."

"Mallomars?" He sounded as pleased as a boy. He came to the table, blinking at the light. "This looks great; I've missed your cooking."

"Can't Jacque cook?"

"Let's not get started."

"Sorry." I felt squelched.

"You know I love you, don't you?" Bruce looked serious.

"I guess. You tell me you do. You say the right words, but you didn't act like it. I believe in the way you act more than in what you say." I looked at him. "You were always a good talker."

"Doesn't my being here prove something?"

"Of course, and I'm here because I want to see what." I ate a few bites in silence. "How does this mean you feel about her?" Keeping my eyes on my plate.

"I care about Jacque. I can't deny that, but I've made up my mind. I want my life to be with you."

"How do I know you won't go back to her?"

"How do any of us know anything? You have to trust me. I've worked through that, and it's over if you'll let it be."

"She must feel awful."

"I don't think I want to talk about Jacque." Bruce was silent. "Of course she feels awful. She cried when I left."

"You were in bed with her last night?"

"Don't."

"I can't leave it alone. It eats at me to think of you being with her."

"I'm not with her; I'm here with you."

"Yes, but I imagine you with her. I can see the two of you making love as part of the tearful farewell."

"You don't know anything about it. Why do you torture yourself?"

We ate in silence. I could barely swallow and thought how much more I enjoyed my meals alone with a book.

He picked up the dishes and carried them into the kitchen.

I stayed at the table, pushing bread crumbs into a line. If I accused him, he got defensive, then angry, and I might as well have stayed home. If I kept quiet, the residual fury boiled like tar inside me. I called to him in the kitchen. "I say these things because I can't not say them. There's a place inside where I hate you for what you did to us. It's like a sore. I rub it to remind myself why I hurt."

"We're trying again." He sat down heavily at the table. "We're supposed to give it a chance."

"I know." I actually felt sorry for him, this man who shattered our life and couldn't understand why a few words wouldn't put it back together. I stood, put my arms around him from behind, and laid my cheek against his head. His hair was thinner on top. "Ready for ice cream?"

"I'm never not ready for ice cream."

Bruce washed the dishes. He had always been good about helping. If I cooked, he washed. When the laundry piled up, we both went to the laundromat. But we couldn't buy a washing machine. That was too materialistic. He'd tell me how many hundreds of loads we could do at the coin laundry before we paid for a washer. I sat in slippery plastic chairs for two hours every Saturday, in air thick with the smell of dirty clothes and detergent, watching our clothes go around.

The first thing I did after Bruce left was order a machine delivered from

Sears. Every time I hung the clothes out to dry, I thought of how much I didn't miss those Saturdays at the laundromat.

At ten o'clock, our old bedtime, I felt suddenly shy. I didn't want to undress in front of him. I went into the bathroom and came out in a long sleeveless cotton gown.

"What is this, an attack of Puritanism?" He lay naked on the bed, legs crossed, reading with that easy way men have of being at home in their bodies.

"I guess so." I turned the bed down on my side and propped two pillows to read.

"I don't want to read." Bruce put his book away. "Take off that silly gown. I want to see you."

"Not yet."

"Why not?"

"I'm nervous. I don't know you anymore in bed. We're strangers, and I can't just peel off my clothes and lie here like a piece of meat. I would feel awful."

"I can make you feel nice very quickly."

"I know you can, but I don't want to feel nice right now. I need to feel good about you in my head before I can be easy in my body. Does that make sense?"

"Making love is not how you want to say hello?"

"Exactly."

"We only have three nights." Bruce's long body turned toward me. He was tan except for the strip his bathing suit covered, the muscular legs propped on top of one another, an exceptional-looking man. Under the light from the bedside table, his face was warm with pleasure, his eyes smiling into mine. Was this the same person who hurt me? He took my hand and moved it down his body.

"If we get back together," I said, "we'll have thousands of nights."

He let my hand go. "Tell me what you want."

"Let's lie here and talk, just be together."

"You got it." He reached up and turned out his light. I turned out mine. The glow from the night sky was enough to see his shape in the dark. Outside, the stars were pinpricks of light in a cloudless sky.

He said, "We could see more stars in the Redland."

"My favorite view is out the loft window." I stared at Esther's ceiling. "After you fell asleep, I'd lie there and look up at Orion. He was our guardian. I felt safe back then, with you asleep and Orion in the night sky, as if nothing could touch us. Now you're not there, but Orion is, so I pretend he's watching over me. Remember how you used to say, 'How much longer do I have to be this happy?'"

Bruce's chuckle sounded bitter. "I took care of that, didn't I?" He was silent for a minute. "It wasn't just me, you know. Nothing is ever one person's fault."

"I took my attention away." I whispered, telling him a truth I hadn't known myself until now.

"I don't know what that means."

"I took my attention away. For all the years we were together, I focused on you. Whatever I was doing, getting a master's degree, teaching—my real focus was you. I saw one of my old students the other night. He said what he remembered most about my class—his first after returning from Vietnam— was the way I talked about my lawyer husband. Your life and accomplishments, your physical being, were more real to me than mine. More worthy. What you were doing in the world meant more."

Bruce propped on one elbow in the dark, watching me. "I never said that."

"You didn't have to say it. You were my teacher. I reflected your tastes and your lessons. Everything about me—the brave new politics, the uncut hair, no makeup, long dresses—all of it was your doing. I became what you wanted."

"You wanted it, too."

"I wanted to please you. What pleased you turned into what I wanted. Things changed when I started working on the doctorate. We went to Maine for my committee work, and I got involved in a project that didn't include you. Nobody up there was interested in your politics or your civil rights stories. You got on your bicycle every morning and rode away. You were distant, and they thought you were a snob."

"They were a bunch of weirdos."

"Maybe, or maybe you couldn't stand being ignored. We came home, and I became co-director of Life Lab. We did something new with the curriculum that fall. I can't remember what, but I was on the phone with Esther and Tim for hours, and reading stuff for my doctorate every other spare minute."

"You wouldn't look up from the telephone when I left for work." Remembering, Bruce sounded angry. "You'd be talking about some stupid thing at school, and you couldn't spare the time to tell me goodbye."

"You're right. When I concentrate, nothing else exists. Before that, I used to watch you dress every day, admiring you from the bed. I watched the special way you looked at yourself, the straight-backed, pleased stare you gave the mirror. When you were done, I told you how wonderful you looked, every day for eight years. And you did look wonderful. I sat on the steps in the mornings, for Christ's sake, and watched you powder between your toes. I made fun of it, but I loved watching. I loved the kind of compulsive attention you paid yourself. And then I stopped. I withdrew my attention because I needed it for me."

"I don't remember that." Bruce sounded doubtful. "I only remember the telephone thing."

"I'm talking about symptoms. You taught me everything. You helped make me into this new person, and then I was made. I wasn't a student anymore. I wasn't the same adoring, needy woman. I withdrew my attention, and you went and found yourself another student."

"I don't see it that way."

"You're a born mentor, Bruce. You love helping people and being the expert. You don't like them as much when they don't need your help."

"People come to me for help."

"Of course they do, and you always have the answer, even when they don't ask. Do you know what my daughter Linden says about you? 'Bruce is always trying to tell me what to think.'"

"I'm sorry she feels that way. I was only attempting to broaden her mind, give her a larger perspective than she might get in Mississippi."

"She knows that, and on some level she probably appreciates it, but people get tired of being students. It would be nice if you'd let us switch roles once in a while."

"It's a theory. If it makes you feel better."

"Don't you see any validity in it? Would you rather think what happened was only you chasing your dick?"

"I hate that word."

"Dong, schlong, pecker. I think it was more than suddenly falling for a law student. I think you needed the adoration of a twenty-five-year-old, and I couldn't give you that."

"Are you saying you can't love me?"

"Of course not. But I can't wipe away what happened because you tell me to. I'll always love you, except for that last year. You are one of the smartest men I've ever known. I admire what you do and the way you love the law. I hate what you've done to us. My feelings for you aren't simple. We were everything to each other, and you betrayed that. You ripped away the veil."

"What veil?"

"The veil of love." I had thought about this. "Early in a relationship, we give our lover a veil that hides the flaws, blinding us to what we don't like and enhancing what we do. It's gone now, and I can see you. I'm not the Mississippi housewife you ran away with. You expanded my world. You opened my eyes and helped set me free. I'm grateful, but I can't adore you like a twenty-five-year-old. I can't give you that kind of total, focused attention, and I think you may need that."

"Then, what's the answer? According to your theory, someday I'll set Jacque free."

"Or you can marry her, have children, and get eighteen years of captive students." I tried to laugh.

"Don't say that." Bruce took me by the shoulders, his face inches from mine, eyes gleaming in the dark. "I want to be with you."

"Why?"

He shook me. "Because she doesn't talk to me the way you do. Because I miss you." He let me go. "Whatever it takes for us to be together, I'm willing to try." He moved closer and kissed me, his tongue in my mouth. "You smell good."

"What do I smell like?"

"Like you."

I was disappointed; I wanted to have a definite smell. We turned. My body curled against his, his knees behind mine, his hands on my breasts.

He whispered. "Doesn't this feel nice?"

"Yes."

I'd forgotten he had knobby knees.

Bruce in his final iteration: beard, but no mustache

53

I woke early. The light outside the window was a pale gray. I dreamed of a party in Mississippi, where I moved down a long buffet line in a room filled with people I knew. They nodded but didn't speak. I felt sad and alone until, across the table, I spotted my mother. I ran to give her a hug. "Mama, I thought you were dead." She shrugged me off, as if death were nothing to carry on about.

I heard gulls calling and felt a heavy warmth against my side. I turned and looked at Bruce, sleeping the way he always had, on his stomach, an arm folded beneath his pillow. I studied his face. I liked the way he looked asleep, the laughing eyes hidden, his mouth softened. He slept as if he deserved the rest. I shifted to see him better, and the eyes opened, instantly watchful, gleaming at me in amusement. Uncanny, that intelligence waiting just beneath sleep, guarded against surprise.

He yawned and raised himself on one elbow, rubbing his head, looking like nothing more than a sleepy man. "Here we are in paradise. What do you want for breakfast?"

"I bought croissants."

"You stay here. He sat on the edge of the bed. "I'll do the honors."

I admired his body as he walked toward the bathroom, the muscular legs and broad back, the brown hair curling on his neck. He was still a beautiful man.

I lay back, wondering why, ten years after leaving Mississippi, I still had dreams of exile and sadness. Maybe the dream was about my discomfort at parties. When I was small, at my friends' birthdays, I hid in their bedrooms and read their books. Once I was hauled downstairs by a mother and made to play pin-the-tail-on-the-donkey. I cheated, peeking under the blindfold, placing the tail close enough to the donkey's rear to win, but not so close as to get caught. The prize was a jar of sourball candies, which tasted sour indeed.

At large gatherings I felt bleak and gauche. In a small group of women friends, sitting around laughing, eating with my fingers, talking about books or politics, I forgot myself, forgot to worry about how I looked or whether anyone liked me.

"Raspberry jam or orange marmalade?" Bruce called.

"Raspberry."

"Come out to the balcony. It's wonderful."

I washed my face and brushed my hair. I looked a lot better than when Bruce left. I'd been haggard then. The circles were gone, and my eyes looked clear. I went to breakfast wearing the long cotton gown, knowing he could see my body through it and not caring.

He had set the small balcony table with a checked cloth, napkins, and two glasses of fresh orange juice. He had on the embroidered Guatemalan pants and no shirt. I watched his eyes move down my gown and tried to pretend we weren't eleven floors up.

"Milk's heating for coffee," he said.

"Everything looks wonderful."

"There was a morning paper outside the door."

"This is a first-class joint."

"The best is good enough for me."

We laughed. We had read Arnold Bennett's novels together, searching them out in used bookstores. Bennett's remark about the best being good enough for him became Bruce's motto.

Bruce hugged me, running his hands up my back and down over my rear, pressing my body against his. He didn't feel as foreign today.

When I edged my chair against the door, he laughed.

We sat looking at the ocean. The air was cool, the sea the color of lettuce. The horizon was stained pink with sunrise, and a gentle breeze blew. A few sailboats were already out where the deeper water turned gray-blue. We read the paper and put butter and jam on the croissants. Bruce filled our cups, pouring hot milk from one pot, black coffee from another, streams crossing the way we'd seen it done at Morning Call in New Orleans.

"You're good at that," I said.

"I'm good at a lot of things."

I studied him over my cup. "When you left, I accused you of stealing the best years of my life."

"I told you they were my best years, too."

"I take it back, they were good, but they weren't the best. Things are getting better all the time."

"I'm glad to hear it." With one hand, Bruce brushed his hair off his forehead, letting me glimpse for a moment the way he would look when he lost the rest of it, like a Jewish scholar. "I told you then," he said, "I was merely the vehicle. I had the car that took you out of town, along with some other attractions. You were always going to leave. I knew it that first night at dinner when I asked about your marriage. If it hadn't been me, you'd have gone off to graduate school and met someone else."

I shook my head. "Fred didn't want me to go to graduate school, and I would never have gotten up the nerve to leave without you."

"Sure you would. You were on your way. It was just a matter of time." Bruce made pronouncements like this with certainty, as if he ran an elevator to the truth.

"It's hard to see ten years later why I left. I thought I couldn't bear it, couldn't stand being a liberal in a town full of racists, pretending to be the good wife, good student, good mother, church worker, volunteer. Screwing around on the side with men from out of town who, with any luck, might show me the secret to decent sex. I felt like a jar with six layers of liquid. One stumble and the game was up."

"That psychologist said you would have gone crazy." Bruce laughed. "But then you were pretty crazy that first year."

"It all seems so melodramatic now. Other people get divorces without that much angst."

"You could have moved out with the kids and taken all the guy's money. That's what most women do."

"I had no idea I could take the children. Fred said if I left him, I would never see them again. I believed him."

"You needed a good lawyer."

Bruce meant like him. "What I regret most is being so afraid: afraid of Fred, afraid of the bigots. I go back to Mississippi now, and things have changed. There are black people clerking in stores and working behind the windows in banks. If I'd had the patience and guts to stay and work for what I believed, the things I hated would have gotten better. I can't stand thinking I ran out of lust and impulsiveness to be with you. If that's true, it's the reason we didn't work. The whole relationship began with rotten motives."

Bruce cleared away the dishes. "Let it go. You did it for a lot of reasons, and all of them seemed right at the time. With hindsight, we could all do better. What it comes down to, finally, is you did it for yourself."

"That sounds horrible."

He changed the subject. "Let's take a walk."

I pulled on a shirt and a pair of shorts and made sure I had the keys to get us back in. The beach was almost empty, the sand damp under my bare feet. I lengthened my stride to keep up with Bruce.

He said, "What do you think your life would be like now if you'd stayed in Mississippi?"

I tried to imagine. "By now I'd probably be drinking in the afternoons like my mother. I can't picture still being married to Fred. Even the first year, when I missed the children so much I thought I would die, I'd visualize the alternative—being back in that house, married to Fred—and know I couldn't go back."

"Look what you've accomplished." Bruce made a large gesture with his hands. "Gotten your master's degree and a doctorate. You're a college teacher—voted the best college teacher. What would you have done if you'd stayed in Mississippi?"

"Maybe if I'd been willing to stay, I could have been a writer. I would have had the time and money to create instead of having to work for a living. That's the trade-off."

"You haven't traded off anything."

"Eudora Welty said if you want something badly enough, you can have it, but you can't have your second choice, too. I chose love instead of writing."

Bruce made a face. He didn't like talking about abstractions. "Fate, choices, goals. I don't live that way. Let's head back."

We turned, stepping in our footprints. I said, "You're a William James kind of guy. No use thinking about results, just go along on your interesting way, and let the results come as they will."

"Is that what James said? That's exactly how I feel."

"I'd like to be that way, too, but I'm always sifting through possibilities, worrying about what might have been, the road not taken, my talents wasted."

"You always did worry too much." He sped up. "What's for supper tonight?"

"I thought I'd let you take me out."

"It's a deal." He leaned down and kissed me on the nose. "Seems like old times, doesn't it?"

"As if we never missed a morning." Did he believe this? I didn't. It was nice, but I remembered those missed mornings.

"Stick with me, kid. I need to go to the University of Miami Law Library for a couple of hours. Do you mind?" He looked genuinely worried.

I shook my head, relieved. I could use the break.

Back at the apartment, he went to shower. On the balcony, I moved my chair flat against the sliding doors and sat watching the boats. How nice it was being on the ocean instead of buried in my jungle. I studied the line where sky met water. South Florida was so flat, I usually glimpsed the horizon only from the top of an expressway, or when I climbed the swaying ladder to our perch between the pines.

Bruce was right; I couldn't fall off this balcony unless I wanted to. I remembered the summer I lived in New York. We went to the top of the Empire State Building, and one of Fred's friends encouraged me to look over the edge. When I did, he gave me a pretend shove, frightening me into tears. He kept saying it was a joke, but that shove confirmed every fear I ever had.

Bruce was back in ten minutes, shaved, dressed in jeans and a shirt. "I'm off." He kissed me on the top of the head.

After the door closed, I reheated the coffee and milk, sat on the balcony with my feet in the other chair, and finished the newspaper. The air expanded without him. I breathed better, which might be because I'd taken my medicine.

The asthma returned after Bruce left, but I had found a good pulmonary man at Mount Sinai. If I used the prescribed sprays morning and night, I was okay.

I smoothed the lace spread over the bed and propped the pillows in place. I put the breakfast things in the dishwasher and wiped down the counters. In the bathroom, Bruce left two signals of his presence: the sink held a fine film of tiny stiff hairs where he'd shaved around his beard; in the clean toilet water, three folded squares of toilet paper floated. Each morning of our ten years together, Bruce folded this exact number and pressed them into the crack of his ass. I laughed the first time I saw it. You can't be too careful, he told me. He was the most compulsive man I'd ever known. His theory of cleanliness included spraying the tops of his shoulders with deodorant, along with the powdering of toes. He said the powder kept his feet dry so he didn't get fungus. The pine straw below our bottom step turned permanently white from talcum powder. Yes, I used to tell him, you can be too careful.

Esther's marble bathroom invited rituals I never found time for at home. I sat in the enormous tub with two packets of lilac bubble bath. I washed my hair and dried it. Hunched in the big bed, I gave myself a pedicure and a manicure, using a kit I found in a drawer.

When Bruce rang the doorbell, I was ready, dressed in an ivory silk blouse and long skirt, with a white, fringed scarf wrapped around my hips.

He looked at me and laughed in delight.

He had always been a noticing man. Little about me ever got by him. At any moment, he knew how much I had in my checking account, my savings account, and my wallet. He remembered how much I spent on my last dress and how often I'd worn it. That kind of scrutiny wore me out, especially after I began earning my own money. We shared expenses using Marxist principles—from each according to his means, to each according to her needs. Since he earned a third more, he paid a third more of the bills. We engaged in fierce arguments over how I spent my remaining money. I did not miss those fights. The nice part of Bruce's noticing was this admiration for my efforts.

"You look splendid," he said.

"I do my best. How was the library?"

"I'm working on a capital punishment case. Trying to keep my client out of the chair."

"Are you doing much of that—keeping clients out of the chair?"

"Quite a bit. I've met some extremely interesting people."

"Do you believe they're innocent?"

"That's not a question I ask. The question is: have they had a fair trial? Have they been denied legal remedies? The answer to that one is almost always yes." He sat on a kitchen stool watching me open a bottle of wine. "I never thought I'd do so well. It all grew out of the work I did with civil rights."

I looked doubtful.

"Not that I did the civil rights work for that reason—to make money, I mean. I never expected to be repaid for what I gave. Do you know why I'm doing so well?"

I put an artichoke appetizer in the oven to warm. "Why?"

"It's not good luck or good fortune, it's good attitude. I've always had a great attitude." Bruce leaned against the counter. "There are twenty lawyers now who respect what I do and recommend cases to me. Major players in jail ask for me. Last week I was interviewed by a team of New York lawyers about handling the appeal of a powerful mob figure, whose name I won't mention."

"Wonderful." I wondered where the line fell between a good attitude and bragging, and how much crime it took to pay for a team of New York lawyers.

He sniffed the air. "What smells so good?"

"I made an artichoke thing for us to have before we go out."

"Let me grab a shower."

I poured two glasses of wine and carried the casserole out to the balcony. I pushed my chair flat against the French door before Bruce got there. The sky matched the dip—artichoke-colored and stained pink from the sunset behind us.

Bruce came out, dressed in white slacks and a starched shirt with the long sleeves rolled up.

The sky was darker now, a line of red stretching like blood along the horizon.

"What are you thinking about?"

I lied. "How much time I spent dreaming about sex when I was young. How I gave up my virginity at fourteen and found it again at seventeen."

"Found it?"

"Twice. First when I went away to college, where all good girls go to find husbands. Fraternities were our stores. If a girl was a virgin and managed things well, by her junior year she had her major and her man. Senior year, she made her debut at Christmas, got a diamond in April, and married after graduation."

Bruce stretched his long legs, tilting the chair. "Did you do it right?"

"I excelled. I found a man by the end of my sophomore year. Finding a man was serious business. I had to re-virginalize myself. No decent man married a woman with a reputation."

"For?"

"Doing it. Men were supposed to do it with bad girls to get experience, so they would be ready to teach the virgins they married. Good girls had to be virgins, so I became one."

"Did it work?"

"Of course it worked. I was a virgin when I married Fred."

"He thought you were a virgin?"

"He still thinks I was a virgin."

Bruce shook his head in disbelief.

In the dark, it was easier to forget our distance from the ground. "A girl in engineering school at Ole Miss got pregnant and had to leave school. According to sorority house rumor, the worst part was, she didn't know which guy was the father."

I was interrupted by Bruce's high neighing laugh.

"It wasn't funny. I lived in a place where an unmarried woman making love to any man had committed a sin, and her only excuse was an immediate plan to marry. To have it known you'd had sex with more than one male, so many you didn't know which was the father—it was the worst thing we could imagine."

"Sounds like the dark ages."

"Doesn't it? Dorm mothers signing us in and out like prisoners. I got restricted once for driving across the county line to bring back a six-pack of beer. The first year, we had to be in our rooms by 8:30. I never saw the end of a movie."

Silence. We sipped our wine.

I said, "You know how I've always wished for big boobs?"

"Your breasts are perfect."

"I mean really big ones. There was a girl in our dorm named Barbara, with breasts so heavy she couldn't get up in the morning without first putting on a bra. She had to lie on her back in bed, and reach behind her to fasten this enormous brassiere—two-inch wide shoulder straps—before she could stand up."

"How big were they?"

"Watermelons."

"Impossible."

"I swear. That was the first time I realized breasts could be too big and wishes might backfire. Not that I could actually wish myself giant bosoms."

"The gypsies' curse," Bruce said. "May your every wish come true. You ready?"

I carried the glasses inside. He brought in the dip and crackers. He gave me a quick hug as we left the apartment.

"What do you wish for now?" I asked him as we rode down in the elevator.

"I don't wish for anything anymore. I wished for excitement, and look what happened."

I didn't answer.

He took my hand. "I wish for more stories. I've known you for ten years, and I haven't heard the end of the stories."

I put on my Transylvania voice. "There is no end to the stories."

"You know, Norma, sometimes you get a little serious. You could lighten up."

I stared at the elevator floor, a complicated pattern of polished parquet. He was right: as soon as things were okay between us, I would lighten up.

We walked to the same restaurant we'd gone to a decade before, to meet the man from the Legal Services board. We sat in the sand that night, but in the years since, the beach had eroded. Tables were now crowded onto a small rectangle of concrete. The sand fleas we called no-see-ums gnawed at my ankles. They came out along the shore after sunset and delivered a powerful bite for their size.

Bruce sent his fish back. "Take a look," he said to the waitress. "You can't expect me to eat that."

I hated the tone he used. Peremptory, as if the grilled fish, still frozen at the center, was a personal affront.

"Very sorry, sir." She took the offending plate away.

"I should hope so." He gave his other laugh, a bark of irritability, propped his chin on his hands, and looked around for validation from fellow diners.

"Do you have to be so mean?"

"I'm not being mean. I'm defending my rights. You should try it occasionally."

I kept quiet. It was true. I hated public confrontation and avoided it whenever possible. My method was sweet reason. The surlier a waiter or clerk became, the wider I smiled. Not a notably successful tactic, but it felt better than my infrequent bursts of anger, followed almost immediately by tears.

According to Bruce and his mother, the world was out to get you, and a smart person kept a sharp eye open. For nine years, Bruce went grocery shopping with me, planting himself, eagle-eyed, at the cash register, watching as each item was rung up. This was before the day of bar codes. Almost invariably, he caught an error and pounced on the cashier like a terrier. Leaving the store, he told me to the penny how much his vigilance saved us. I wondered how much daydreaming through grocery stores had cost me since he left. I suspected Bruce could tell me, but I didn't bring it up.

We walked back to the condo along the sand. At night, the beach reflected white in the darkness, like a road in a fairytale, the one leading to the castle where the princess lay enchanted. There were no enchanted princesses, I had learned, only women who had not woken.

Bruce put an arm around my shoulder, hugging me against him. "I love you."

"And I love you." I heard myself say the words and wondered where they went, these I-love-yous. I love you, I love you. We had said it daily, often many times a day, as if to seal our relationship. I knew how to say I love you in six languages. How many men had I said it to, and what happened to all that love? The sky must be thick with it, a layer of discarded emotion, the eros-sphere. I walked on, taking large steps to match Bruce's.

He said, "Do you remember the night on the beach in Vero when you got scared?"

It came back instantly. We'd been walking along the water in the dark, with the sea pounding blackly on one side, empty sand in front and behind. Bruce had hissed, "Two went out, but only one returned."

I had stared up at him, trying to read his expression. He'd laughed, but all I saw were teeth gleaming. He wanted to drown me, and who would know? He'd go back to the motel, dripping wet, crying: his wife had waded out into the water and been pulled under. "I tried to find her," he'd sob, "but the water was too dark." He was a lawyer. He could talk anybody into anything.

I remembered pulling my arm from his. "You want to kill me." He tried to grab me, claiming he was only kidding, but I ran toward the lights of our motel, yelling back. "Remember what Freud said: there are no jokes."

Tonight I laughed. "I was truly afraid of you." Yet here I was, on another beach, walking in the shelter of his arm.

"But why? You know I would never hurt you. I've never physically harmed anyone."

"What about that first year when you beat me up?"

"You hit me first. You made me do that."

God, ten years later, and he still couldn't admit that I'd hit him once, but he'd punched and kicked me. I unhooked myself from his arm and walked faster. The white sand was scalloped with black seaweed. "When I die," I called back to him, "I want to be composted."

He caught up. "What are you talking about?"

"Instead of buried. We aren't meant to be sealed inside boxes. We're meant to rejoin the elements. In this climate, if you put me in the compost pile, after a month I could be pushing up a mango tree."

"That's disgusting."

"You can't stand any mention of death."

Bruce kicked at the seaweed. "I don't see the point in dwelling on it."

"You think the angel of death is listening. If you say his name, he'll come." I gripped his arm and lowered my voice. "You called, Bruce Rogow?" I answered in a falsetto. "Please, not yet, Mr. Death. That was my wife."

"Don't be ridiculous." He shook my arm off. "I simply don't want to waste time while I'm alive thinking about being dead."

I ran ahead of him down the beach, turned around and walked backwards. "I talked you into buying life insurance, remember? You watched me for weeks, waiting for me to murder you?"

"I did not."

"Yes, you did. Admit it."

"I don't like talking about it, that's all. You dwell on it. If you had your way, we'd practice our funerals. You used to wake me up talking about being dead."

"Only when you slept late. I'd say, 'There'll be sleep enough in the grave.' That's Benjamin Franklin."

"Well, it's depressing."

"I don't think so." I took my sandals off and ran over the wet sand, darting away from the foaming water. I misjudged a wave and got the bottom of my white skirt wet. "God, that's cold."

"Look what you've done to your dress."

"It'll dry, but it feels creepy. Like a shroud."

"There you go again."

"My mind leans that way. Besides, death is natural. We should treat it the way we do being born. We don't remember anything before we were born, but we weren't miserable. When we die, we won't be miserable either because we won't *be*."

"You find that reassuring?"

"Not particularly, but it's better than believing I'm going to roast in hell or be divided like sheep and goats by some heavenly father who's kept track of my every misdeed. I'd like to believe we die and become sentient particles of some great light." I spread my arms and looked up at the dark sky. "The golden realization of an infinite connection."

Bruce said nothing.

I couldn't see his expression. "I'd like to believe that, but I'm afraid the truth is, we become nothing, the same as before we were born. The only immortality is in our genes, our children carrying a miniscule record of us into the future."

"Then I'll leave nothing," Bruce said.

"Not yet." Not with me was what I meant.

After leaving them, the only honor I could give my children was to not have more. They were my children. They would be my only children. Bruce and I talked about it, and he agreed.

I linked arms with him now, wishing I were taller. I'd like to swing along shoulder to shoulder with a man instead of reaching only the top of his arm. I wondered if I chose tall men because they kept me feeling like a child. What a disheartening thought. "Tell me what you believe."

Bruce shook his head. "I'm too exhausted to believe anything. I'm just treading water. I don't have the strength to wonder what will happen when I die."

"You used to say you didn't know how to spend the rest of your life. You'd done everything you wanted, and you couldn't imagine just going on being happy."

He stared out over the dark water. "I think sometimes I went crazy. That's what Uncle Louie said: 'Son, you are too old to be acting this crazy.'"

I smiled. I was glad Uncle Louie told him that. I wanted everyone in the world to let Bruce know what a mistake he'd made, since he appeared unable to say it himself. I wanted him to writhe in his bed at night with sorrow and never find happiness away from me. This was a foolish wish. Bruce never doubted himself. Whatever he did was the right and perfect thing.

Back in the bedroom at the apartment, I lowered the window overlooking Honeymoon Harbor to stop the wind from blowing the pages of my book. Bruce lay beside me, more subdued than he'd been the night before.

He said, "Are we ever going to make love?"

That gave me a jolt. I knew he would ask. I'd been waiting for it. He didn't come back to walk on the beach. "Sure."

"When?"

I put down my book. "Whenever you want."

He turned, brown eyes inches from mine. A line of white curved around the top of his pupils. He said the missing pigment had been caused by childhood measles. It looked weird. I switched off my lamp. Bruce's hands slipped along my body outside my gown. Such familiar hands, the long fingers sliding along my back, palms carressing my sides. He moved me closer, pressing himself against my thigh. His breath smelled of Listerine. He kissed me, his tongue wandering in my mouth like a dental hygienist: how's this tooth, and this one? I stopped. If I didn't quit thinking, making love would be terrible. I needed to empty my mind like a glass of water and focus on my body.

I rode him as I did in the old days. I heard myself cry out, then Bruce, the sounds mingling. I came back to my body, hanging above him, braced on my arms, head drooping.

I found him watching, smiling. "Was it good?" he said. "Did you come twice?"

"God, Bruce." I pulled myself off and lay beside him.

"What's wrong?"

"Why would you ask that? You act like you're the chef, and sex is a dish you've prepared. 'Was it good?' As if you're watching from the kitchen, and making love isn't something that happens to you."

He stared at the ceiling. "You're never satisfied."

"I am satisfied. It was good, and I came once."

We lay in silence.

I said, "Is that what you say to her?"

"What?" He sounded sleepy.

"Was it good? Did you come five times?"

Bruce groaned, and I laughed, taking his head in my arms. His hair was warm against my skin. "Kidding," I said. "I'm only kidding."

54

On Saturday morning we went shopping at the Key Biscayne Winn-Dixie. Bob, the librarian from college, was coming for dinner and to watch the fireworks. Clay, soon to be a senior at the University of Miami, was coming, too, along with his girlfriend, Kim, she of the enormous breasts, breasts that floated like untethered balloons beneath her shirt.

"Clay's bringing Kim." I pushed the cart. "Try not to stare at her chest."

Bruce snorted. "She should just unbutton her blouse and give us a good look. Get it out of our systems."

I nodded. "Disgusting, but not a bad idea. Bob is coming, too."

"Does he still have the girls?"

"He does." The girls were Bob's two cats, living in luxury in his small South Miami house. Bob was my ideal single friend. He kept an interestingly decorated house and a lush garden. He made complex, sauce-covered meals from scratch. Each year he planned a vacation to a different foreign country, traveling alone, sending me postcards from his stops. When he was home, we went to movies together. He seemed perfectly content with his life, and whenever I ran the bag lady movie in my head—nobody will love me, I will wind up under a bridge with a grocery cart—I thought of Bob. We could be bag people together.

I pushed the cart past the canned vegetables and up the aisle by the pet food. Bruce walked ahead, deciding what we needed.

"Have you tried this cat food?" He held up a small can. "It's just big enough for one meal. You don't get those open cans stinking up the refrigerator."

"Is that the brand you and Jacque use?"

He rolled his eyes. "Please."

"We have three cats, remember? Leftover cat food is not my problem."

We decided on steak for Clay and his girlfriend, who did not eat seafood. Bob, too. I wanted filets, but Bruce said they cost too much.

"We can get small ones. Nobody needs a lot of meat."

Bruce shook his head. "The T-bones are only half the price."

"But only that one little piece is tender."

"They won't be picky. They'll be happy with whatever you serve."

"I cook steak about once a year, and I'd like to use a good piece of meat." I had a great recipe with shallots, butter, vinegar, and lots of black pepper. I served it with Yorkshire pudding, and the smell made me want to be a carnivore again.

"Have it your way, but this is why you'll never have any money."

"You're probably right." I did not want to be reminded of my finances. Since Bruce left, it took every penny I earned to live. Doing without his salary had been a shock. I thought he would keep paying his share of the mortgage, but he said I asked him to leave. He didn't go voluntarily, so he didn't owe me a penny. He was letting me use his half of the house, he said, and that took care of his share of the mortgage. He even laid claim to my doctorate, asking me how much it cost me, and demanding half. I told him I had paid for that with my own money. He said if I hadn't gotten the degree, we'd have that much more in the savings account, and half would be his. I couldn't fight reasoning so twisted. I remembered screaming, "Over my dead body," which made him laugh and added to my anger.

Here I was, forty years old, with two husbands, and nothing to show from marriage but the modest salary I earned teaching. How did women do it, the ones who came out of bad marriages with cash, jewels, houses? I obviously didn't have the touch, not even when I lived with a man. It made me squirm to ask for something I could perfectly well buy myself.

I was confused and angered by the connection men made between money and love. Bruce said when we got back together, everything he had would be mine. If he loved me, why did I have to belong to him to get the money? He was making $80,000 a year now, a sum so enormous I couldn't imagine how he spent it.

Bruce said, "How much have you got in your savings account?" We were standing in front of the fresh shrimp while I tried to decide if a pound of medium was enough.

"I don't remember."

His voice became stern. "Of course you do. It was $4,000 when I spoke to you last."

"Must be about that much."

"You need to keep track of these things. You treat money too casually."

"A pound of medium shrimp, please." I spoke to the man behind the counter and turned to Bruce. "Why? If we get divorced, you'll take my savings for your half of the house, and if you come back, we'll be rich."

"I'm not rich. You've got to stop thinking rich. I'm doing well."

"I'm doing okay, too." I tossed the brown package into the grocery cart.

"Look at you, shopping in this store. The prices here are ridiculous."

"It's the only grocery store on Key Biscayne." I picked up a can of sweetened condensed milk for a key lime pie.

"It caters to rich people, and they're robbing you."

"It's only for this one weekend." I got limes, thought about it, and added a pint of strawberries at $2.99.

"What are those for?"

"To put on top of the pie."

Bruce made an impatient sound. "I'll bet if you concentrated, you'd know how much you have in your savings account. With interest, it should be close to five thousand by now."

I started laughing. "Remember how you used to do that? You'd sit on the toilet in the morning and give me numbers through the door: I have $8,000 in my savings, and you have $3,500. That's almost $12,000. You have $260 in your checking account, with another check coming next week, that's $800. I have $900 in mine. You're carrying about twenty dollars, and I'm carrying twice that. We have twelve thousand in the house. We're worth—whatever it added up to. You'd call out the total through the bathroom door, sounding happy."

Bruce provided the total. "Thirteen thousand, seven hundred sixty dollars." I could tell from his voice he was angry. "I was watching out for us."

I kissed him on the mouth in the aisle between toilet paper and napkins.

I had always enjoyed kissing him in grocery stores. Other women had to push carts through by themselves. I had a handsome, funny man shopping with me.

We checked out. I had spent $42.00. Bruce looked disgusted and handed me a twenty. I took the other twenty-two out of my wallet. He didn't say a word, but I felt him thinking how extravagant I was on my $20,000 salary.

I spent the afternoon in the kitchen, putting the pie together, mixing batter for the Yorkshire pudding, washing salad greens. I hummed with happiness. Making a dinner for people was fun, often more fun than eating it. While I cooked, I envisioned each person's face. Clay would smile when I put a steak in front of him and reach for butter to slather on his pudding. Before he took a bite, he would ask if there was more in the kitchen, so he'd know how fast to eat. Bob would smack his lips over everything, saying, "Honey," in a surprised voice, as if he'd never seen such food in his life. Bruce would compliment me on each new thing he tasted. I didn't know Kim well enough to predict.

Bruce went to use the condo's weight room and returned sweating to show me how broad his back was getting.

"Fantastic." I poked at a muscle through his shirt.

"I try to work out four times a week."

"That's great." I licked lime filling off a finger.

"I'm more fit now than I was in high school." He took off his wet shirt and flexed at himself in the hall mirror.

"I don't doubt it."

"What does that mean?"

"I didn't know you in high school, but I don't doubt that you're telling the truth."

He came up behind me, cupped my rear in his hands, and spoke in a mock-ferocious voice. "Don't fuck with the falcon unless you can fly."

"Right." I ignored the hands, and bent to put the pie in the oven for twenty minutes at 350 degrees.

The few minutes before the guests arrived were the best. The lights were dim; the living room looked warm and welcoming. Dinner was prepared, or as much as I could do ahead. I was clean and dressed in a yellow sundress and long turquoise earrings. I studied myself in the bathroom mirror, spraying White Linen on my neck. I didn't look bad for a middle-aged woman, or almost middle-aged. I planned on living longer than eighty.

Bruce complained from the bedroom. "I don't know why we had to invite people over. This was supposed to be our weekend."

"I told you they were coming, and they're not people. They're my son, his girlfriend, and our best friend. They're dying to see you."

"I hate planning things in advance. When the time comes, I'm never in the mood. I hope they don't stay late."

"They won't."

I disliked this part of Bruce, the squasher of joy. One night in the Redland, my friend Fran and her boyfriend got lost and arrived late for dinner. Bruce was angry when they got out of the car and practically shoved them out of the house at ten p.m., before they'd had coffee or dessert. "Getting late," he said. "Party's over." Standing to show them what he meant. I could still see their confused faces, the awkward goodnights. Bruce was already locking the door when they went down the steps.

Once, Bob drove twenty miles down to visit us, and Bruce told him goodbye after an hour when our favorite television show came on. "Time for *M.A.S.H.*," he said, standing and motioning toward the door. Bob never forgot and reminded me of it periodically. I hated myself for not being braver, for not insisting my friends stay and letting Bruce go watch his show. There was a part of me, though, that admired his nerve, and I wanted to see *M.A.S.H.*, too.

"Very few things are worth spending time on." Bruce leaned against the kitchen counter watching me. "Work, reading, riding my bike. Everything else usually turns out to be a waste."

I didn't agree. I loved spending time with my children and my friends. I liked cooking food for people and making the house look nice. I had to admit, there was a moment during every party when the room got loud and I was running around. A quiet voice whispered in my head, wouldn't you rather be reading? The answer was almost always yes. Maybe this was the difference between men and women. Men were allowed to act on these feelings, while women were expected to keep quiet and be good.

Clay and Kim arrived promptly at 7:30. I tried not to stare at the girl's breasts under the thin, pink shirt. My pneumatic woman, Clay called her. She had a wide, friendly smile, which urged you to look at her face instead.

"What a place." Clay walked around, whistling between his teeth. At eighteen, he was longhaired and thin. He wore his tight jeans low on his hips and sported a single turquoise earring. I watched him laugh, but noticed he seemed slightly uneasy around Bruce, doing that nervous thing with his hands.

I felt a flush of love for my son, along with an emotion not quite as pleasant. He was so much like me. Charming to see my virtues repeated and horrifying to see the flaws. When I was small, I used to pull my hair back to see what I'd look like as a man. Here was Clay, tougher, taller, definitely a man, but with my mannerisms, telling stories the way I did, smiling the same smile when he lied.

He and Kim went out to the balcony and leaned on the rail, talking and pointing. I wanted to go hold onto the backs of their shirts.

"Amazing view," Clay said.

Bob arrived forty-five minutes late. He was always late, coming in the door breathless to let us know he'd hurried. He brought a box of chocolates, opening them to show me and eating one.

"Wait for dinner."

"I want to be sure they're okay."

We sat in the dining room at the handsome fruitwood table. Bob was ecstatic over the steak and had three helpings of Yorkshire pudding, washing it all down with ice water. He was in A.A. and didn't drink. Clay looked more relaxed, and Kim's face went pink from the wine. I glanced around the table, smiling. I made this happen: brought them together, prepared the food, and everyone was having a good time.

Bruce looked hooded and fierce at the far end of the table. He made us laugh with stories about law school. In spite of his dire predictions, he usually had fun with people. I took another swallow of red wine and let it warm my throat. Was this how love returned? I watched Bruce. Did it come sliding in, the way the wine went down, gradually warming you until you forgot it ever left? I felt the alcohol smoothing over the torn places inside me. The horrid words were distant, spoken in wrath by other people and long ago. I snapped out of my reverie. What was Bruce saying?

"I made you bury it." He neighed a laugh.

Bob looked miserable.

I said, "What are you two talking about?"

Bruce flashed me a black look. He hated it when I didn't listen. "That Thanksgiving Bob came down to the house, the time you invited the Israeli students. Bob crept muttering out of the bathroom, and I finally got it out of him: he had stopped up the toilet. He took me in to show me, and my God." Bruce laughed, indicating with his hands the size of what he'd found.

Bob's face turned an ugly brick color.

"Bruce, please. Not at the dinner table." I tried to look stern enough to make him stop. I sounded like my mother.

"There was only one thing to do." Bruce was talking to Clay and Kim, who laughed. "I got a bucket and a big spoon and had him fish the turds out. We carried that bucket through the living room, and I made him bury them outside under a pine tree."

Clay and Kim roared. Clay slapped the table, coughing his smoker's cough.

Bob laughed weakly and asked if he could be excused.

"Careful in there." Bruce yelled at the closing bathroom door. "It's a long walk downstairs."

Clay whinnied, and I laughed, too, hating myself.

"How can you be so mean?" I whispered.

"It happened." Bruce shrugged and turned to Clay. "How's school?"

My son stiffened. "Fine."

"Still not driving, huh? Lucky man to have a woman like this chauffeuring you around." He stared at Kim's breasts.

Clay nodded, saying nothing.

I said, "I'll get dessert." I stacked the plates and took them into the kitchen. I didn't want to hear Bruce begin on the accident. Clay had gone home to Mississippi after the hearing. Back in Miami, he would graduate from UM next June. He still lived with Kim, who drove him everywhere.

I'd found peace with Clay. Once we no longer shared a house, I didn't have to fret over the nest he built around himself: the dirty clothes, candy wrappers, torn books, cigarette butts, and ashes. From a distance, we got along great.

Bruce hadn't forgotten. I carried slices of key lime pie into the dining room. The fireworks were just beginning, and I opened the French doors wide so we could watch them from the table. No one looked at the colorful display. Clay was stony-faced. What could Bruce be saying?

"Still thinking about going to law school?"

Clay nodded.

"When you apply to the Bar, you realize they're going to want a complete disclosure of your past."

Clay just stared at him.

"No sliding by the accident. You'll have to tell them."

"Good grief," I said. "That will be years from now." I stared angrily at Bruce. "He doesn't have to write the letter tonight."

Bruce's mouth turned down. "He'd better think about it. The incident hasn't gone away, and he can't afford to ignore things that affect his future."

I looked over at Clay. He pushed his pie away and looked back at me, raising his eyebrows. He'd been happy when I told him Bruce would be here for dinner. He didn't look happy now.

"Got to go," he announced.

Kim swallowed her last bites of pie and stood up. "Just a fabulous meal."

I walked them to the door.

Clay gave me an awkward hug. "Yeah, Mom, great eats."

Before the door closed, Bob was there. "Another marvelous meal, my dear. Fun seeing you two in these glamorous surroundings."

"Maybe we can go to a movie next week." I rested my head on his shoulder, wishing I were leaving with him.

55

Bruce ate Clay's pie while he cleared the table. "Bob's gained weight, don't you think? He ought to exercise more."

I said, "Why did you have to bring up the accident?"

Bruce stacked the dessert plates. "I'm interested in the kid's future."

"No, you're not. You're interested in tormenting him."

"That's simply not true. He thinks he wants to be a lawyer. I'm a lawyer, and I am familiar with the process. Clay is not known for telling the entire truth. He doesn't talk about the accident, treats it like it never happened. I want to be sure he knows, when it comes to the Florida Bar, there's no fudging. He's going to have to tell them everything. He had an accident. He was charged. He killed people." Bruce clattered the dishes together.

"Be careful with those. This isn't our house. If you don't want to help clean up, don't, but don't break Esther's dishes to give me the message."

"I want to help clean up. I always do, don't I, even for parties I didn't want to give?"

"The accident was almost three years ago," I said, "and I'm sure Clay thinks about it. He probably talks about it, too, but not with us. It changed his entire life. He hasn't driven a car since that night. He has almost four years before he graduates from law school. Why can't you let it go?"

"That's why he had the accident, because you let it go. You let him drive when you knew he was irresponsible."

"You taught him to drive, not me." I sounded defensive. "I can't believe we're starting on this again. Can't you ever forget? It wasn't your accident. You didn't kill anybody. It was Clay's. He did it, and he wears the scars, not you. Let it go, for God's sake." I hated the sound of my voice.

"Calm down." Bruce smiled the way he did when he thought he'd won.

"You don't need to get so angry. We're just talking."

I scraped dishes into the trash, thinking over what we'd said, going over all the conversations of the past two days. I hadn't felt this bad for months.

I knew what I had to do, and the certainty made me feel as if I'd swallowed a stone. "You're right," I said to Bruce. "We're not going to talk about it anymore."

"Good." He stopped banging dishes and looked pleased.

"Because I'm not going to be with you."

The words rang into silence. Bruce put the glass he held on the counter and stared at me. "What do you mean?"

"You heard me."

"Just like that? Just like that, you decide. You get to announce what the future's going to be? No discussion?"

"I am exhausted by being with you, and we've been discussing it all weekend. It's what we've been saying under everything we talk about. I can't be with you. I love you, or I did love you, but you eat me up."

"It's someone else. You've found another little simian boyfriend." He meant the curly-haired professor.

"If I never find another man, I can't be with you. Can you hear that? I haven't been this angry in a year, and I hate it."

"You're upset about Clay. You've never been able to accept what he's really like."

"And what do you think he's really like?"

"He doesn't apply himself and probably never will. He's one of those bright people who manage to slip by on their wits, but he doesn't really care about anything."

Bruce could be describing himself: all wit and no caring. Knowing his temper, I was not tempted to say this out loud.

He was still talking. "All those years living with me, and does he care about justice? No. Does he feel any obligation to people who have nothing? No."

My face got hot. "You could talk about how much you care about poor people when you made $9,000 a year. Not now. You earn $80,000. You're getting rich off the money of criminals."

Bruce bristled. "Just because I finally earn a decent living from the law doesn't mean I don't help people. What you refuse to see is that Clay is lazy, and he's always been lazy. He'll never put forth the intellectual effort to amount to anything."

I gave up arguing. The wind had grown stronger. I closed one of the French doors. Far off to the north, fireworks exploded over downtown Miami in silently expanding circles of gold, green, and red. I was bone tired. The days with Bruce felt like a marathon, and I was almost to the finish line. I longed for the peace of the house in the woods. No arguing, no battle of wills, no defending my right to think.

I said, "You've known Clay since he came to live with us, for what—five years? From age thirteen to eighteen? I don't think you have the right to pass judgment on someone's life based on five teenage years."

"I wasn't like that as a teenager," he said. "I was never that thoughtless."

"You were perfect, Bruce, your mother says so." I smiled to myself. I would never have to eat another one of Jeanne Rogow's terrible meals again.

Bruce poured soap powder into the dishwasher and closed it. "I don't see Clay suddenly filled with zeal for work, or for anything else. He's wasting his brain. He shouldn't even be in college. What's he making, Cs? He'll never get into law school."

"You don't have to worry about it, do you? You're not going to be around."

"You're really going to leave me?"

"Let's get it straight, Bruce. You found another woman, and you left me. We came together for a few days to see if it could work, and it can't."

He slapped the dishcloth against the counter, making me jump. "Just like that, huh? You get to decide just like that?"

"It's not just like that. I've been deciding for three days."

"Oh, have you? And when did you make up your mind?"

"It's not black and white. I didn't make up my mind in any one moment. I watched how I felt being with you, and I feel—not all the time, but too much of the time—less."

"Less than what?" He was being sarcastic now, leaning against the counter, arms folded, eyes narrowed.

"Less of a person than I am by myself."

"That's the stupidest thing I've ever heard."

"See?" I heard my voice rising and took a breath. "That's what I mean. I'm stupid, my son's lazy, Bob's fat. You're always defining the world."

"And you never enjoyed a good dissection after a party?"

"Of course I enjoy it, but it's not a part of me I particularly admire or want to encourage, and it's not nearly as much fun when the dissection is turned on people I love."

"You never could stand criticism, could you?"

"I admit it, I hate criticism. I'm hard enough on myself." I laughed. "The worst part of being criticized is realizing I didn't think of it first."

Bruce laughed, too, and tried to take me in his arms. "You can't leave me. You're too funny. We have such good a time together."

I wriggled away. "I'm not leaving you. We're each going back to the house where we were three days ago."

He shoved me, and my heart stuttered with surprise. "Stop it."

"You stop it." He pushed me again, not as hard, giving me little shoves to emphasize his words. "What gives you the right to upset my life like this? Bring me here thinking we have a chance?" Another shove. "That we'd make a decision together. Then you announce it won't work." Shove. "What gives you that right, huh?"

I sat down in a kitchen chair so he couldn't push me anymore. His eyes were black and hard. I hadn't seen him so angry since that first year we were together. Was he going to beat me up? I felt my heart thumping against my ribs. "We can talk about it all night, Bruce, but you can't make me want to be with you."

He fell to his knees in front of me, his head on my lap, his voice soft. "Don't do it like this. Don't throw it all away."

I touched his dark hair. "I'm not throwing it away. It left. It's been leaving since you told me about Jacque. I can't bring it back just because you want me to." I stroked his hair. "Are you crying? Please don't cry."

He stood and pushed me so hard the chair wobbled. His smile was bitter. "You'd like that, wouldn't you? Seeing me cry? Fat chance, my friend. You want to go, go. You'll be sorry for the rest of your life."

I got up, trying not to cry myself, and walked into the bedroom. I took the basket out and began folding clothes into it. Bruce followed me, and stood leaning in the doorway, watching.

"You're leaving now, are you? It's after midnight."

"I'm not leaving now. I'm packing now. I'm leaving in the morning."

He picked up the basket and dumped my clothes on the bed.

I said, "What are you doing?"

He didn't answer. I put the basket on the floor and began refolding the clothes. Bruce sat on the bed saying nothing. I felt his eyes on me. When I finished packing, I carried my hanging things into the living room and put them over a chair. Bruce followed, picked up the hangers, and threw them on the floor.

I screamed at him. "Stop it. You're acting crazy. Leave me alone."

He took me by the shoulders. "I will not leave you alone. You don't deserve to be left alone. You've treated me like shit, and now you're going to know how it feels."

I tried to relax under his fingers. "Bruce, let's just go to bed. We'll both make more sense in the morning."

He released me and followed me back to the bedroom, where I turned down the bed. He threw the covers on the floor. "You'd like that, wouldn't you? Go to sleep, wake up, get your stuff and leave. All so easy."

I picked up the covers, got my nightgown, and locked myself in the bathroom. I heard Bruce through the door, banging my basket around. It got quiet. "I'm not coming out until you act like a human."

"Come on out. I'm okay." He sounded worn out.

I opened the door a crack. He sat on the far side of the bed in his undershorts, looking defeated. My clothes were on the floor again. I dropped my dress on top of them and climbed into bed. I spoke to his back. "Good night." I closed my eyes. I was so tired.

His hands were on my shoulders, shaking me awake, his voice angry. "Don't think you're going to sleep." He paced the room. I sat up, watching him dully. "What makes you think you can do this to me? What gives you the right?" I shook my head, not answering. "We never even talked about it. You decided. You announced. We were supposed to have a few days together and then talk about it." His voice was pleading.

"We did talk. We both talked. I listened, and we lived here together. How else are we going to tell how our life would be?"

"That's not what I mean." Bruce walked a path from the armoire to the bathroom, gesturing with one hand as if this were a courtroom. He stopped and pulled on his Guatemalan pants. "I mean, we should sit down and talk about what we like about living with each other, about any problems we may have, and what we want to do about those. You shouldn't announce a decision."

"I'm sorry." I didn't feel sorry at all. "You want to go through all the steps. Okay, here's how I see it." I sat up and crossed my legs. "I loved you very much. Love was like the veil I told you about, and it hid everything but your good qualities. You could do no wrong. If we fought, it was my fault. I had done something to destroy the serenity. Then you hurt me. You took a mistress, and that hurt horribly. Even that I thought was my fault."

"I told you I was sorry."

Had he told me he was sorry? It didn't matter now. "Let me finish. When you hurt me, the veil got ripped away. I see you now, and I feel warmth toward you, even desire. What's missing is the veil. Without it, I see the small ways you diminish me every day, the things you do to control me, telling me I'm wrong, I'm unreasonable, criticizing my friends. I see how unkind you are in the name of honesty. You always have to be King of the Mountain, Bruce. You want to own me, and I don't love that."

"You never gave me a chance." Bruce stopped pacing, folded his arms, and watched me from the end of the bed.

"Life is the chance. Every minute of the day is the chance. We each got to be who we are for these three days. Too much of the time I felt bad about myself, wondering what I'd done to make you cross, feeling guilty about money, about buying filets or strawberries, blaming myself for spoiling your moment. At home, I don't do that anymore. I go days now without giving myself a hard time. Do I want to be with someone who is never quite pleased? It makes me anxious, and I don't like that." I got out of bed and began picking up my clothes. "I'm tired. I want to go to sleep."

He stood over me. As fast as I folded things and put them in the basket, he threw them out again. "You're not going to sleep, I can tell you that. You're damned well not going to sleep. Do you know what you are?"

"What?" I gave up on the clothes.

"You're a second-rater. You go through life half-doing things and walking away. Leaving wreckage behind you. You gave up on your marriage. You had four children and left them. You got a second-rate doctorate that you didn't have to work for. You teach at a second-rate college, and now you're walking away from me. You never stick anything out and do a first-rate job. Never."

I walked into the living room. The sky was dark now over the ocean. I was about to cry, and I would not let him see. Was that how I was? Second-rate? Was that how I'd always seemed to him? What he said hurt. He took my worst fears and turned them on me like a knife. I never knew he felt I was second-rate or that I hadn't rightfully earned my doctorate. I worked so hard on it. I didn't go to the best school, but they let me keep teaching, and I slaved over it for years. Bruce sympathized then, but this was what he really thought. During all our years together, this was what he was thinking. Tears dripped off my chin onto the front of my gown.

He was there, behind me, twisting me, holding my shoulders too tight. "Crying? Cry, then, but don't think you'll get any sympathy from me. You want to cry? I can give you something to cry about." He shook me. "You deserve to be squashed like a roach." He pushed me hard, and pushed me again.

One of the French doors was still open. Was he going to throw me off the balcony? My skin prickled with terror.

"Scared, aren't you? You'd better be scared." He pushed me again.

Did he hate me enough to kill me? I moaned when he shoved me.

"Cry. Who's going to hear you? You are despicable, Norma. Do you know that? All your talk of women's rights, your so-called independence. It's shit. What's it doing for you now, huh?"

I should have waited until morning to tell him. We could have spent a safe, reasonable night in the same bed. Impulse again. Impulse could get you killed.

He shoved me harder. "Like a roach."

I ducked and darted past him into the bedroom, anything to get away from that open door. I ran into the bathroom and slammed the door, locking it. If he tried to break it down, I could push Esther's antique chest against it.

The small gold clock said five after four.

Bruce stood on the other side of the door, his voice angry. "No use hiding. You're going to hear everything I have to say."

I was scared shitless, but I had to laugh. "There's more?" On the back of the door hung my bathing suit and shorts. I pulled them on. I didn't have to stay until morning. I would leave now. No shoes. That was okay. Forget my clothes. Esther could bring them to me, or maybe Bruce would throw them off the balcony the way I once threw his. My face in the mirror looked as pinched as a mouse. I spoke to the reflection: hold on, kid.

I opened the door quietly and peeked out. Bruce stood at the bedroom window, his shoulders slumped, looking down on Honeymoon Harbor. I tiptoed by the bed, out the door and up the hall. He called my name as I grabbed my purse and the car keys off the entry table. I was out the door before he caught up.

"Where do you think you're going?" He stood in the doorway watching me.

I pushed the elevator button. "Home."

"This is typical, a little criticism and you run away."

"Yeah, well." I wanted to laugh, but a choked sound came out. When the elevator door opened, I stepped inside.

He ran and held it. "What about your stuff?"

"You keep it. It's second-rate stuff anyway."

"I'll ride down with you." He got in and let the doors slide closed.

My heart pounded so hard, I wondered if Bruce could see it. When the doors opened on the first floor, I practically ran toward the front entrance. The man who was supposed to be at the desk was nowhere in sight. I was afraid Bruce might try to kill me outside in the parking lot. I spotted the faded green Volkswagen, parked between a Cadillac and a BMW. Almost crying with relief, I ran, opened the door, slid in, slammed it behind me, and pushed the lock button.

Bruce stood on my side. He gestured for me to roll the window down. I did—an inch. "So, this is it?" he said.

I put the key in the ignition. "I guess so." I turned the key and pressed the accelerator.

Nothing. The Volkswagen's engine didn't make a sound.

I tried again, staring fiercely at the dashboard, willing the car to start. Silence.

Bruce's laugh was a bark. "You take care of it." He turned away, speaking to me over his shoulder. "That's what you're good at, isn't it? Figuring things out." I watched him walk toward the building, his long frame outlined by light.

On the eastern horizon, the sky was beginning to pale. I relaxed against the seat, limp with relief. I would figure things out. It was almost morning, and there was a service station on the corner. When it opened, I could walk over and ask for help.

Sitting in the locked car, I breathed in and out, letting my heart slow. The sun rose over the water. My hands still shook, but I felt oddly unafraid, or maybe I was light-headed from lack of sleep. I got out and counted up to Esther's floor. The windows were dark. Knowing Bruce, he was back in bed, enjoying the sleep of the self-justified. In a few hours, he would awaken and return to Jacque in his best of all possible worlds. Tell her he tried, but Norma was too filled with bitterness, and he couldn't take it. I didn't mind. I might be what his mother called me—that woman from Mississippi—but I was no longer his woman.

I remembered learning to ride a bike when I was nine, with my father holding the seat, and the feeling of freedom when I realized his hand was no longer there. I was on my own, and I didn't fall. I wouldn't fall now either, not off of Esther's balcony, anyway. I tried to smile at my joke, but a part of me vowed to keep away from high places.

In 1966, I ran away from one man, looking for freedom with another, unable to see the irony in that. Ten years later, for the first time in my life, there was no man. When I was nine, having wheels felt almost like flying. I had wheels now, and I was in the driver's seat, or would be when I got this car running. In charge of the only life I could save.

AFTER THAT

When I left Mississippi, the Episcopal priest told me I would suffer from guilt for the rest of my life. He has not been wrong, but guilt can generate constructive change, and pain has a way of revealing what is important.

Maya Angelou wrote, "Have enough courage to trust love one more time." I loved my work and hoped to love another man. It took me three tries to find one willing to love me without owning me.

Freud said love and work are all we need, but having those can't repair the past. To live my own story, my quest, I broke the conventions of my society, and broke hearts as well. The children have forgiven me for leaving, but I have never quite forgiven myself.

I read about string theory with its multiple universes. In an alternate reality, perhaps I didn't make the same mistakes. Instead of running, I stayed in Jackson, Mississippi, and fought for the change I believed in. In that universe, I used feminism to help women instead of taking that post-pill, pre-AIDS moment as an invitation to a big helping of free love. Maybe Eudora Welty helped me become a writer.

To a Southerner, home is where you were born, no matter if you leave the next day. If you take yourself away, don't think your accomplishments will impress the people you left behind. Anything you do outside that center of the universe is suspect. I went home to Mississippi once, swollen with my new doctorate and my professorship. My old college roommate said, "We heard you left here on the back of a motorcycle and went into real estate." Uncle Doug's wife, Leigh Latimer, took me down another peg. On one of my trips home, she cast an appraising eye at my flowing hippie gear: "You used to be cute enough to wear those cheap clothes."

Exile is a funny thing: you can take your body away, but the mind is more reluctant. I have been gone for five decades, but Mississippi remains the home of my memories and the heart of my stories.

Allison's Wells, the hotel where I grew up, stood for everything good and bad about the South. In 1963, in the middle of the civil rights turmoil, it burned. One tradition ended, but a new world opened for the servants, the people we called only by their first names.

Women learned from the power of the civil rights movement and formed a movement of their own, breaking free between the arrival of the birth control pill in 1960 and the passage of *Roe v. Wade*. Freedom might have its terrors, but I doubt many of us would willingly climb back on that pedestal.

Despite Bruce's dire predictions, Clay graduated from law school, was made partner in a large Miami firm, and was named, year after year, as one of the best lawyers in America. Allison surrounded herself with children, animals, and beautiful things. Linden took her love of learning and animals to vet school and teaches veterinary pathology at the University of Tennessee. Thomas studied architecture and became a builder like his father. When the 2008 recession hit, he and his wife, Kay, transformed the ground floor of their office building in Highlands, North Carolina, into the Ugly Dog Pub, the town's most popular watering hole.

Bruce did not remain an enemy. Unlike Fred Craig, who despised me until he died, Bruce refused to let either of us hold onto bad feelings. After our unfortunate weekend, he married Jacque and fathered three children. We get in touch on our birthdays. Whatever we did to one another, and however badly it ended, this was the man who started me on the long road to freeing myself.

Allison at fourteen

Thomas at fifteen

"When Sleeping Beauty wakes up, she is almost fifty years old."

— Maxine Kumin

Time and trouble will tame an advanced young woman, but an advanced old woman is uncontrollable by any earthly force.

— Dorothy L Sayers

Acknowledgements

I want to thank Ron Goldfarb, my agent, who did not give up on me; all the folks at Nautilus Publishing—Neil White, Sinclair Rishel, Carroll Moore, and Karen Bryant, who guided me through the process and corrected my commas; Scott Manning and Abigail Welhouse for helping spread the word; Susan Bono, who found the title; and, most fervently: Ginny Rorby, Katherine Brown, Kate Erickson, Ginny Reed, and Lynn Courtney, fellow Mixed Pickles. Week by week, they read, commented, and turned me into a better writer.

Made in the USA
San Bernardino, CA
08 September 2017